Emmanuel Levinas and Maurice Blanchot

Emmanuel Levinas and Maurice Blanchot: Ethics and the Ambiguity of Writing

William Large

First edition published Manchester 2005

Published by Clinamen Press Ltd
Unit B
Aldow Enterprise Park
Blackett Street
Manchester
M12 6AE

www.clinamen.co.uk

A catalogue record for this book is available from The British Library

ISBN 1 903083 33 8

Typeset in Times New Roman

Printed and bound in England by Antony Rowe Ltd, Chippenham, Wiltshire

For my father, who knew
that the only truth
the philosopher needs to learn
is how to die well

Contents

Acknowledgements

I would like to thank the College of St Mark and St John for granting me research leave in order to write this book. I would especially like to thank Doctor Geoff Stoakes, Vice-Principal of the College, for all his support. Without the commitment to research of my colleagues in the theology and philosophy department, this book would never have been finished. Special thanks go to Professor Adrian Thatcher, and above all to Doctor Paul Grosch who read and re-read the manuscript more times than he would probably care to remember. Finally thanks also to my friends who read this work whilst it was being written and were unstinting in their encouragement: Arthur Bradley, Robin Durie, Lars Iyer and David Webb.

Note on translations

I have used English translations throughout this work. If they were not available, I have translated the work myself in parenthesis. If occasionally I have disagreed with the English translation (either because it goes against the sense of a sentence, or because it differs from the standard translation), then I have indicated this in the endnotes.

Introduction: have we the power to think the Other?

We cannot begin to get an adequate grasp of Levinas's ethics unless we understand its phenomenological origin.[1] Most importantly of all this will prevent us from sentimentalising it, succumbing to this 'Respect and veneration,' as Žižek calls it, 'of a kind of vacuous Otherness *à la* Levinas' (Žižek 1999, ix).[2] All this talk of the Other, the face, 'widows, orphans, and strangers,' and even, if I might say it, the victim, can be quite philosophically uninteresting and banal. I am reminded of one of my favourite quotes; Lacan's humorous warning to the uninitiated about the new fangled concept of the Other:

> One of our colleagues, our ex-colleagues, who used to hobnob a bit with *Les temps modernes*, the journal of existentialism, as it is called, told us as if it were news that in order for someone to be analysed he had to conceive of the other as such. A real smart Alec, that one. We should have asked him – what do you mean by the *other* – his fellow man, his neighbour, his ideal I, a washbowl? These are all others (Lacan, 1998, 7-8).

'What do you mean by the other?' How can we answer this question in relation to Levinas? We can answer it without reflection and hurriedly by saying that the Other is the other human being who faces me, who calls into question my self-satisfied and content egoism and so on, but philosophically speaking this does not really say anything at all. For the important and decisive question that we must ask ourselves is; what makes the other person different from the washbowl or any of the other 'others'? The way into the question for Levinas is through a phenomenology, even if this path leads to a phenomenology which would be paradoxical and to a certain extent impossible to complete; a phenomenology whose very success would be measured by its failure. Levinas is not a phenomenologist in any simple sense. He is not merely a disciple of Husserl discovering a method with which best to describe alterity, or even, as some would like us to believe, giving a new depth to phenomenological analysis.[3] On the contrary, Levinas's work brings phenomenology to a *crisis*, which does not mean that it escapes phenomenology or even invents a new method beyond it.

We might falsely believe that Levinas is merely contrasting and opposing the ethical situation with phenomenology, the former somehow, though in a very mysterious and enigmatic way, signalling the excess of the Other over representation, and the latter the work of representation. Here we have the obvious and often repeated opposition between the *numinous* and *thought* which has characterised every discourse of transcendence, and which, rather than escaping the limits of reason, is reason's own self-definition. It is quite easy to get lost in Levinas's discourse and to believe that the same opposition operates. For example, in *Otherwise than Being*, Levinas writes that thematisation 'destroys' or 'undoes' the *face* and only 'ethical language' can truly 'indicate' its 'absence' (Levinas 1991, 94). Well it is obvious, is it not? On the one hand, we have the laborious work of thematisation, and on the other, ethical language, the wondrous immediacy of suffering which requires not the slightest bit of thought at all to communicate its pain and distress to us, a veritable anti-philosophy. The difficulty with this opposition, however comfortable it might be, is that it is impossible to imagine how this ethical language could indicate anything outside the work of thematisation. Is not the language which Levinas uses in *Otherwise than Being* still thematic, constructed from propositions, statements and arguments which need to be defended, even when it speaks of an ethical language?

Perhaps the ethical language of the trace is not exterior to phenomenology, but interior? This does not mean that first of all we have a phenomenological description from which an ethical meaning can be deduced in the same way, for example, as an intentional meaning can be arrived at from the description of perception. On the contrary, the ethical meaning interrupts, deranges or throws into disorder the phenomenological description. This does not mean that the ethical language contradicts, opposes or negates it, as though the relation between ethical language and phenomenology were dialectical. If this were the case, the ethical language would either be one more stage in thematisation, of which the phenomenological descriptions would be a lower order, or it would indicate some inexplicable experience. Such an experience, however, would be utterly contentless. We could say nothing about it, for as soon as we spoke we would betray it. There is no doubt that Levinas can be read as though he were saying the latter, but this would lead to an absolutely vacuous, empty meaning of the Other. If he does speak of the betrayal of the language of thematisation, then this is a necessary betrayal both of thematisation and the unthematisable. What cannot be thematised only has meaning within thematisation and not outside. This does not mean that the unthematisable is determined by thematisation in advance. The unthematisable only appears in that moment in which thematisation is pushed to its limit. Phenomenology is not opposed to ethical language; rather, ethical language marks its interruption so that it does not congeal in the proclamation of its own certainty and intelligibility.

This does not mean that there can be a phenomenology of ethics in which the Other would function as some kind of ideatum of an intentional analysis. This would dissolve the paradox of which Levinas speaks. Phenomenology, if it wants to bear witness to the *excessive* meaning of the ethical, must 'read' it through the trace of that which escapes any phenomenological description or any other thematisation without at the same time taking the easy way out of falling into silence or a mock and empty profundity. It must tell us *why* the Other is not the same as a washbowl or even any being at all and that it *appears* as such, even to the risk of incoherence. The phenomenology of the ethical, however much it might threaten and undermine the clarity of and logic of a phenomenological idealism that only interprets experience through the meaning that consciousness bestows upon it, still has its own *positive content*.

A positive content, however, that has its own paradox, for it outstrips its description. Such an eccentricity seems to justify an appeal to an experience beyond the labour of words, or that such a labour could point and indicate to it without compromise. At this point we need to read Blanchot. He saves us from the mystical and numinous Levinas, who is his own worst enemy. In *The Book To Come*, Blanchot writes that what is beyond the work is the very reality of the work, since the force of the attraction which seems to carry the reader outside of the work, as though it were a matter of verifying the status of the work in the external world, which is somehow meant to stand outside of the effect of words, is in fact the very movement which impels the reader towards its centre, to 'the secret of itself' (Blanchot 2003, 90).[4] The descriptions of the Other, which appear to point to something outside of the work, outside of the work of writing, of bearing witness and accounting for experience, actually carry or propel us back into the work, because without the paradox that befalls phenomenology there would be no way of attesting to experience or justifying it.

To think the experience of the Other, which is nothing less than to think suffering, is to refuse to allow this thought to fall into the image of thought. Thinking always makes use of images, but this does not discount the distance between thought and the image of a thought. The power of thought is measurable by its ability to exceed the images that it produces.[5] This power of thought Levinas defines as metaphysical desire, which is 'a thought that at each instance *thinks more than it thinks*' [italics in the original] (Levinas 1969, 62). There is a power to thinking that exceeds the representation of an object or image of an object of thought. This explains the sensation when reading Levinas that nothing he writes can capture the experience of the Other. This is not because the experience of the Other is beyond thought, but the power of the thought of the experience of Other is beyond the image of that thought. Words are not only images of things; rather they can evoke things by keeping their distance from them. To transpose a word into an image of a thing is to already to lose the power of words, their fascination and in turn their power to evoke and attract further thought.

As Thomas Wall reminds us, we can already find this difference between the power of thought and the image of thought in Kant's explanation of the transcendental imagination and especially in the distinction between a rule and a schema (Wall 1999, 138-55). Images are the product of rule that belong to the delineation of an empirical concept (the concept 'dog', to use Kant's example, traces 'the figure of a four-footed animal in a general manner'). Schemata, on the contrary (and which, therefore, are in no way images at all), belong to the transcendental function of categories. If a category is not an image what then is it? It is a temporal unity. The schema of a category is a temporal determination which is true of the object in general (the transcendental object x) and not the image of the object.

We are all very aware of the different intentions behind Kant and Levinas's philosophy, though they are sometimes over-exaggerated, but what delights me in Kant's description of transcendental imagination is the difference between the power of thought, in this case the power of thought to unify experience, and the image of the object of thought that it makes possible. The power of thought to unify experience, and which Kant himself admits is 'an art concealed in the depths of the human soul', belongs to the unity of time. The schemata are the elucidation of this temporalisation of experience, the anterior integration of the sphere of pure intuitions and concepts that makes possible individual experience. Perhaps what is really at stake in Levinas's thought is the possibility of another time, one that disrupts and deforms the time of representation, a time which is out of phase with itself, out of joint and dismembered. Instead of thinking of the Other as an image of an object of thought, why not think of it like a schema, which unlike Kant's schemata, would be the disfigurement of thought's formality and thus the increase of our power to think?

The aim of this book is twofold. One is philosophical and the other philological. Let us start with the philological first, because it is the easiest. My thesis is bold and stark. You cannot read Levinas without Blanchot.[6] In relation to this argument, the most important chapter of this book is the fifth one, 'Writing'. This is not because I believe that Blanchot has unique insights into Levinas's work so that he can inform us what it really means. On the contrary, after reading Blanchot reading Levinas, I am less sure that I understand Levinas than I did before. But that is precisely where I want to be. The opening essays of *The Infinite Conversation* must be required reading for anyone who lazily appeals to the experience of the Other. What is at the heart of these pages is the movement from an obsession with the transcendence of the Other, an ineffable, secret and mysterious experience of the other person, to the impersonality of the ethical relation. This brings us to the more difficult philosophical thesis of this book. Ethics has nothing at all to do with people if one understands people as individuals, units of resource, or even inexplicable mysteries but with the *logic of relations*.

The asymmetry of the ethical relation can be either inclusive or exclusive. Now in the end this is a matter of thinking about the difference between transcendence and immanence. Since Hegel, we might think that the aim of philosophy is to overcome transcendence. In this picture of the history of philosophy, Levinas's thought would be a regression, a return to 'unhappy consciousness' and a projection of the 'good beyond being'. How would this distinction between the inclusive and exclusive relation answer this judgement against Levinas? In the exclusive relation, the Other is external to the self and determines it from the outside. In the inclusive relation, the Other is internal to the self and determines it from within. The difficulty of the second relation is to how to demonstrate that the Other does not disappear or dissolve in the immanence of the self. The argument of this book is that this indeed is Levinas's question and not the separate existence of the Other. The problem of ethics is the problem of the subject. Levinas's answer to this problem is to demonstrate that the Other is not lost in the inclusive asymmetrical relation, because such a loss would presuppose that the self-identity of the subject precedes its relation to the Other. What if the subject were always more than the existence of a self? This is the basis of Levinas's phenomenological method. Its aim is to show that the self, at the very heart of its existence, is other to itself. The problem then becomes not how the otherness of the Other is preserved in its relation to the subject, but how the subject is already substituted by the Other before it has even become a self.

This book is organised in a linear manner. The first chapter is a description of the exclusive relation to the Other, which concentrates on the transcendence and distance of the Other. This is the Levinas that I want to leave behind, but which has had the most power influence on the cultural production of ideas. The next two chapters explain the inclusive relation to the Other following some of the more esoteric and exotic phenomenological descriptions in *Totality and Infinity* and progressing to the less well known, intricate, and difficult analyses of *Otherwise and Being*, whose focus is the idea of substitution, the Other-*in*-the-Same, and not the Other-*to*-the Same. We then proceed to the two chapters which describe Blanchot's reading of Levinas's work, which is so important to any understanding of the difference between the inclusive and exclusive relation to the Other, and the rejection of any anti-philosophy, which is the subject of the last chapter.

The common thread that holds all these chapters together is the difference between ethics and writing. Ethics outside of writing is the appeal to a pure experience outside of philosophy. This is Levinas's temptation, and the temptation of some of his readers. The demand of writing demonstrates the impossibility of this appeal, which has always been the fantasy of an anti-philosophy, even in the very moment in which it is written.

Notes

1 This is not a startlingly original thought. There has recently been a book published whose topic is wholly this. See, John E. Drabinski, *Sensibility and Singularity: The Problem of Phenomenology in Levinas* (Drabinski, 2001).

2 All those who are inspired by Levinas might also profit from reading the chapter on his work in Badiou's admirable book *Ethics: an Essay on the Understanding of Evil* (Badiou 2001, 18-29). Although it is clear that Badiou has read little of Levinas, and his remarks should therefore be taken with a pinch of salt, his critique of a certain kind of Levinas reader, who perhaps has more to do with cultural theory and what has come to be called 'post-colonialism', than philosophy, seems to me to be spot on. 'For the honour of philosophy,' as he writes, 'it is first of all necessary to admit that this ideology of a "right to difference", the contemporary catechism of goodwill with regard to 'other cultures', are strikingly distant from Levinas's actual conception of things' (Badiou 2001, 20).

3 As Stephen Strasser writes, '*Levinas a changé l'optique phénoménologique en y ajoutant une dimension de profondeur*' [Levinas changed the phenomenological optic by adding a dimension of depth] [italics in the original] (Strasser 1977, 124).

4 The important essay here, which is rarely commented upon, is 'The Secret of the Golem'. We shall return to it in the last chapter of this book in the section 'The Symbolic', pp.150-3.

5 This notion of the power of thought is deeply inspired by Philip Goodchild's book *The Price of Piety: Critical Theory and Philosophy of Religion* (Goodchild 2002).

6 I am not the first to suggest this and no-one more than Paul Davies has pointed out the importance of Blanchot to reading Levinas. This is not just a matter of personal history, but of opening up Levinas's text to a more subtle, ambiguous and perhaps even dangerous influence. See especially his essay, 'A Fine Risk: Reading Blanchot Reading Levinas' (Davies 1991, 201-26).

1

Language

The importance of dialogue in philosophy is perhaps inseparable from its Platonic origin. To engage in philosophy is to speak to another, and it is also to prevent those who do not have a legitimate claim to philosophy from speaking. To speak to another is to address them directly and through friendship, as Socrates speaks to his fellow Athenian citizens, but also to speak through truth to the extent of risking one's life. Even the principal of contradiction, where it makes no sense to assert two opposite opinions, and which for many is the very bedrock of philosophical logic, is portrayed by Aristotle in terms of a conversation. You cannot have a proper dialogue with someone who continually changes their mind, saying one thing at one moment and something entirely different at another.[1] And yet for all the emphasis that is given to speech and dialogue in philosophy, which furnishes the political and social setting of its practice and without which it could not exist, for all their metaphysical splendour, language itself, the materiality of the word, is forgotten. For what matters in philosophical dialogue and speech is not the tone and timbre of the voice or even the beauty and sound of the words, but the truth that is spoken through them. It is this commitment, which is an ethical and political one, that distinguishes the philosopher from those pretenders, such as the poets and the sophists, that would take his place; do not listen to the words that I utter, but only the truth spoken through them, for which they are only a necessary avatar. Without these words I would not be able to communicate my thoughts to you, but what is most important is the thoughts themselves, which are utterly and complete distinct from them.

The idea that expresses what something is, is not the same as the word which refers to it. Words are merely carriers of ideas which have no effect on what they transport. The privileging of speech and dialogue in philosophy has as its corollary the purification of language of all external influences which would disturb the uninterrupted flow of information, whose impossible ideal would be to cancel out the very words, the very phonemes of speech. Impossible, because no conversation could be without words, but it must deny their significance and importance, otherwise they would contaminate the spirituality of the relation between the two interlocutors, a spiritual relation which takes place beyond words even though it only happens through them. Attend to the *truth* of what I say, not how I say it.

Of course, we should not avoid the paradoxical nature of this struggle. Philosophy needs words as much as it wishes to do without them, and it is continually resisting the temptation of poetry. When we think of the relation between philosophy and poetry, or philosophy and literature, we should not think of this as merely a struggle between two disciplines (though philosophy might wish to portray it this way, as it always displays its superiority over any other discourse), but as a question addressed to philosophy from within. This is really what is stake in the relation between Levinas and Blanchot, the ancient quarrel between philosophy and poetry, though it is not quarrel in the sense in which either wants to prove himself right over the other. For Blanchot will not deny any of Levinas's philosophical concepts; rather in their contact with his work they undergo a metamorphosis which brings them into proximity with what Blanchot will call the 'demand of writing'.

Language without words

What is at stake in this contact is language, for literature contests the Platonic heritage to which Levinas clearly belongs. Take for example the essay 'The Dialogue', which appears in *Of God Who Comes to Mind* (Levinas 1998, 137-51). We might first expect that Levinas is leaving this tradition behind, for in the opening pages of this essay he contrasts the meaning of dialogue in philosophy with its significance in the ethical relation. In the former, dialogue is only a pretence, because reason only feigns to be dependent on the words which utter its truth. To be really dependent on words would mean that reason would be subject to language which existed before it, and therefore could not claim to be the ultimate explanation of reality. On the contrary, from the perspective of this long tradition, the externality of language is merely an empirical fact which does not touch upon the essence of thinking. The ideal of this dialogue, as Plato described, would be a dialogue addressed to oneself, where thought thinks itself, and whose highest limit would be Aristotle's definition of God, in the *Metaphysics*, who is nothing but 'thinking as a thinking on thinking' (1074b). It is this dialogue of reason with itself which is the precondition of all other dialogues, as if the exchange of conversation, of question and answer, were merely co-ordinates within the unity of thought. For all these responses, if they are spoken in truth, could only be reason speaking to itself. There can only be *one* reason and not two, even if for the sake of dialogue there must be two speakers.[2] To this dialogue of reason, Levinas contrasts the relation of speech in which the I addresses the Other and what matters is not what is said, but the distance between them. The fact that in turning to speak to you, I address you without making you one more theme in a discourse. At this moment the unity of reason, where every part is part of a whole, is broken. Neither you nor I, as addresser and addressee of speech, belong to the same plane. Moreover, it is this relation that is the true condition of the dialogue of reason. Without the unique relation of one human being to another, without this primary sociality, there would be no space for thought and the content of what is said.

Even this priority of the ethical dialogue, however, makes no difference to the status of the word. For just as the unity of reason subordinates language to knowledge, so the ethical relation suppresses it for the sake of transcendence. Ethics is speech, conversation or dialogue, but what is significant is only the relation they express, the terms in the relation, and not the words which are spoken. It is at this more fundamental level that Levinas is Plato's descendent. Again, if Levinas does evoke certain expressions to capture the ethical significance of this relation, such as Abraham's reply to God, 'Here I am', then like reason, it is not the words which matter, but what is spoken through them. So even though in the priority of ethics over reason, reason must be subordinated to language, and not language to reason, this leaves the function of the word as a carrier of higher significance unchanged. Even for Levinas, what matters about language is how it can be the servant to a higher master, so that this reversal of reason to ethics, is not a reversal in favour of language, but a subordination of the latter to the encounter with the Other, which, like reason, is also beyond the words that are spoken. The latter are always secondary, since what is important is only the relation they attest.

The same denial is also present in the pivotal essay 'Language and Proximity', which acts as a bridge between *Totality and Infinity* and *Otherwise than Being* (Levinas 1987a, 109-26). Here language is interpreted, first of all, from the point of view of structuralism, where its meaning is reduced to the function of a system of signs, in which all meaning is captured within interlocking chains of signs. There can be no sign that is truly unique or ineffable, for every sign points to another sign and so on. Reason is made up of a system of signs which is fully describable, even though it might be invisible to the speakers of the signs from within the system itself. Thus every religion speaks of the mystery of the Divine, but for the ethnologist this is just one more example of a system of signs which needs to be interpreted. But structuralism, for all its claim to be a new science, cannot be separated from the long tradition in Western thought of reducing experience to meaning. For though the sign does not immediately relate to things, since its immediate relation is to the system of signs, which already sets up the relation to the world, things only make sense through the sign that signifies them. This relation is the same one which has always pertained between language and being. There is no manifestation of being without language. Things remain mute and lifeless without the word which animates them. Even when we speak of the relation between consciousness and experience, it would be absurd to think that experience simply strikes against consciousness, and then somehow has to be refashioned into something meaningful, as though I first of all hear a sound outside my window, an utterly meaningless sound, which I then bestow with meaning. Is it not more correct to say that I hear a car outside my window, or the sound of human voices straight away?[3] Experience is already meaningful prior to being taken up by someone, and it is the system of signs, which are in no way constituted by me or by any other individual, or even an aggregate of individuals, that gives experience this meaning. In a more phenomenological language, we would say that an intention always precedes a sensation, or that it makes no sense to talk of sensation having a sense outside of the intentionality that gives it life. It gives meaning to experience not because it is dependent upon it, or even logically and temporally prior to it, but because it is wholly and utterly outside of it. There is no meeting place of meaning and experience.

Meaning, Levinas writes, is the statement of identity, the naming of beings, a *kerygma* (Levinas 1987a, 111). It owes nothing at all to experience, but the latter only has a sense or direction through it. The identical is not an addition of different experiences. No matter how many different aspects of a thing I see, it only makes sense through the reference to an identity, which has no aspects or profiles. I see a box, Husserl says, and as I twist and turn this box in my hand I see different sides of it, but in seeing these different sides I nonetheless continue to see one and the same box. No matter how much I look and search, however, I will not find this 'consciousness of identity' within experience, for identity belongs not within multiplicity, but outside of it (Husserl 1970, 565-6). This 'outside' is the system of signs, which make up our historical and cultural space, and which are separate from experience. The relation between them is not reciprocal. The systems of signs is not dependent on experience, and this is why Levinas describes it as a *kerygma*, but experience is only latent and suspended without it. The sign does not describe experience; rather it brings it into existence: 'Every phenomenon,'

Levinas writes, 'is discourse or fragment of a discourse' (Levinas 1987a, 112). The formalisation of experience, therefore, necessarily follows from this relation. For if there is no experience without the unity of the system of signs, then there is no experience as such without unity. Although this unity does not come from experience, without it it is not possible. Every experience, therefore, if it is meaningful, takes place within a system. This is no doubt the meaning of Kant's famous deduction in the *Critique of Pure Reason*, when he argues that the *a priori* conditions of experience in general are the conditions for the possible objects of experience (Kant 2003, 138, A 111). The unity of the understanding is not something that takes place over and upon experience, as though first of all you have an experience and then you add an act of synthesis to it; rather, without the act of synthesis first of all, there would be no object to experience. This would mean that identity is the condition of multiplicity, rather than multiplicity identity, which is the idealist position *par excellence*. Language takes the form of judgement not because it follows the logical form of thought, but the logical form of thought follows it. Predicative judgement already expresses the unity of language as the manifestation of beings within a system of signs. Logic, in the restrictive sense, is secondary in relation to the prior unity of language and being.

What is lost in the naming of a thing is the latter's singularity, which must be sharply distinguished from its individuality which has always been thought in terms of the universality of identity. What is at stake is whether sensation is merely the content of an idea, or whether it has a significance of is own. We take for granted, from within this perspective, that without meaning granted to it by consciousness, sensation is merely mute, or like Descartes that it is purely a mechanical process of the body that affects the mind, but has no intrinsic meaning of its own. We should not confuse the object with the sensory perception, since the latter is purely an intellectual operation (Descartes 1985, 81). But even this picture seems to leave a small remainder, even if the model cannot itself enable us to think it: the mute, lifeless and dead object, which stands outside the sphere of ideas, but grants it its content, however transformed and changed this might be. For without the causal operation of the sensible object upon the eye, even if this object is unknowable, there would be no sensory perception. As Levinas writes, 'in sensation something *comes to pass* between the feeling and the felt', which is not the same as the disclosure of the sensed through sensation [italics in the original] (Levinas 1987a, 117). I can be touched by things before knowing or intellectualising them, and this 'touch' is in no way a stepping stone towards insertion within a system of signs. The world does not just offer itself as something to know or be understood, whether in a theoretical or practical sense, but as a palpable presence that is exterior to my place within a culture. The touch of hand against skin, before I ask who this person is, or whether this touch is permitted. Of course, this palpable world is not exterior to the cultural world as a 'world behind this world', rather it lies beside it, and thus can at every moment be inserted back within this cultural world, and the system of signs that constitute it, and likewise, the cultural world can be disturbed and interrupted by its unnerving concreteness.

What is significant within this context is that this contact is also language. There is another sense to language than naming things and Levinas writes something very surprising here that we might not expect, given our description of his views in the essay 'The Dialogue'. When language expresses this different relation to things, in which things are not reduced to an identity, but have a palpable presence which exceeds any description or knowledge of them, language becomes poetry: 'the proximity of things is poetry' (Levinas 1987a, 118). This is the relation to things, for example, the cup on the table, the tree outside of the window, as might be embodied in the poetry of Francis Ponge. Or as Raymond Carver writes,

> It is possible in a poem or a short story, to write about commonplace things and objects using commonplace but precise language, and to endow these things - a chair, a window curtain, a fork, a stone, a woman's earrings - with immense, even startling power
> (Carver 2000, 89).

In this turn from the language of naming to poetry, a crack emerges, where the word becomes visible. What is poetry but the presence of the word, the sensibility of things captured by the sensibility of language? And yet, as soon as we move to the ethical relation, this fissure is closed over, for the word has no more significance in the ethical relation than it had in the relation of the system of signs. For the true significance of poetry, which is a tenderness towards things, is the presence of the Other. The aura that surrounds things, this palpable and impalpable presence which resists any conceptualisation comes not from things in the world, but from another presence. I speak about things to someone. Even God needed Adam to name things, and Crusoe his Man Friday. This presence of the Other, which is the condition for poetry as its ultimate reference, is not poetic. This is why Levinas can say, even though the relation to the Other takes place within language, it is 'without words' (Levinas 1987a, 119). 'Without words', because it is both the condition for the language of naming and poetry, but not reducible to either.

We might, therefore, speak of two disappearances of the word. One at the level of nomination, where the word is reduced to the status of a carrier of information, and the other, which is at a completely different level, since it is the condition of both forms of language, poetry and thought, in the ethical relation. Even though *what* I speak to the Other must be words, *that* I speak is wordless. To use Levinas's own formulation, it is a 'pure communication' (Levinas 1987a, 119). It is, however, only because the word is understood as the conveyance of information, as a sign within a system of signs, that the relation to the Other is also wordless. To admit that the word has a presence outside of the idea that it expresses would undermine the opposition between ethics and culture. It would insert a third possibility between them, which would be neither ethics nor culture, and which, to certain extent, Levinas announces, but passes over too quickly, when he writes of the poetry of things.

Although this 'language without words' is a thread which runs throughout Levinas's work, we might find its most detailed formulation in *Totality and Infinity*. If this language has little to do with words, it is because its true function is to represent the transcendent spatiality of the ethical relation, which is the distance that separates the I from the You. For a word already crosses over this distance, since it implies an ideality that we hold in common. When I speak to you I use words that you understand, and you understand them because we belong to the same cultural horizon. For Levinas, there is another space that has nothing to with the immanence of communication, it is the *distance* between the speakers in the conversation, and this distance cannot be spoken by any word, but just by the fact of speaking. It is precisely because this distance cannot be spoken through a word, but only through speaking, that it is completely outside any thematisation. For thematisation only understands speaking through the said, through the idealities that are expressed in words. When we think of speaking ethically, it has more to do with space between the speakers, than the vocalisation of any word. Speaking, here, does not express what is said, but simply the relation between the speakers, the distance that separates them and which is outside the cultural horizon of what is said. It is only this distance between speakers which is ethical and not anything that they might say to one another.

This space is the ordering of desire, an orientation in language which takes place before any word has been spoken. If we read the opening pages of *Totality and Infinity* that introduce the concept of metaphysical desire, we see that it is initially described as being without any predetermined goal, in a certain sense, aimless (Levinas 1969, 33-5). This is what distinguishes desire from need. When I need something, I know what particular object can satisfy this need whatever the obstacles which might be placed between me and it, or even make its reach beyond me. The impossibility of desire is quite different from the impossibility of need. The impossibility of desire is its very expression, the impossibility of any object satiating it, rather than the impossibility of this or that particular object. The relation to the object is a need, whereas the relation to the Other is desire. For if the Other is to remain truly other, then it is stripped of its status of an object. No doubt it is possible to need others in the same way that I need any other object. I can want another in the same way that I need food to appease my hunger. An object can never become an Other, but it is possible for the person I desire to exceed any satisfaction I gain from them, to the extent that even this possession dissatisfies me, which is not a dissatisfaction of disappointment, but a kind of sadness associated with the realisation that they will always remain untouched by my possession. This distance of the Other from my grasp is the measure of the impossibility which is *intrinsic* to desire, as opposed to the *extrinsic* impossibility of need.

At first Levinas describes desire as being without any goal or direction, for to assume that desire had an aim would be to confuse it with a need. This aimlessness, however is relative, to the order of need. Rather than being without measure, desire has its own measure, its own 'dimension'. In need, the terms of the relation are coterminous and symmetrical, since something is needed to the extent that it satisfies a need in me. To need something is bring it within your orbit, and to satisfy a need is make something part of oneself, just like the food which assuages your hunger. In desire, on the contrary, the terms are illimitable and asymmetrical. What is desired is forever outside of my reach, but not because of some inadequacy on my behalf. The exteriority belongs to the desired, and not to me. It belongs to the very space of the relation rather than the terms in the relation. This space Levinas describes through 'the dimension of height' and the 'Most High' (Levinas 1969, 34).

We move from a distinction between need and desire, where what differentiates these two relations is that one appears to have a direction and the other not, to a specific direction which belongs to desire. The function of language is to give desire this direction. Language is the expression of the height of the Other, this distance of the Other from me, which is not the same as the distance between myself and an object. We might think of the difference between these two relations as the difference between negativity and transcendence (Levinas 1969, 40-2). What is negated belongs to the act of negation. Even what resists me is determined by my relation to it. Its resistance only makes sense within my weakness. The life which I wish beyond this life only makes sense in terms of the life which it refuses. Even the attributes of God are merely the inverse image of my own imperfections. But perfection

8

might not necessarily be understood as negation, nor infinity the negative image of the finite, but as a distancing from the finite, a 'trans-ascendence' rather than simply transcendence (Levinas 1969, 41). The relation to the infinite, therefore, would be a crossing of this distance which would not abolish it. Such an illogical relation is produced in speech where two speakers are both brought together and kept apart. To address another is both to relate to that speaker, but also to maintain a distance from them. We might believe that this distance is something that the speaker sustains by respecting the listener, but for Levinas this respect is dependent on a different respect which belongs to the relation itself and not the address. Already before a conversation, there is the *space* of conversation which precedes the speakers. It is this space that is broken by violence, and upheld by the address, but only because the speaker is already *orientated* towards the Other before they have spoken, only because there is this orientation of language before any word.

It is Plato's philosophy which sustains this transcendence of language. In *Totality and Infinity*, references to this philosophy far outnumber any other. Plato's name legitimises the exclusive separation of the Other. The dimension of height, which designates the spatiality of the ethical relation, is introduced by a quotation from the *Republic* (Levinas 1969, 34). The absolute being of the Other, its separation from the interlocutor which addresses them, is described in the language of *Parmenides* (Levinas 1969, 64-5). The denial that writing can have an ethical meaning, which we shall see is decisive to the absolute separation of the interlocutors within the relation and the reduction of language to 'pure communication' and thereby the rejection of the word, is supported by the famous denial of writing in the *Phaedrus* (Levinas 1969, 73, 181). Reference to the same dialogue also underlines the absolute inequality of the interlocutors in the Other's proximity to God, as though the distance expressed by language were essentially theological (Levinas 1969, 297).

The denial of the significance of the word is a repetition of Plato. Despite appearing at first glance to have nothing at all to do with the old history of the dialogue in Western philosophy, since it overturns the primacy of reason, the ethical dialogue is in fact a more subtle imitation. What is identical both to the Platonic dialogue, and Levinas's depiction of the relation of ethical speech is the suspicion of the word. For Plato, the word is merely the avatar of truth, and what is significant is only the idea which it contains. For Levinas, the word only bears witness to the transcendence of the Other, the separation and height of the Other over and above the interlocutor who is addressed by them. For Plato, the truth, the idea of the Good is the source of all meaning, for Levinas, the Other. In both cases, the immanence of language, this confusion, hubbub and tumult of words, is flattened out by reference to

9

transcendence.

Transcendence

The ethical relation, in *Totality and Infinity* is expressed through speech. I do not regard the Other, I respond to them, and this response is the essential meaning of responsibility, prior to any system of morality and the rationality sustaining it. That the relation to the Other is one of speech, rather than vision, marks out the specificity of this relation. Every other relation to the world is visual, and if I do speak of things, then it is only because I have first of all been addressed by the Other. I speak of things to someone, and even if I speak to myself, it is because others have already addressed me about the world. We need, however, to be very careful about the status of speech in Levinas's ethics. We need to separate attentively its function from what we might call *empirical speech*, from what is uttered. Its jurisdiction is transcendental, enunciation, the possibility of speaking, rather than what is spoken.

No one has brought this difference out more clearly than Etienne Feron in his book *De l'idée de transcendance à la question du langage*. He too argues that Levinas's ethics cannot be separated from language, and even more importantly stresses that we should not confuse this priority with the concrete relation of speech. It is not that there is first of all the relation between the interlocutors and then they speak, but that without language there would be no relation at all. Appellation, which is the specifically ethical relation to the Other, is not one of many cultural forms of speech, but the condition for speaking at all and thus the condition of any culture. Language *founds* ethics. It is not the reality of the words spoken, but the possibility of speaking, of being addressed and responding to this address. Before any word is spoken this 'original dimension' is already in place. It is this 'dimension' which is ethical, and not the words that are spoken. Or if these words are spoken, then it is because of this 'dimension' which stands above and prior to any word and any 'system of signs'. 'Le langage,' Etienne Feron writes, 'est la dimension transcendantale de l'éthique' [language is the transcendental dimension of ethics] (Feron 1992, 93). It might be true that the meaning of this transcendence is not the same as the metaphysics of subjectivity, and when we say that language founds ethics this does not mean that ethics is merely a gesture of transcendental subjectivity. The founding activity of language unseats the priority of subjectivity, it does not maintain and support it. The transcendental dimension of language for Levinas is appellation, not nomination, judgement as justice, not predication. Nonetheless, the relation between the transcendental dimension of language and the spoken word is a typical transcendental relation. Without this dimension no word would be ethical and this relation is irreversible: the word is conditioned, not conditioning. If I speak to the Other, it is not the words which I speak that attest to my responsibility, but the bearing witness to the Other already before I have opened my mouth. What is essentially ethical about language, its transcendental function, is not discourse as the spoken word, but the beginning, the origin of the word.

Every word has its place in a 'system of signs', belongs to a given culture and a history, but even this order has its origin in the commencement of speech, a beginning that takes place in the relation between the interlocutors that language makes possible, a silent origin out of which the first word is spoken. What concerns Levinas is not the words themselves, but the relation in which they are spoken, and it is this relation which gives the words, even as a 'system of signs' (for I speak them to someone), their ethical import. Language is first of all ethical not in its content, but in the relation of appellation which it makes possible. The essence of language is inseparable from this appellation. The first word is a response, but a response to the order and demand of the Other for me to speak. This command, even if the Other speaks, must be separated from the word, for what gives the word its force is the subordination of the terms in the relation. It is this dimension of language which is transcendental and not at all anything that is spoken. Etienne Feron writes,

> *Le sujet n'est pas parlant parce qu'il serait "éthiquement" responsable au préalable; il est responsable parce qu'il est fondamentalement parlant et que la modalité originelle de la parole est la réponse*[the subject speaks not because it would be "ethically" responsible beforehand; it is responsible because it is fundamentally a speaking being and in that the original modality of speech is the response] (Feron 1992, 96).

This is why we must clearly distinguish this transcendental dimension of language from the empirical fact that as speaking beings we are all inserted within language, for the latter concerns only the words that are spoken, and not the anterior interval of speech which is already a response to the Other.

It is this interval, 'the curvature of intersubjective space', at least at the time of writing of *Totality and Infinity*, which expresses the truth of being (Levinas 1969, 291). Afterwards, Levinas will be reticent of speaking of ethics and ontology in the same breath, but here, precisely because of the transcendental function of language, he does not hesitate to bring them together.

11

Being is first of all exteriority prior to the division between the inner and outer world of the subject. There is a more fundamental exteriority than the externality of things that somehow abrupt against a subject that is closed off from their inner essence. More fundamental even than the space of the visible in which things come to presence, and which philosophy takes to be the being of things. This exteriority is the space of language. It is that space which grants to speech its truth, or its sincerity, to which the truth of things is subordinate. For I speak about things and the world to someone, and the truth of the content of my discourse is given by the possibility of being sincere, which in turn has its origin in my orientation towards the Other. Even before I speak, speaking is a response anterior to any statement. Things come to be in language, but language is already directed towards the Other. The truth of being is not the visible, but the 'subjective field' of speech, in which even that language which addresses things and the world is first addressed to the Other.

The distance between me and the world, which is a distance that is crossed over in language, since in my words the reality of the thing is negated, is subordinated to another distance, which is the space between me and the Other in which speech takes place. Without this distance, without this 'curvature of space', the truth of the language of things would not be possible. Judgement is the servant of candour, and candour obligation. My relation to the world as truth is interior to the ethical relation which is its condition of possibility. In the absence of the relation to the Other, there can be no truth. My world would then be a world of equivocation and appearances. It is language which gives meaning and direction to the world, and this 'sense bestowal' is originally a response to the Other. Even though I can grasp the world in its totality as a 'system of signs', the condition of this totality is the relation to the Other in speech, which as this condition cannot be a part of the totality. This relation to the Other is the condition not because the Other stands outside of the totality as an ultimate cause, but because meaning arises in a 'subjective field' which is anterior to it. The truth of every word I speak is preserved in the ultimate address to the Other. Without this address my words would dissolve into emptiness and nullity. The truth of things is dependent on me speaking the truth, but speaking the truth is dependent on the relation to Other. Truth, first of all, is not a property of something, rather it is produced in the demand, in the appeal, of the Other upon me. I speak the truth about things because the Other demands that I do so. To refuse this demand is already to deny the truth even before you have spoken. The sincerity of discourse has its source not in my wish to tell the truth, but in the appeal of the Other that I should do so.

Here we reach the crux of the matter; it is this transcendental status of language which explains Levinas's commitment to the phenomenological method in *Totality and Infinity*, even though he was already suspicious, in his thesis, *The Theory of Intuition in Husserl's Phenomenology*, of the latter's 'intellectualism' (Levinas 1973, 155-8). Philosophy begins, for Husserl, with the phenomenological reduction.[4] This movement, Levinas writes, only discovers the meaning which animates our lives by stepping back from it. The philosopher becomes a spectator. He or she views life from afar, and though it is true that phenomenology, and this is its anti-metaphysical stance, is only concerned with the meaning of concrete life as it appears; it appears only to a consciousness which must divorce itself from its own existence. The meaning of life is to be found in a life represented and not in a life lived. What is 'intellectualist' about Husserl's phenomenology is not that he takes science as the method for philosophy, but that philosophy is seen as belonging to the same 'metaphysical destiny' as the pure sciences, and is thereby as divorced from the 'historical situation of man' (Levinas 1973, 155). It seeks the meaning of life in what is eternal, in the pure essences of those acts that constitute it. To reject the eternal basis of life is not to return to a positive conception of philosophy that is critically dissected in the first part of Husserl's *Logical Investigations*. Nothing in Levinas allows us to think that to be critical of intentionality means simply to return to the naturalist thesis, still less that to read Levinas carefully, and be aware of the paradoxes that emerge and evolve in his work, permits us to return to this position. Levinas's ethics is not an empiricism in this sense, nor is his scepticism the same as the scepticism that phenomenology refutes. 'Scepticism itself,' Levinas writes in a footnote, and in words that prefigure his comments on scepticism in *Otherwise than Being*, 'need not necessarily be anti-intellectualist' (Levinas 1973, 156). There would be a scepticism beyond scepticism and an intellectualism beyond intellectualism.[5] The historical critique of phenomenology is ontological, not empirical. History is not a property added to a human being that already exists, but belongs to the way of being of every human being, no matter what their particular histories might be. Such an historical understanding of human existence, which Levinas notes is central to Heidegger's phenomenology, cannot appear in Husserl's work because of his continued commitment to the atemporal gaze of philosophy, to which even history must be submitted.

In *Totality and Infinity*, the step beyond Husserl's 'intellectualism' is no longer supported with reference to Heidegger's concrete phenomenology, but with another judgement that is part of the estimation of Husserl's method in *The Theory of Intuition in the Phenomenology of Husserl*. Again the source of Levinas's unease is the priority that Husserl gives to theory, but this time the object of criticism is not the reduction, but representation. Levinas asks whether it is the case that every act, theoretical or not, must have, as its base, an act of representation, in which, 'the characters of usage, value etc., can exist only as grafted on a being that is the correlate of a representation' (Levinas 1973, 94-5). It is this theme which is picked up, and which is perhaps constant to Levinas's work, in *Totality and Infinity*. Such an intellectualism presumes that to wish for something first of all means that you have to represent that thing to yourself, for without that act of representation, you could not wish for anything at all. The same could be said for sensation or any act that is not initially an act of representation. Representation has a unique place in Husserl's phenomenology: every act implies an act of representation, but representation does not imply any other act. What would it mean to reverse this relation, to argue that representation were only one act amongst many, and not the general basis of every act? Or to argue further that life preceded the 'act-character' of intentionality? The latter is a bigger step, for even if representation were the condition of every act, it would still be conditioned by life that exceeds it. Its transcendental status would be called into question, and it would only be one more element in the flow of life. Levinas does not deny the posteriority of representation, that all theory is *après coup*, but resists the temptation of falling into empiricism and thus the impossibility of any transcendental method. Empiricism cannot be the alternative to intellectualism, because it is *intellectualism's* own alternative. To go beyond intellectualism must mean to also to overstep its empiricism. Levinas does this by situating the source of representation not in contemplation, but in the relation to the Other. If all theory is *après coup*, then it is so with respect to ethics and not life conceived of as merely a concatenation of impressions which somehow find an organisation after the event. Thought is not an addition to life, one part added to another, it is an 'extraterritoriality', it completely changes my relation to life, and in this sense it is 'anterior', even though it comes afterwards (Levinas 1969, 169-70). This anteriority, or deterritorialisation, this 'transcendental energy', can only be accounted for if representation has its origin elsewhere than life. The distance between me and things, this other space than the space as mere living and possession of things, has as its condition the space between the Other and I, and it is this space which is the conditioning condition, which gives to representation its anteriority. Without the transcendence of the Other, there would be no transcendence of thought. In describing Levinas's method as transcendental, we therefore need to be careful. It is not transcendental in the sense that the frameworks of Husserl and Kant are, in which experience is constituted by the anteriority of the subject, for this anteriority is posterior for Levinas. It is conditioned by the relation to Other that interrupts my world and thereby opens up a distance between me and things, a distance that thought inhabits. This relation to the Other is not a postulate of thought, it is not an idea, but a *concrete event*. In *Totality and Infinity*, this concrete event is language, but not language as the words spoken; rather it is the interpellation of the Other. This transcendence which is the hidden horizon of every spoken word, and thus of every representation.

Levinas's method is transcendental to the extent that it attempts to uncover the unconditioned condition of every condition, but only to the degree that it finds this unconditioned in the concrete event of language rather than the *a priori* structures of subjectivity. And yet this concrete event, precisely because it must have none of the positivity of a fact (otherwise Levinas's method would fall into a crude empiricism), must be purified of any materiality, so as to find the invisible within it. It is not the concrete fact that these words are spoken which is the unconditioned, but what within these words is not a word. Just as in Husserl it is not the subject which is the unconditioned, but that within the subject that is which is not subjective. We move from the transcendence of the subject to the transcendence of the Other, from representation to language, but what is identical to them both is an erasure of the materiality in which they adhere. In the first case it is life itself, and in the second the materiality of the word. If we follow Levinas's argument whereby the anteriority of representation is posterior to the relation to the Other, then we might add that the true unconditioned would be the materiality of the word, for what would the concreteness of language be in the absence of the word? It is this reversal which is forbidden by Levinas in his absolute separation of the ethical sense of language from the word. For Levinas the ethical space of the dialogue is anterior to the word that is spoken; this is because the Other has a relation to language which the self does not have, and this relation is anterior to any concrete act of speech. Anterior, not in that it comes before this act, but that it could only be called ethical because of it. When Levinas says that the concrete event of language is the unconditioned of every condition we need to go a little further and see that the unconditioned lies in the interpellation of the Other and not in the words spoken, and that interpellation is not a word, but a relation prior to every word. This is how we should understand Levinas's statement that the method of *Totality and Infinity* should be understood as the attempt to discover the invisible within the concrete, and thereby remains loyal to the phenomenological method, despite the latter's intellectualism (Levinas 1969, 173).

Teaching

The Other has a relation to language quite distinct from mine. Although ethics is described as a response, it does not come unbidden. To respond to an Other means first of all you must be interpellated. A response is something demanded. The first word, therefore, belongs to the Other. Yet this first word, as we have seen, is not a word at all, but a relation that is prior to any word which is spoken. It is a shaping of a space between the speakers, as, for example, a courtroom already shapes the space between the accused and a judge before any word is spoken between them. We should not confuse this space with the space of things. The courtroom exists in time and space, was built at a certain date, and no doubt will also disappear, but the interval of speech is what makes sense of this space. Without judgement, there would be no need for courtrooms. You can imagine a different relation between speakers, where the courtroom would no longer be a courtroom, though nothing of the actual room had changed at all. The judge becomes the accused and the accused the judge. The space of things would, therefore be secondary in relation to the space of speech. We can think of this space through the horizon of a culture, and this is no doubt what the social sciences hope to achieve. You could imagine a meticulous historical and sociological analysis of the subtle shifts in the meaning of punishment, as for example, is hinted at in Nietzsche's *On the Genealogy of Morals*, when he says it would be quite absurd to think that the function and purpose of punishment had remained the same throughout the ages (Nietzsche 1967, 76-9). Levinas, however, is not concerned with this social space of speech as a positive fact. Rather, as we have also seen from the previous section, he seeks to reveal its transcendental constitution. Before any particular speech act, to use the vocabulary of ordinary language philosophy, the space of speech is already determined by the relation to the Other.[6] Indeed, it may be the effect of many speech acts, even the relation between the judge and the accused, to cover over this *a priori* alignment of the interlocutors in the ethical dialogue. When Levinas comes to discuss the relation of teaching in *Totality and Infinity*, we would be making an error if we thought that it was on the same level as any other speech act, such as promising or judging. Rather than one speech act amongst others, teaching describes the fundamental orientation of ethical space in which any particular speech act takes place. In this position the Other has a relation to language which is quite separate from the interlocutor. It is a relation which is prior to any spoken word, and which already orientates the direction of speech in interpellation. The immanent relation of language, communication, dialogue and speech, will be completely dependent on an originary relation to language which only the Other has. Interpellation is not a speech act, but the condition of every speech act.

The relation between a word and a thing is secondary to the relation of speech. It is because the world is spoken about, thematised, and written down that things have a meaning and not the other way around. The one who speaks, who describes this world in signs is not themselves a sign. I can speak of myself as a sign and I can speak of the Other as sign too. Both of us can be themes of a discourse, but the one who addresses me cannot be a sign. It is not the Other as such that cannot be a sign, but the address. It is not what can be said in the address that cannot be a sign, but the *addressing* itself, whose significance lies not in the spoken word, but in the *speaking* of it. But do I not also speak? I speak because I am spoken to. This is the fundamental meaning of the address. Without first being addressed by the Other, there would be no speech. Language, prior to nomination is a dialogue. Things have names because we speak to one another, but speaking for Levinas is first of all, prior to thematisation, an address. We speak of things to someone, but this 'to someone' is already a response to an address. 'Attention', he writes, 'is attention to something, because it is attention to someone' (Levinas 1969, 99).

When Aristotle famously says in the *Metaphysics* that philosophy begins with wonder, this wonder would be meaningless if it were not expressed to someone, and, Levinas would add, I would not express it if I were not first of all addressed, if I did not first of all have a relation to the Other.[7] This relation to the Other is the beginning of all communication, which is the precondition of all knowledge, but it itself cannot be a theme of communication. This address, which is the condition for all discourse, also reveals a relation of the Other to language, which is not repeated from the side of the interlocutor. It is this specific relation to language Levinas calls 'teaching'. If I speak to the Other, then this is only because the Other has first of all spoken to me, and if the world has a meaning, then this is because the Other has already taught me this meaning. It is not the content of teaching which is significant, but the relation itself, and more specifically, through the relation the Other has to the words they speak *prior* to speaking to me.[8] There is an inversion of the monologue as the highest essence of language. It is no longer the monologue of the I, but the Other. In teaching, Levinas writes, the Other 'attends' or 'assists' (*assister*) the words they speak (Levinas 1969, 98-100). It is this attention or assistance which is the surplus that goes beyond the word, and it is this surplus, rather than the words spoken, which is the ethical significance of language, and let us not forget, the transcendental condition of any speaking at all. It is a surplus that only comes from the relation of the Other to the spoken word and not the one who is interpellated. This is why Levinas calls this assistance or attention 'teaching'. Only the Other attends or assists the words they speak, not I. It is the relation of the Other to the word that is the condition of the relation between the word and the object. Without the Other, my relation to the world is obscure and confused. It is only through nomination that things take on the consistency of a definition, and that I can see through things to what they mean, but the origin of what is meant does not come from me. It comes, rather, from the relation that the Other already has to the words they speak. If signification, thematisation and objectivity arrive only with speech, which requires that my world is interrupted by the presence of the Other, then I cannot, as idealism purports, be the origin of the meaning of the world. It is because I am already addressed by an Other who speaks that the world can be thematised. 'The presence of the Other,' Levinas writes, 'dispels the anarchic sorcery of the facts: the world becomes an object' (Levinas 1969, 99). It is important to note here that it is the 'presence of the Other' which fractures the world of facts, and not the *word* of the Other. It is first of all the presence of the Other which is the condition of words meaning anything at all, and brings it about that I too can understand and speak these words in a language community, but this presence is itself not a word and must clearly separated from the existence of words. There are two domains of matter. One is the materiality of the world prior to objectivity; the brute experience of the world which Levinas describes in *Totality and Infinity* through enjoyment, where the I bathes in the elements (Levinas 1969, 132). The other domain (that is not at all discussed in this book, but remains at its margins), is that of word. The word stands to the presence of the Other, as the elemental stands to the I. The word is a pure materiality, it has no reality except that given to it through the presence of the Other. Without this presence it is a dead letter.

We understand why, therefore, for Levinas, ethical speech is opposed to writing.[9] The inspiration of this denial is again Plato. In the *Phaedrus*, Socrates argues that writing cannot belong to true dialectics, because it is external from the original author (274c-277c). Unlike the situation in speech, the writer cannot respond to the questions of the reader, nor come to the aid of his or her words. They remain lifeless on the page. In speaking, on the contrary, you can defend, or retract what you have said and participate in the dialectical progression of knowledge. Socrates compares writing to painting. The images seem to be living beings, but if you ask them something they remain silent. It is just as much an error to think that words have 'intelligence'. No matter how many questions you put to them, they always remain mute stubbornly saying the same thing over and over again. Worse, once a word has been written down, it can be repeated from one person to the next, and they, having read the word, think that they know the truth, whether or not they have any real connection to it. Words, Socrates says, need a 'father' (πατρòς) (275e). They need to be placed in the mouths of those who love the truth. Against this illegitimate word, Socrates compares the genuine writing that is written in the soul. This genuine writing is the origin of the 'living and breathing word' of which the false writing is merely an image, twice removed, like the reflections of the divided line in the *Republic*, from the truth. The pretenders to philosophy are those who confuse the image with life, who substitute the living presence of the word with its lifeless copy, place writing above speech. It is not that Socrates is wholly denying writing, rather it must be placed under the superiority of speech. We must accept writing as a copy, only authentic when animated by an intelligence concerned for the truth, but to be distrusted when separated from it.

We can understand this distrust of writing through the antithesis of presence and absence. What is distinctive to speech is the presence of the speaker, the presence of an *intention* behind what is said. In writing, on the contrary, where the speaker once was, there is only an absence, or pretence at a presence. There seems to be a real person behind the words, but when we try to discover who this person is, we find nothing. This is even the case when the writer writes a preface or introduction to her writing, for even in the preface, the writer is absent. She would have to write and preface to the preface and so on in an infinite regress. Levinas compares this absence to the marks left in caves by long dead civilisations (Levinas 1969, 181). There is a presence there, but it is a presence of an absence. It is not just that writing is absence, and speech presence; rather, writing is a dissimulation, because it pretends to present an absent present, the author or civilisation who or which is long dead and gone. It is only as this simulacrum that it is dangerous and harmful and its absent presence should be exorcised by the proper presence of speech. Every word refers to a thing, but only in the thing's absence. There is always the possibility that the relation between the word and thing can become broken, that the word can go astray. It is this absence that is made up by the sincerity of the speaker who offers the word, by the intention they maintain behind the words that they say. I mean this when I utter this word. The surplus of the speaker's intention holds the word to the thing which it signifies. 'This assistance,' Levinas writes, 'measures the surplus of spoken language over written language, which has become again signs' (Levinas 1969, 182).[10]

Levinas rejects writing in *Totality and Infinity* because of the particular form of the ethical relation presented there, where the terms of that relation are exclusively separate from one another. The relation of speech expresses this distance which keeps them apart. For only the Other has a relation to the ethical meaning of language in exceeding the words they utter when demanding a response from me. This is the cornerstone not only of ethics, but the very possibility of sharing a common world through which any intellectual achievement is possible. Language is the condition for objectivity, but the condition of language is first of all the address, the invocation of a response from another. The invocation is irreversible. It is the Other that addresses me, not I the Other. The response of responsibility is only possible through the antecedent relation of the Other to language. It is only the presence of the Other which gives to language its surplus over the written word. This antecedent relation is extra-linguistic, in the sense that it has nothing at all to do with what is said, the words uttered or spoken, but the *position* from which they are spoken. This position is always marked in *Totality and Infinity* through the metaphor of elevation and height. The centre of language is no longer the word, but the position of the speakers, the distance between them and the height of this distance. Language has become a metrics. Only the introduction of this elevation, this lengthening of the space of speech, prevents the contamination of the ethical dialogue, which is the condition of every dialogue, by the word, because the assistance given to the word, this non-linguistic surplus to language, is only attested by the relation's asymmetry. What we witness here is a curious reversal of the position of the speaking subject. It is no longer the origin of the speech, as is taken for granted in linguistics, but the Other. It is only the origin of speech, however, to the extent that what it speaks is unimportant. What gives it this antecedence is extra-linguistic, this 'dimension of height' (Levinas 1969, 75).

Beyond the face

Every book is like a labyrinth in which there are many ways to enter the maze. We are tempted to offer a unified reading of the book, because we think this is what the work itself demands. Yet the more that we reflect on the activity of reading, the less certain we are that any such identity is possible. This is not because we have failed on our part, and someone with much more intelligence and sensitivity could find this unity, and thereby redeem the work, but that even the most carefully constructed work, and perhaps only the most, is always fragmented. Such a loss of unity is not merely a result of the psychology of the reader, as though this disruption were caused by the simple fact that there are many readers with many different interpretations of the same work, since for all these readers this work would still be one, but that for the single reader, if they are attentive enough, and not swayed by the opinion that the work must have a single truth, its supposed integrity will unravel. This is true of philosophical works as of any other, though philosophical reading tends to obscure it. We are quite happy to unify the work of a philosophy through a proper name. We say that Plato means this, and Spinoza that. The proper name becomes a talisman for a theory, and the complexity of the texts, which to some extent might run quite counter to the direction of this theory, is forgotten. We need to read the texts with a little more attention so something new and unexpected can arise for us.

If both sides of the ethical relation absolve themselves from the relation, and thus break with the traditional logical choice between either unity or opposition, then they do so in a different way. The Other might not annul the self, but this does not prevent there being a difference between them, and this difference, whatever Levinas might say, is not wholly empty of negativity (Levinas 1969, 40-2). It cannot be so, because the Other has a constitutive function in *Totality and Infinity* which replaces the usual position of subjectivity. It is the Other which is the foundation of the world through the originary relation of ethics. It is not the ethical relation itself which is this foundation, but the assistance which the Other gives to the words they speak. This means that despite the fact both terms absolve themselves from the relation, it is the Other which founds the world of meaning and objectivity and not the self. It is true to say that for Levinas this relation of constitution and foundation is not to be thought of in terms of a totality in which a whole constitutes a part, in which my freedom, like Kant's moral law, would be raised up to a higher level through negation. 'The relationship between me and the Other,' Levinas writes 'does not have the structure formal logic finds in all relations' (Levinas 1969, 180). Nonetheless it is not a relation of equals. The speakers in the relation do not absolve themselves from that relation in the same way. This inequality is expressed in the metaphors of height. Part of the impact of *Totality and Infinity* is to demonstrate the independence of the self from any totality or system, but this separation is secondary with respect to the constitutive function of the Other. Unlike the self, the Other is separate before and after the relation. It is 'absolute', to use Levinas's expression. It conditions both my relation to the world, and my relation to the 'hyper relation' of ethics, which commences the relation to the world by exceeding it. I, on the other hand, am not the condition of the relation of the Other to me. My relation to the elements is outside my relation to the Other, and even to the world, whose condition is found not in my subjectivity, but in my relation to the Other.

There is no analogical symmetry between me and the Other. It constitutes the objective world of the self, the world in which things and people have a sense. I, however, in no way constitute this ethical surplus of the Other, both over my elemental being, and the world, which it commences by forcing me to break with the first existence. The Other, to use a faintly absurd formulation, is more *separate* than me. There is a 'difference in level' between us, since 'the Other measures me with a gaze incomparable to the gaze by which I discover him' (Levinas 1969, 86).

How is this gaze to be conceived in light of Levinas's insistence that the ethical relation should not be thought through the priority given to vision in Western thought (Levinas 1969, 187-93)? In the *Republic*, Socrates asks Glaucon how we see things (507c-509a). His reply seems obvious enough. We see things because we have sight. Socrates replies that it cannot be that simple, for we see things not just because we have eyes, but because there is light to illuminate them. This light is a 'third type of thing' which is neither our eyes, nor the things seen. For Levinas, this 'third type of thing' is so different from the other two that it is not a thing at all. It is the space in which things are revealed, but which is outside them. It makes things appear by getting rid of darkness, chasing away the shadows, illuminating the hidden places. As this space, it is the origin of the appearance of things, for without it they could not appear, but it itself is not a thing. The eye does not first relate to the thing, but to the openness which allows the thing to be seen.

Unlike the ethical space of dialogue, the space of vision is transversal. Sight crosses over the illuminated space of the visible to reach the object seen. In vision, I bring the object to me, it becomes part of me, I grasp it. The eye and the hand are intimately connected; they work with one another. Because vision brings the eye and the thing together, makes possible their union, it can never be a relation to something other. In vision, all things are correlative to the position of the eye, there is only a 'lateral signification of things' (Levinas 1969, 191). Speech, on the other hand, is a relation of incomparables. In responding to the address of the Other, I do not regard them as an object in my field of vision, but I reply to them. The face of the Other is not a perception, but an interpellation. In responding to the Other, the distance between the terms in the relation, unlike vision, remains. In speaking, the speaker turns towards the interlocutor, but this paying attention or turning towards does not abolish the distance between them; rather it intensifies this distance. In vision, the exteriority of things is transformed into interiority, like the image which is produced on the back of the retina. Even if I speak of this relation from the outside, and thereby treat it as something to be contemplated, I speak of it to someone, so that the same separation is repeated.

It is possible to read Levinas's work as only the description of the absolute separation of the Other, where the word is subordinated to the presence of the Other in speech. This is the ethical meaning of speech. But there is also, marginal for sure in *Totality and Infinity*, but significant later, more ambiguous relation to language, where writing rather than speech is the sign of an ethical surplus over representation, and where the separation of the Other becomes uncertain and equivocal. The marginality of writing in *Totality and Infinity* eats away and disturbs the portrayal of the absolute transcendence of the Other, and yet the apparent lack of unity and coherence, which is not a weakness, but the real evidence of thought, is perhaps even more straightforward. The first and most obvious fact about the structure of *Totality and Infinity* is that it is divided into two parts marked by the subtitle 'Beyond the Face'. Many commentators get beyond this difficulty by simply ignoring it, as though this section were merely a supplement to the main argument of the book, but does not change it substantially.[11] We are then faced with two possibilities: either the last section does not add anything, or if it does, then it leaves the rest of the book substantially unchanged.

Our argument is very different. The last section of *Totality and Infinity* changes everything for the reader. It means that she has to read the whole book again from this new vantage point and in so doing the whole meaning is changed and transformed. The book is written as though it should be read as a linear narrative. First we have the separated existence of the self, then we have the ethical relation to the Other, and finally Eros and fecundity, which in some uncertain way exceed the ethical relation, but leaves it untouched. But if we read *Totality and Infinity* twice, starting from the the last section, this uniformity begins to disappear and evaporate. Would this second reading merely confirm our first, which allows us to see the last section as an addendum, or would it make the ethical relation more ambiguous, since the supplement of the description of Eros and fecundity now represents the beginning of our second reading, rather than the end of our first? The second reading might force us to conceive of speech as the repression or exclusion of a more uncomfortable and equivocal relation to the Other.

The section 'Beyond the Face' is not the exploration of an origin which was absent in the first part of the book, as though the evacuation of the condition for the ethical dialogue had not gone far enough, and behind the Other which assists the words they speak, stood the true unconditioned, the Other of fecundity and paternity. Rather the section 'Beyond the Face' admits a wholly different logic of alterity than the spatial orientation of language, and, to a certain extent operates against it. This division is not a split that organises *Totality and Infinity* into two separate parts which would either work together or apart from one another, but a tear that ruptures the unity of the book. It is not a matter of how the book is organised, but how it disorders itself through writing, through the *ambiguity* of a transcendence, which 'goes both further and less far than language' (Levinas 1969, 254). On the one hand, Levinas will assert that the ethical dialogue has nothing at all to do with eroticism, but on the other, eroticism has to be ethical, for what distinguishes eroticism from the love of things is that it concerns the Other as other, who, in the very impulse towards possession, cannot be possessed. Eroticism is less than ethics, because this relation can always be transformed from a longing for an Other to a unity of lovers, a double self-obsession, and yet it is not merely the love of things; it requires a human presence more troubling than the scintillation of any spectacle. Even in this ambiguity between immanence and transcendence, between self-absorption and opening out to the Other, there is a more excessive movement towards that which 'comes from beyond the face', a light which Levinas describes as 'obscure' and which echoes his descriptions of the *il y a*. That which comes to the face, enigmatic and vague, from beyond the face, is the future. The 'beyond of the face' is temporal not spatial, and has nothing at all to do straightforwardness of ethical speech. It invades this space from the outside. The significant ambiguity lies not *within* eroticism, as the ambiguity between passion and possession, but *between* ethics and eroticism. It evokes a different logic of alterity, a filiation to writing rather than speech, which we shall begin to examine in the next chapter.

Notes

1 As Paul Davies explains in his essay 'This Contradiction', the scene of the principle of contradiction in Aristotle's text is a conversation. 'Until and unless,' Paul Davies writes, 'the disputant respects the *arché*, there is no need to respect the disputant. A condition of speech, here and now, will be that it be bounded by this principle and that the question of these bounds be, in turn, ruled out of bounds.' (Davies 2001, 22)

2 'Le dialogue philosophique,' as Catherine Chalier writes in *Levinas: l'utopie de l'humain*, 'permet de confronter les idées et de s'élever à un savoir universel dans lequel les singularités s'abolissent comme telles en se reconnaissant dans l'unité de la Raison' [The philosophical dialogue permits the comparison of ideas and elevation to a universal knowledge in which singularities, as such, are abolished and recognised in the unity of Reason' (Chalier 1993, 98).

3 This example is Heidegger's. 'We never really first perceive,' he writes, a throng of sensations, e.g., tones and noises, in the appearance of things - as this thing-concept alleges; rather we hear the storm whistling in the chimney, we hear the three-motored plane, we hear the Mercedes in immediate distinction from the Volkswagen. Much closer to us than all sensations are the things themselves' (Heidegger 1977, 156).

4 The reduction is fundamental to understanding Levinas's relation to the phenomenological method, and we shall return to it later on in this work. See chapter six, 'Ethical language', pp.146-50.

5 We shall also return to this theme of scepticism at the end of this work. See chapter six, 'Scepticism', pp.153-8.

6 It is tempting to describe the ethical relation in Levinas in terms of speech act theory, and more specifically performatives. As, for example, Jan De Greef does at the end of his essay 'Scepticism and Reason' in *Face to Face with Levinas* (De Greef 1986, 171-75). Performativity undercuts the priority given to the sign, or what Austin and Searle would call meaning or reference. Nonetheless, it is difficult to see how the interpellation of the Other could be described as a performative in a strict sense, since all speech acts imply an intention, and thus, as is the case with linguistics, the priority of the first person. '[a] performative,' Austin says, 'should be reducible, or expandable, or analysable into a form, or reproducible in a form, with a verb in the first person singular present indicative active (grammatical)' (Austin 1962, 61-2). No doubt there is some confusion by Levinas in this regard. By committing himself to the priority of speech in *Totality and Infinity*, he makes intention a mark of alterity, but this intentionality would be the same both for the

Other and me. This is the crux of Blanchot's difference from Levinas, and is most visible in his essays on Levinas's work in *The Infinite Conversation*, whose complexity and subtlety we shall investigate in chapter five.

7 'For it is owing to their wonder that men both now begin and at first began to philosophize' (982b).

8 We shall see later that Blanchot's reading of Levinas in *The Infinite Conversation* also begins with teaching, but it is precisely this characterisation of language as speech that he wants to move away from. See the section 'The teaching of philosophy' in chapter 5, pp.107-10.

9 This antagonism is the key to Levinas's work. See, chapter five, 'Plato', pp.110-14, for a further account of this passage from the *Phaedrus*.

10 Lingis translates *l'assistance* as 'attendance' (Levinas 1961, 157). There is no reason not to use the closer English word to the French.

11 Surprisingly, one of these readers is Derrida, who insists upon his determination, in a footnote to his essay 'Violence and Metaphysics' (perhaps the most substantial and influential interpretation of Levinas's work), to stick to the face-to-face relation. 'We will not go beyond,' he writes, 'this schema. It would be useless to attempt, here, to enter into the descriptions devoted to interiority, economy, enjoyment, habitation, femininity, Eros, to everything suggested under the title 'Beyond the Face', matters that would doubtless deserve many questions' (Derrida 1978, 315). Why it would be 'useless' he leaves unexplained. Though it is clear in his later writings on Levinas that all these themes, especially habitation and the feminine, become the focus of his attention. See especially his latest work on Levinas *Adieu to Emmanuel Levinas*, which has a long discussion of habitation, hospitality and the feminine (Derrida 1999, 21-45).

2

Relation

Alterity does not describe a being, but a relation.[1] What matters to Levinas is not what the Other is, what properties or attributes it might have, but a relation to the Other whereby through the relation itself we can no longer speak of properties and attributes, since the terms in the relation have ceased to be objects of knowledge or ideas of reason. In these instances, what is known or thought has its condition in the knower or thinker. What the object or idea *is* is what I have already placed there in advance. It is not just that without knowledge and reason the world could not be known, but in their absence there would be nothing at all. This is why we should not confuse the subject of knowledge or thought with the individual person. The interiorisation of the world within the knower or thinker, whereby the possibility of the world is discovered in that being which is no longer part of it, is not merely accomplished through one of the terms of the cognitive relation, but by the relation prior to these relata. It is not the subject alone which determines the known world, but the *subjectivity* of the subject. The subjectivity of the subject is universal and not particular, transcendental and not empirical. This is why Levinas writes that there must be a 'third term' which mediates between the subject and object (Levinas 1969, 42). This 'third term' (which strictly speaking is not a term at all, but a relation) is consciousness.

Subjectivity is the expression of Being, which is neither the perceiver nor the perceived, the seer or the seen, but the space of the visible, which is no-one and nothing. Without the illumination and disclosure of Being, no individual consciousness could grasp and comprehend an object. This is why the relation of knowledge cannot be understood simply through the relata, but must, first of all, be thought through the ontological status of the relation. This is why, for all the difference between Levinas and Heidegger, their antagonism can never be reduced to the simple reversal of the relation between Being and beings.[2] To simply assert the priority of the Other over the self, without changing the logic of the relation between them is not to escape the scope of ontology, but to remain firmly inside it. If an ethics beyond ontology is possible, then ontology must be open to a critique that exceeds it. There must be a critique of critique, a 'meta-critique' of reason that goes further than reason. Before we can make any appeal to pre-philosophical experience, as the possibility of the unseating of the ontological relation, we must be certain that these experiences rest upon the higher possibility of a non-ontological relation.

Identity and multiplicity

For Levinas, the key to the difference between the ethical and ontological relations lies in the neutrality of the latter. What does it mean to say that Being is neutral (Levinas 1969, 298-9)? It means that the relationship between the terms in the relation is always impersonal, even if one of the terms of the relation is the Other who addresses me. It means that this address is reduced to what is spoken, and can be spoken by everyone and no-one. It means that the presence of the Other is reduced to the meaning of Being, to the 'human habitation between Heavens and Earth', which is common to both speakers, but belongs to neither of them, and is 'the word of no one', which speaks through them both (Levinas 1969, 299). To break with the impersonality of Being is to face the Other before they have been comprehended through Being. It is to go in the opposite direction of Heidegger's thesis of *Being and Time*, where the relation to 'someone' is reduced to the relation 'with the Being of existents' (Levinas 1969, 45). But the possibility of relating to 'someone' before their insertion within the comprehension of Being, rests on the occurrence of another relation. To return to the Other does not mean simply asserting the independence of the 'other person' or the 'other human being', since such an assertion still belongs to the comprehension it seeks to refute. The answer to the question 'what is the Other?', at the very moment it gives its response and searches for its ethical meaning, cannot but express the very ontological language it is hoping to avoid. This other relation is not the relation of comprehension, even an ethical one, but the *immediacy of speech*, as we saw in the previous chapter, where I am addressed by the Other who accompanies the words they speak. Speech is ethical, not ontological, because interpellation precedes interrogation. Even the words I speak in response to the question 'what?' are spoken to a 'who', who addresses me prior to the question. The play of question and response that characterises thought is posterior to the appeal which summons it. 'The *quis-nity*,' Levinas writes in

28

Otherwise than Being, inventing a neologism, 'of the *who* excepts itself from ontological *quiddity* of the *what* sought which orientates the research' (Levinas 1991, 25).[3] Only in speech, where the Other is present absolutely, καθ' αὐτό, and *in person*, is the presence of the Other not mediated through the impersonal presence of Being (Levinas 1969, 67). This explains Levinas's rather shocking phrase that speech is a 'relation without a relation' (Levinas 1969, 295).[4] The 'without a relation' refers to the absence of a mediating third term. The terms in relation relate directly to one another without detour through another term which would constitute the relation itself prior to the relata. If I perceive an object, this perception is already determined by the form of perception. Even if I knock a nail in a piece of wood, this activity is defined in advance by the structure of involvement. Every relation is already constituted prior to its accomplishment by its *form*. Thus, every relation is doubled: there is the relation between the terms themselves, and the relation which makes this relation possible. The source of this second relation is in one of the terms of the relation, but is not reducible to them. In Plato the relation to the forms is the condition of the relation to beings, but this form is not the same as the beings which participate in it. In Kant, the pure categories and intuitions are the condition for the relation to the phenomena, but are not the same as the phenomena. This relation, which is the condition of the relation between the terms in the relation, and which for philosophy has always constituted the truth of every relation, Levinas names 'totality'. It is this second relation, the relation to the third, visibility, as opposed to the seer and the seen, Being as opposed to beings, which gathers the two terms in the relation into a unity and whole. Ethics, as the disruption and interruption of this unity which precedes every relation, would then be a relation without this relation, 'a relation without relation'. Levinas calls this other relation a 'multiplicity' (Levinas 1969, 295).

The phrase 'relation without relation' does not mean that there is not a relation between the terms, but it is not a relation of unity or wholeness. In the relation of totality or unity, the terms of the relation are already constituted in advance through a third term, which might belong to one of the terms in the relation, but only to the extent that it is abstracted from it. The visible might belong to the seen, as the Idea of the Good in Plato, or to the seer, as the general structure of subjectivity in Kant, but in each case it functions only to the extent that it diverges from the term in which it finds its birth. This defines the incipient dualism of philosophy, which is not primarily a dualism between the mortal and the immortal, or even idealism and materialism, but between the terms in the relation, on the one hand, and the relation which makes this relation possible, on the other. In this second relation, the difference, the distance, between these terms must be annulled. For even the possibility of their difference is predicated upon them belonging, first of all, to this identity, to this relation which constitutes both of them.

The relation of multiplicity is completely dissimilar to the relation of identity, because it is the difference between the terms, internal to the relation itself, which determines the form of the relation, and not some prior identity. In the relation of identity, the mediating third term joins the other two across the distance which separates them. The eye sees the object, because the light of the visible nullifies the separation between them. The relation of multiplicity, on the contrary, rather than annulling separation, maintains it. The terms in the relation act across a distance, where paradoxically this 'crossing" does not extinguish the distance traversed. The hand that touches the flesh does not find contact but anguish, or even if it does find contact, the toucher and the touched remain separated, and this separation is the very sense of their proximity. But touch, as we shall see in the phenomenology of the caress, is ambiguous for Levinas. It can still fall back into the relation of identity, of wholeness and unity (though it remains unclear to what extent this identity is the same as the identity of comprehension and knowledge). The only relation in which multiplicity is confirmed unequivocally is speech. In speech, and more specifically 'teaching' the terms of the relation remain *in* the relation without becoming a totality (Levinas 1969, 295). This is because the Other who speaks to me does not offer themselves first of all as something to be comprehended, but as someone to *respond* to. The Other remains exterior, at a distance, different from me, without this difference being thought in advance. In the relation of identity, typified for Levinas paradigmatically as the relation of vision, the exteriority of the second term is reduced to the interiority of the first. It is this reduction which is the very work of the relation of identity. It transmutes or translates the exteriority of terms into an interiority. In comprehension, it is impossible to conceive how it might happen that the exteriority of the thing could be held onto, since even this exteriority, like Kant's 'thing-in-itself' is an idea of reason. It is not possible to get behind the subject so as to relate to the thing as it is, because the thing and the subject are already related to one another through the relation of identity. Any thing is only a thing for me (which is the same as saying that the thing is an object), because it is already constituted by the essence of subjectivity. The categories of thought do not represent the object, they *constitute* it. To know the thing as a thing would be to become a thing in turn, to become absolutely bereft of any subjectivity. But then the subject would become something dead and petrified, absolute passivity, receptivity without spontaneity, part of the universe rather than apart. In speech, on the contrary for Levinas, I do not relate to the Other as an object, where their exteriority must be subsumed into an interiority; rather, the exteriority of the Other invades and infracts my interiority without either abolishing its exteriority or my interiority. 'The exteriority of discourse,' Levinas writes, 'cannot be converted into an interiority' (Levinas 1969, 295). In responding to the demand of the Other, I do not abolish the distance between us, but maintain and support it. Even in speaking about this relation, and thus once more totalising it by making it an object of comprehension and the understanding, I speak about it to someone, and this 'speaking', rather than the words which are spoken, is a relation of multiplicity, rather than identity.

For this relation to be a true multiplicity both terms would have to be equally separate from one another. In other words, there would be no relation which precedes the terms in the relation. And yet, in the previous chapter, we precisely questioned whether this is the case, since the relation of the Other to the words they speak has a transcendental function which is absent in words of the response of the I to the summons of the Other.[5] Interpellation precedes response, and without it the response would not be possible. The Other has a relation to language anterior to the ethical relation, and it is this relation which first of all makes ethical speech, as opposed to ordinary communication, possible. The ethical relation takes upon itself the same structure of the relation of comprehension, but in a reversed form. No longer does the pure interiority of the subject constitute the exteriority of the object, but the exteriority of the interpellant constitutes the interiority of the response. It is interpellation, the presence of the Other in the words they speak, which makes a response ethical, and nothing else. This presence would, then, would be the mediating term of the ethical relation, in the way that Being, for example, is the mediating term between beings.

Moreover, we might ask whether the appeal to transcendence and multiplicity are mutually exclusive. Multiplicity is defined as the equal separation of the terms in the relation, but the transcendence of language implies that the Other has a different relation to language than the interpellated subject, and that this relation constitutes the orientation of the ethical relation in advance. It is the presence of the Other in speech which allows for the self to be a separated being. 'The I,' Levinas writes, 'disengages itself from the relationship, but does so within a relationship with a being absolutely separated' (Levinas 1969, 215).[6] It is only the Other which is 'absolutely' separate, and not the self which enters into this relation, for the possibility of the ethical response has its condition in interpellation. This must mean that there is a relation prior to the relation of multiplicity which makes it possible.

If we conceive of the ethical relation primarily as the relation of speech, then it does not seem possible to think of it also as a multiplicity, if multiplicity is thought of as the mutual separation of the terms in the relation. This does not mean that Levinas falls back into a relation of identity, which he thought he had escaped, since even if ethical speech is determined through a prior relation of the Other to the words they speak, this does not make the interpellated and interpellatee equivalent. It does mean, however, that the difference between them is *exclusive*, rather than *inclusive*. This is because the difference, just as in the form of identity in the relation of comprehension and knowledge, lies on the side of one of the terms in the relation, and not *between* them. It is clear that Levinas is aware of this problem, when he insists that the difference between the Other and the self should not be seen as produced by any properties or attributes of the terms in the relation, but by 'the I-Other conjunction' (Levinas 1969, 215). Yet it is difficult to see how this could be the case, when it is only the Other which has a unique relation to speech and not the 'I'. Speech, as ethical dialogue, is not, first of all, a 'conjunction of I-Other', but the presence of the Other in the words they utter. Levinas goes on to confirm our hesitation, when he adds that this conjunction also implies the 'inevitable orientation' of the I to the Other, which has a 'priority' over the relation of the terms themselves (Levinas 1969, 215). Does not the Other, then, become like a third term which mediates between the terms of the ethical relation, by diverting from itself, just as in the traditional form of the epistemological relation, the subject becomes the condition of relation by transcending its own particularity? What then is the status of the separation of the self? Can we think transcendence and multiplicity together?

Transcendence within immanence

It is not enough just to think the terms in the relation as mutually separate. Their relation can either be inclusive or exclusive. In the first case, the transcendence of the Other determines the relation from the outside, whereas in the second, it is interior to the relation. Alterity, rather than the relation between two different realities enclosed in themselves, breaks the identity of the terms from within, even the self-identity of the Other. In the first relation, transcendence is an upward movement away from immanence, operating upon it from a distance, and determining it in advance. In the second, transcendence is a downward movement, shattering immanence from within, but also thereby changing its own temporal status from an anteriority to a posteriority.

Such a new meaning of transcendence is evidence of the subtle influence of Jean Wahl on Levinas's work, to whom *Totality and Infinity* is dedicated. Transcendence is at the centre of the former's thought, but it is a 'transcendence indifferent to hierarchy' (Levinas 1993, 81). It is a transcendence whose very height is also a descent, where that which is most subterranean is also the most exalted. At this point the negativity of transcendence, its supposed opposition to immanence, goes beyond the Hegelian negativity, for the self does not find its essence in it, its own ability to be, but only its own destruction. And yet the abjection is the very hidden uniqueness of the self, an individuality beyond that of the objectivity of Nature and Spirit. The self finds itself not in going outward, but inward. And yet, in the intensification of this inner movement, the self finds that this 'itself' becomes 'other to itself', as though the heart of the inner self was other to itself. 'Will the philosopher,' Levinas writes quoting the question which ends Jean Wahl's *Traité de métaphysique*, 'have the strength finally to transcend transcendence itself and to fall valiantly into immanence without letting the value of his effort of transcendence be lost?' (Levinas 1993, 82)[7] For Jean Wahl, transcendence falls back into immanence, because the source of the beyond is within man himself. This is the lesson of finitude. Finitude is not the denial of transcendence, but its interiorisation, its falling back into immanence. This is not to deny transcendence, but to overcome its opposition to immanence. This does not mean, as in the classic Feuerbachian analysis, that we discover all along that transcendence was merely a disguised immanence, for here the interiority of consciousness is merely exteriorised. Rather, what Levinas sees in Jean Wahl's thought of a transcendence falling back into immanence is an exteriority *within* interiority, as though consciousness were turned inside out like a glove. Levinas will call, in 'From Consciousness to Wakefulness' (one of the most important of his late essays on phenomenology) this transcendence, a *transcendence within immanence* (Levinas 1998, 24).

Philosophy, Levinas argues in this essay, enters a decisive transformation in the idea of critique. It ceases to simply accept the evidence of reason, but submits its apparent lucidity to the 'wakefulness' of self-criticism. This new beginning has its origin in Kant, who denounces the 'transcendental illusions' of dogmatic metaphysics. This 'sobering up' of reason against its own excesses is seen as a return to immanence. Phenomenology travels in the wake of this Kantian revolution, and takes this idea of critique even further, for it returns not to an 'unconditioned principle of the deduction', which would have its source in a subject outside of appearance, but to the appearance itself that cannot be separated from lived experience. Even transcendental philosophy needs to come to its senses. It is in this lived concrete experience where you find the true meaning of the world. At this point, Levinas finds in Husserl's thought, where critique has been pushed to its limit, a certain ambiguity which would allow phenomenology to escape the 'identity of the same', where the reduction would not halt at the 'ideal of certainty', which calls into question the naivety of the evidence of common sense, but go further towards a 'significance of meaning - contrasting with the norms that command the identity of the Same' (Levinas 1998, 21). Levinas refers to a passage in *The Cartesian Meditations*, where, within the presence of the self to itself, intuition can no longer fill the act of signification, since the past horizon of the object reflected upon exceeds the 'immediate object of experience' (Levinas 1998, 22). For Husserl this inadequation of intuition and the act of signification does not undermine the ideal of apodicticity, since it can be grasped as something certain at a higher level of reflection. Nonetheless, however apodictic this certainty of certainty might be for Husserl, it can never be adequate. It is an ideal only in the Kantian sense of an infinite approximation, which must be continually repeated. Levinas interprets it as continual re-awakening at the heart of the wakefulness or 'sobering up' of the critique begun by Kant. Reflection on reflection then becomes not only a consolidation of identity, but an opening up of it from within, as an 'I-that-holds-itself-at-a-distance' (Levinas 1998, 23). Since the movement of this reflection is infinite, and cannot be filled by any act of intuition, the distance between the first and second reflection cannot be crossed. It is as though the I, in the very moment when it seeks an apodictic foundation of certainty, becomes out of phase with itself. This structure Levinas describes as a 'transcendence in immanence', whereby, at the very heart of identity, the I is turned inside out (Levinas 1998, 23). For Husserl, this transcendence is still interpreted in terms of intentionality. It is in terms of the understanding and comprehension of the world that my consciousness must sober up, and reflection reflect upon itself. But this analysis, Levinas insists, 'must be pushed beyond the letter of Husserl's text', where the identity of identity is torn by a difference irreducible to identity (Levinas 1998, 25). Husserl covers over this difference by labelling it as an idea, and even though it is an 'idea in the Kantian sense', this infinity is still apodictic, even if approximate, and thus the difference between reflection and the reflection of reflection still belongs to the act of reflection no matter how many times it is repeated. For Levinas, on the contrary, underneath this doubling of reflection, there is a more profound structure of subjectivity, which cannot be reduced to any act of reflection, and which is difference itself, the being out of phase, out of joint, of subjectivity, wakefulness and its continual re-awakening; a difference which he calls (recalling his earlier analysis in *From Existence to Existents*) insomnia. Insomnia is not one possible state of the subject amongst others, but names the very getting out of phase of itself, which philosophy conceals by subjecting it to the activity of reflection. For the subject to be out of phase with itself, and for this asynchronism not to be synthesised at another level of reflection, it must be interrupted by transcendence from within. This would mean that even the certainty of certainty, concealed in the hidden depths of the subject, would already be deposed by the Other, as though this certainty would require a restlessness which would be beyond the amphibology of certainty and uncertainty, where common sense finds its uneasy repose. Levinas's philosophy would then be a reduction of a reduction, going back behind the Husserlian reduction, in which, as he writes, there would be an 'explosion of the Other in the Same' (Levinas 1998, 29).

Atheism

This different structure of transcendence within immanence is already in operation in *Totality and Infinity*, despite the centrality of the metaphysics of language which we have already analysed in the first chapter. This is no more clear than in the idea of infinity. *Totality and Infinity* has two significant philosophical sources. The first, as we have already seen, is Plato, but the other is Descartes. For the sake of the unity of the book, Levinas must think of these two as mutually supporting one another. He attempts this by separating the Platonic dialogue, as a model of ethics, from its Socratic origin. If the relation between the Other and the self is to be seen as teaching, then it is to be differentiated from maeiutics (Levinas 1969, 180). This is because in the latter, the speakers are unified through a truth which is anterior to the conversation. Socrates is not concerned, for example, in the *Meno*, with the presence of the slave boy in the words he speaks. Rather, what matters to him is only the truth spoken through them, which is common to all men, Athenian or non-Athenian. To teach in the ethical sense, on the contrary, is not to bring out the truth already existing in the interlocutor, and which would exist even if they did not, but to place a command or injunction upon them. In this manner, the Platonic dialogue is grafted onto the Cartesian idea of the infinite, for in addressing someone it is always a matter of placing something more into something less. It is not the I who understand the command before it is addressed to me, but in the command my ethical existence, and thus my existence *tout court* for Levinas, becomes possible. Yet hidden in the idea of the infinite is a much different meaning of transcendence. Rather than an isolated self breaking out its identity by responding to the Other from a distance, its self-sufficiency is already broken, shattered and fragmented from within. Teaching is the relation of an interiority to exteriority from the outside, to the presence of Other, which precedes ethical speech in the command they utter. The idea of the infinite, on other hand, is an *interiority exteriorised*, turned inside out, folded over, and containing more than it is possible to contain.

None of this stops Levinas from trying to Platonise the idea of the infinite, thereby substituting an interiority exteriorised for an exteriority interiorised, imposed as it is from the outside, and this step is never more apparent than in the description of the separation or autonomy of the self as an atheism. What lurks beneath this idea of atheism is the relation of the creator and created. The peculiar consequence of this is that the 'death of God' is subordinate to the existence of God, since it is the contraction of God which allows for the independence of the creature.[8] The independence of the creature exists only to the extent of the withdrawal of the infinite. Its atheism is secondary to the original contraction of God's existence, and multiplicity would be a secondary effect of this dependence rather than a original inter-penetration of the terms in the relation. Separation is conditional on the primacy of the Other, whether as a demand, or in this case, a contraction, which comes to the self from the outside. It is, therefore, impossible to say that both terms *equally* absolve themselves from the relation. Or to put it another way, the 'relation without relation', multiplicity, where the terms in the relation relate directly to one another without a mediating term, is conditional upon another relation which is not a relation of multiplicity, but interpellation. Interpellation is the *superiority* or *ascendancy* of the Other over the Same. Only because the God contracts; that is to say first of all relates to itself, can the I be separate from God.

This does not mean that relation between the infinite and the finite, as it is conceived in the idea of creation, is the same as a totality, where the finite is merely a part of the infinite, but neither is it a relation of pure multiplicity, if the latter is defined as the separation of terms in the relation, what Levinas calls their 'reciprocal exteriority' (Levinas 1969, 293). It cannot be mutual separation, since the relation of the self to the Other is dependent on the anterior significance of the Other, which determines the ethical relation (if we might use this Kantian expression) as the condition of its possibility. The exteriority of the Other, in relation to the self, is *more* exterior than the exteriority of the self in relation to the Other. Rather than a 'reciprocal exteriority', as Levinas describes it, the exteriority of the Other is an *exteriority of an exteriority*. It is in this sense that we begin to see why Levinas can write that the Other 'resembles God' (Levinas 1969, 293). This exteriority of exteriority does not transform the separation of the terms in the relation to an opposition, where the difference between the terms is conceived only from the position outside of the relation itself. The exteriority of exteriority is not the vantage point of a theoretical gaze which would see both terms in a glance, and understand that their opposition is the expression of a deeper unity, rather it *produces* their exteriority to one another from the outside. This is the conjunction between the idea of creation and speech. Both implicate a relation to the Other outside of the relation of multiplicity implied by Levinas's expression of a 'relation without relation'. It is the self-identity of the terms in the relation that constitute the difference between the terms, and not the difference itself. Moreover the identity of the self is dependent on the identity of the Other. We mean by the 'identity of the Other' not what Levinas means by the identity of the Same, which is the idea of totality, but that the Other is defined by its *self-differentiation* from the Same. Again this logic is most visible in the idea of atheism. For atheism is not at all possible, and this is the strange consequence of Levinas's argument, except as an aftereffect of God's withdrawal. Atheism would then be the best proof of God's existence. It is only because God differentiates itself, contracts His own essence, that another identity, which is not God, is possible. What initially appears at first glance as an 'reciprocal exteriority' is not at all, since the exteriority of the terms in the relation is dependent on the external self-differentiation of God, more exterior than the exteriority of the world. The separation of the world is not reciprocal to the transcendence of the God. In other words, it is not simply the negative image of this transcendence. Yet without transcendence there could be no atheism. The separation of the I is dependent on the self-separation of the Other. Only the transcendence of the Other is utterly independent and absolute, whereas the independence of the I is dependent.

Descartes

The assertion of the primacy of the infinite over the finite gives a precedence to the logical, as opposed to the chronological, relation between the terms. Again, referring to Descartes' argument for the existence of God in the *Meditations*, chronologically speaking, the evidence of the *cogito* precedes the idea of the infinite (Levinas 1969, 54). For Levinas, this temporal distance, within the order of discourse, between the cogito and the idea of the infinite, expresses the mutual separation of the terms. The I is independent of the Other, and is utterly complete and self-sufficient. What we come to discover, however, in the unfolding of the argument, is that the primacy of the cogito is an illusion. The order of discourse is reversed by the order of reasons. The evidence of the cogito, though it appears first in the series of the meditations, is logically dependent on the existence of God, since without God's existence, I would not exist at all. The chronological unfolding of the argument is subject to the logical conclusions, and much of Descartes dispute with the objections to the *Meditations* has to do with his correspondents failure to differentiate between the superiority of the logical over the chronological order.[9] The same is true also of *Totality and Infinity*, at least in the way that Levinas wants us to read it. Though the separation of the terms in the relation appears first, the independence of the self is in fact logically dependent on the prior absolution of the Other from the relation. It is only because the Other attends to the words they speak in its own unique relation to language that the self can be autonomous at all. Without the speech of the Other it remains immersed within the world, and hardly distinguishable from nature.

What is significant, however, about Levinas's Cartesianism, is that it allows us to read the meaning of this relation in quite another way. This is to be found in the actual detail of the argument for the existence of God, rather than the coherence of the *Meditations* as a whole. What is at the heart of Descartes' proof is the non-correspondence of the idea of the God and its *ideatum* (what is represented in the idea). Their divergence is not determined by an opposition between immanence and transcendence, or even the infinite and the finite, but by the *interruption* of the *cogito* from within. What distinguishes the idea of God from any other, such as the idea of an external or imaginary object, is that even though the idea of the God is immanent to the *cogito*, an interval nonetheless remains between it and what it is meant to represent. This means, unlike any other idea, whose origin could be in myself, I cannot be the origin of the idea of God. For if I were its origin, then I would be able to represent the content of this idea to myself, as I can with any other idea. Although I can understand the idea of God, as Descartes writes in the first set of objection and replies, this does not mean that I know what God is (Descartes 1984, 81). The idea of God is, therefore, in my mind, but it cannot come from within me. Such is the paradox that the mind can contain more than it is possible for it to contain. Such a paradox subverts the exclusive relation between the infinite and the finite, since the distance between the idea and the *ideatum* is *internal* and not external to the idea. Yet even though it is internal to the idea, it does not belong to the idea as such, otherwise the *ideatum* would be perfectly representable in the idea (Levinas 1969, 48-9).

The 'in' of the infinite is not a sign of negation, but inclusion. The surplus of the infinite over the finite is internal, not external to the finite. Because the idea and the *ideatum* are not one in the idea of the infinite, we cannot say that there really is an object that corresponds to its idea. The idea of the infinite appears to have the same form as all the other ideas within the *cogito*, but because I cannot grasp what the infinite is from within the *cogito*, I can give it no objective representation. All I can think is the difference between the idea and the *ideatum*, but I cannot think what this *ideatum* might be. I can think the idea of the infinite, but not the objective content of this idea. This means that the idea is, at one and the same time, immanent and transcendent to the *cogito*. Nonetheless, at least in the first stage of Descartes' argument, this surplus does not point to some reality external to it. The difference between the idea and the *ideatum* belongs internally to consciousness, similar in structure to the immanent transcendence Levinas discovers in Husserl. The idea of the infinite is, therefore, an *involution* of the *cogito*, rather than an externalisation. We say 'at the first stage', because of course Descartes will later, in the same priority of the order of reasons over the order of discourse, subordinate the fold of the infinite within the *cogito* to the objective existence of the God. Since I cannot be the origin of the difference between the idea and the *ideatum*, it must have an external source, which corresponds to the content I cannot represent.

What concerns us here is not so much the legitimacy of Descartes' proof, but the model of alterity it seems to imply: the peculiar moments in Descartes' argument where the cogito becomes involuted, turned inside out around a surplus it cannot comprehend, which then becomes uncoiled and flattened out by an exterior transcendence this surplus is meant to signify. *Totality and Infinity*, itself can be read in the tension of these two moments. On the one hand, there is the immanent difference between idea and the *ideatum*, and on the other, the transcendent difference between the very same idea and its external reference. Levinas attempts to think these two moments together, whereas we might ask whether they are completely different relations. The idea of the infinite and the metaphysics of language operate by a completely different logic of relations. The first is an inclusive, and the second an exclusive separation of the terms in the relation. In the first the Other is within the self, and in the second it is external to the self. Levinas obscures this variance, in a similar way to Descartes' proof, by subordinating the internal difference between the idea and the *ideatum*, to the external difference of the absolute Other. The idea of the infinite then becomes the desire *for* the infinite, and the involution of the self is only for the sake of the presence of the Other in language. And yet, although the logic of inclusive separation is marginalised and rejected in *Totality and Infinity*, it becomes the model for alterity in the idea of substitution in *Otherwise than Being*. Before we reach the discussion of this idea in the next chapter, however, we need to see how, by using the notion of inclusive rather than exclusive separation, we can give a completely different importance, significance and meaning to the status of the feminine in Levinas's work, than perhaps he himself does. For the feminine, (more than any other description in *Totality and Infinity*), and this probably explains both its importance and marginal status in the argument, is caught between these two different meanings of alterity.

The feminine

In lectures that Levinas gave immediately after the war, and which bear the title *Time and the Other*, he told his listeners that the only other that can be truly other is the feminine (Levinas 1987b, 85). This would mean that the difference between the sexes is not a specific difference in the way that 'rational' distinguishes human beings from animals, but a 'formal structure' breaking up the unity of human existence as a whole. The difference between the sexes is not merely a distinction between them that can be understood empirically, as any other difference between a species, but the very possibility of a 'reality as multiple' (Levinas 1987b, 85). This is because this difference is not merely the opposition of one sex to the other through distinguishing marks and characteristics, in a way, for example, that the botanist might speak of the sexual parts of a plant, but a very split within human existence. Sexuality is not merely a definition of human existence, but the very way in which that existence *is*. This is why sexual difference is not something that befalls human sexuality from the outside, as though first of all there were a neutral human existence, and then, in a second moment, this neutrality becomes either masculine or feminine.

If human existence is sexual, then it cannot be one, but must be, at least, a multiplicity of two. This multiplicity must not be confused with a duality, for the latter is dependent on a unity that precedes it. The difference between the sexes is not the difference between two things, for number requires a common measure. Sexuality is not something inert. It is not simply the counter position of two dissimilar objects; rather it is a way of existing. Human existence is multiple, cannot be thought of as one, which is really to say, cannot be thought as masculine, because the feminine withdraws itself from the masculine gaze. It is 'a mode of being,' Levinas writes, 'that consists in slipping away from the light' (Levinas 1987b, 87). The feminine interrupts the general unity of being in which all things and persons are made visible. The feminine is not mysterious or obscure, as merely the play of light and shade, which has been its resonance throughout Western culture, but the very absence of the visibility of the visible, a darkness more dark than the rhythm of day and night. This is why the alterity of the feminine is not to be confused with the 'object's simple exteriority' (Levinas 1987b, 87). An object might or might not be difficult to grasp, but this difficulty rests upon the side of the perceiver, who might fail to see it. Every object has the potential to be seen. It makes no sense to speak of an unseen object, for an object that is not given to the senses is no object at all. The feminine escapes my gaze not as an object within my field of vision, but as outside of this field of vision altogether. Nor is the relation between the sexes one of equalities, for again both terms would have to be thought through a third term which would be common to them, and which on further analysis would be discovered to have its origin in one of the terms in the relation. Are not liberty, freedom and equality masculine ideas, which hide their neutrality in supposed objectivity and reason? And if they seek to abolish the difference between the sexes, do they not do so through masculinity? A strange abolition which would preserve one of the terms in the relation by disengaging it from the reality of its sex. To preserve the multiplicity of sexual difference, we must begin with the difference between the terms first of all, and not think this difference in terms of an identity which precedes them. The feminine is not different from the masculine because it is *not* the masculine, rather it is *other* than the masculine. 'The other,' Levinas writes, though he will cease to use this kind of expression after *Time and the Other*, 'bears alterity as an essence' (Levinas 1987b, 87-8). This already suggests the logic of the 'relation without relation' of *Totality and Infinity*. The terms hold their difference within themselves. Alterity is not a comparison between terms, as though the Other and Same were recto and verso of the same page, but they are absolutely different from one another. Their difference precedes any identity.

Added to the precedence of difference over identity, is the requirement that difference always comes from the side of the Other. What permits multiplicity is the alterity which the 'other carries as its essence', and if the same is also 'absolved' from this relation, then it is because of this 'first' alterity. The logic of separation, as we have seen, hides within it an inequality of terms. It is important to stress, however, that this superiority of the Other is not the same as the domination and submission which governs the relation of identity, where everything is reduced to the same. In this case, it is the identity between the terms which precedes the relation, and not their difference. The inequality lies at the level of what we might call a condition without which multiplicity, the rupture of the totality of being, would not be possible. The terms in the relation do not absolve themselves at the same level. The separation of the same is conditional on the verticality of the Other, the 'Most High' (*Le Très-Haut*). The alterity of the Other precedes the separation of the Same. The verticality of the Other threatens that the ethical relation will fall back into a relation of identity, determined in advance by the uniqueness of the Other, and not by the mutual differentiation of the terms in the relation.

In the idea of the feminine, the logic of separation also implies that the break with the unity of being never happens from the side of the masculine, but only from the feminine. Alterity determines the Same, if the masculine ideal is defined in this way, and not the other way around. The masculine by itself is the unity of being. It is the alterity of the feminine which reveals the fiction of this unity by demonstrating in her very existence that being is more than one, and thus the masculine belongs to the multiplicity of being as much as she does. She is, or not even 'is', if 'is' is what he is, always more than he can say about her. She is an exception to his being, but it is only this exception which proves that being is not one, not even his. What is important however, and what differentiates the feminine from the idea of atheism, is that this exceptionality of the feminine does not repeat the exclusive separation of the terms which we find in *Totality and Infinity*. This has to do with the very ambiguous status of the feminine in this work. Negatively, because of the very priority given to the exclusive relation, the feminine is given a marginal status, even placed outside the very argument of the book in the section 'Beyond the Face'. Positively, however, we can read the marginalisation of the feminine as postulating a new idea of alterity, one which is inclusive rather than exclusive, and indeed becomes the dominant modal of alterity after *Totality and Infinity*. This gives a whole new meaning to separation. It is not the Other which differentiates itself from the Same from afar, rather this region is already split; it is already differentiated from the very beginning.

When Simone de Beauvoir read *Time and the Other*, she was quite horrified because she misunderstood alterity to mean exactly the opposite to Levinas's own conception, as merely the debased form of masculinity.[10] For her, the relation between the sexes is to be thought in terms of reciprocity. Just as much as the woman is determined by the man, the man should be determined by the woman. But what would count as the neutral operation between these differences? To what would we appeal to be the common measure for this reciprocal action? For Levinas, on the contrary, the relation between the sexes is one of difference prior to reciprocity, and rather than there being a mutual 'reciprocity of a subject and object', it is the man who is determined and differentiated in relation to the woman. The absence of difference belongs to the history of the man, not the woman, and equality is the culmination of this history.

And yet, despite Simone de Beauvoir's hasty judgement, we might feel that we are rushing to Levinas's defence a bit too quickly here. For the status of the feminine in *Totality and Infinity* is not the same as in *Time and the*

Other. She still has the status of the Other, but not the ethical Other. She appears within the familiarity of the home, but is excluded from the seriousness and importance of ethics, and in eroticism, she is excluded from fecundity. You can caress or be comfortable with her, and the 'you' here is definitely masculine, but you should not take her too seriously. She is not, you might say, responsible enough.[11] So it would seem that eventually Simone de Beauvoir is right, though not in the sense that she had originally intended. Levinas's ethics does exclude the feminine from what is 'essential', not because it rejects her status as a subject, but as a figure for alterity.

The meaning of alterity is first marked by sexual difference, which is the expression of the relation itself and not a term in the relation, only to be remarked by an ethical indifference, where the feminine becomes identified with a sexual description which does not seem to be very dissimilar from the most predictable ideological content, where the woman is a either a domestic presence or an erotic plaything. In the first case, the feminine is detached from the woman to become the general expression of the plurality of being. In the second, the feminine falls back into the social role of the woman, as it is defined in opposition to the man. She *is* only to the extent that she is not a man, whereas the man is the measure of what it means to be. Her definition is only to the extent that she differs from man, but it is man who acts as the measure through which everything else gains its meaning. This is why man can appear as a neutral objectivity, whereas everything else is a specific difference. This only works, because the specificity of man, which is an historical and social reality, remains concealed in discourse.

Nonetheless we might hesitate for a moment here in our indictment of Levinas. As we have argued, *Totality and Infinity* is crossed by a double meaning of alterity. On the one hand there is the metaphysics of language, where the Other is opposed to self, and on the other, the idea of the infinite, immanent transcendence, where the Other interrupts the subject from within. If we read the feminine from the perspective of the first meaning, and it is certain that Levinas wants us to read *Totality and Infinity* in this way, then the idea of the feminine is subordinated to the ethical relation, whose supposed neutrality conceals a masculine bias. But if we read the idea of the feminine through the second meaning, then, against Levinas's intentions, we could understand it as the interruption and dislocation of the neutrality of the ethical relation. To read *Totality and Infinity* in this way is to detach the idea of the feminine from its reduction to a content of sexual difference, where the feminine is opposed to the masculine, so that it becomes the image of subjectivity *tout court*, without at the same time, as is the case in the transcendence of the masculine, concealing its sexuality. It is as though, beneath the ethics of responsibility, and the neutrality of the Other, there subsisted the enigmatic and ambiguous presence of the feminine, one which the text both exposes and conceals.

This ambivalence is present in the passages devoted to the description of the dwelling in *Totality and Infinity*. Even before the relation of speech, the interiority of the subject is hollowed out from the inside by the Other. This other relation is not a relation to the Other which stands above me, but one in which the exteriority of the Other is interiorised. Levinas writes of my enjoyment of the world being disturbed by an uncertainty and inquietude from within, which is the mark of the difference between the human being and the animal (Levinas 1969, 149). This disturbance of enjoyment happens within enjoyment. It does not occur after I have enjoyed the world, but accompanies enjoyment from the beginning, and if it is this restlessness which distinguishes human from animal enjoyment, it must also be its very condition. Without this restlessness, there would be no *human* enjoyment. The source of this inquietude, whose ultimate end would be suicide, that I am never satisfied within satisfaction, that pleasure, happiness and consumption are never enough, is the Other. It is only because my interiority is already interrupted by the Other, prior even to speech, that my own existence is not enough for me. My existence is not only called into question from the outside, but also from within. The source of my conscience is the other person. 'Suicide,' Levinas writes 'appears as a possibility to a being already in relation with the Other, already elevated to the life *for the Other*' (Levinas 1969, 149). Such a relation to the Other, Levinas describes as intimacy. If it is an emotion or mood, then it should not be comprehended as something merely psychological. Intimacy is first of all a relation to the future. There is an insecurity that belongs to enjoyment which is not disquietude or restlessness, but is the 'concern for the morrow' (Levinas 1969, 150). Being concerned about the 'next day' is not egotistical, because it opens up, from within interiority, the self to Other. Being with others is not one possibility of mine amongst many others, which I could choose or not; rather the relation to the Other is the condition of the future in which something like having possibilities is possible. The future is conditional on the relation to the Other, and not the other way around. The future is not my possibility at all, it is the time of the Other. The Other of speech, who is exterior to my interiority, is sexually neutral (though of course we might be suspicious that like every neutrality it is really masculine), but the Other of time, who is interior to my interiority, *intimate*, is feminine, a 'extraterritoriality' within man's territoriality (Levinas 1969, 150).

There is a real problem here. How are we to fit this relation to the Other, which is a relation of sexual difference, to the other relation, which is sexually neutral? Levinas immediately surmounts it by referring the relation to the feminine to the logic of the 'relation without relation', but this is merely an abstract and formal description, which in itself has nothing at all to do with sexual difference. When Levinas writes that we must understand the non-dialectical and non-oppositional force of the idea of the infinite through 'feminine grace', he says something much stranger. Does he mean that every relation to the Other must also be a relation to a woman, or is there a more general concept of the feminine which would displace the neutrality of masculine discourse, in which women themselves are defined in opposition to men? This seems to be the case when Levinas adds that 'femininity' has nothing to with the 'empirical absence of the human being of the "feminine sex"' (Levinas 1969, 158). The extraterritoriality of the feminine would be something much stranger than merely the ideological repetition of sexual difference, it would be the contortion of this relation itself, whereby the extraterritorial difference of the feminine would pass between the sexes, just as the territoriality of the masculine has always passed between them.

If this were the case, then this extraterritoriality would be as much a question to Levinas as another philosopher. Is it not also a problem for the neutrality of the ethical relation in speech? The problem is circumvented by denying the feminine the proper status of alterity, as though there could be degrees of alterity. What would be the common measure of alterity which could determine whether something was more or less other? The answer is language. The feminine is not a true alterity, or at least not absolutely other, because it does not enter the relation of speech, where the Other is unambiguously and directly present in the words spoken. 'This alterity,' Levinas writes 'is situated on another plane than language' (Levinas 1969, 155). How can there be two alterities each with their own level? Is it not really the case that the alterity of the feminine is less than the alterity of the Other in speech, because the latter determines what a proper alterity might be? Does not Levinas confirm this when he compares the alterity of the feminine to Buber's 'I and Thou', since elsewhere he had distinguished this relation from his own account of alterity, because it did not sufficiently emphasize the distance between the two terms in the relation (Levinas 1969, 155)? The feminine, even though it is exterior to the self, is not exterior enough. Because its exteriority *inhabits* the interiority of the self. It is, to an extent, compromised by it. It is too close to the self, its intimacy conveys too much familiarity, and it lacks the necessary distance and height of the proper alterity of speech.

This is puzzling. How can the feminine be other and not other enough? Why does Levinas step back from permitting it to be truly other? One answer is to appeal to the ideological content of the descriptions, and posit that

Levinas is merely importing within a supposedly concrete phenomenological description of human existence, the content of a conservative conception of the social roles of men and woman, perhaps shaped by his orthodox Judaism. The description of the extraterritoriality of the feminine, however, might make us hesitate from making this judgement. For all their ideological content, these descriptions nonetheless break through the opposition of sexual difference, by granting a generality to the idea of the feminine which exceeds the supposedly empirical fact of being a woman defined in opposition to the logic of the masculine. Why Levinas steps back from granting the feminine the true status of alterity is not just because of these ideological prejudices, but because to do so would undermine the exclusive logic of the ethical relation. An interesting thought experiment would be to link the inclusive logic expressed in the idea of the infinite to the idea of the feminine, and thereby *feminise* the idea of the infinite. This does not mean to make the Other a woman, since the extraterritoriality of the feminine passes between the sexes, but it would mean to make the woman the starting point of the relation to the Other. To do so changes the whole status of alterity. It would no longer be defined through the height and straight-forwardness of the interpellation of speech, where the Other is fully present in the spoken word, but an enigmatic and ambiguous alterity of contact, touch and emotion. It is significant that it is this alterity, and not the alterity of speech, which increasingly becomes the model of the ethical relation after *Totality and Infinity*. If we hold onto the generality of the idea of the feminine, then we might say that this Other is progressively feminised.

This does not prevent us from recognising that at this point the alterity of the feminine threatens the formal argument of *Totality and Infinity*. Its ambivalent status, and perhaps to a higher degree, is repeated in the description of eroticism at the end of the book. Heightened, because Levinas will write that the transcendence of the feminine 'goes both further and less far than language' (Levinas 1969, 254). In habitation, the feminine is, first of all, before its degradation below the proper alterity of speech, an equivalent description of the relation to the Other. If it is discovered later to be less transcendent than the Other of speech this is not because previously it was more so. Levinas interrupts the phenomenological analysis of eroticism by reminding us of the ethical 'signification' of language (Levinas 1969, 261). The face does not signify like any other object in the world. It is not granted its meaning by an act of consciousness. It already 'signifies itself' before any bestowal of meaning. It does so not because, like some mysterious sign, it hides a meaning within itself that can only be read by an initiate. The Other is not a palimpsest. The Other has its own meaning, because it is the origin of all meaning. 'One does not have to explain it,' Levinas writes, 'for every explana-tion begins with it' (Levinas 1969, 261). The Other is not a sign, but the beginning of all signs. The world has a meaning, because I speak of it to someone. Comprehension, thematisation, reason is already orientated by this prior relation to the Other that takes place in speech. I do not speak of the Other, first of all, but I am addressed by the Other, and this address, interpel-lation or command is the condition of speaking about anything at all. Objectification is not primary, for first of all there is the relation to the Other in which something like objectification or sense would have a direction. Levinas is not denying representation, but its possibility of grounding itself. The image of the world in representation is something which is given to the Other, who is not part of this image. To signify is not, first of all, to present a sign, but the presentation of the Other in speech to whom I respond. This means that the Other is not to be understood as a mysterious sign which I cannot under-stand, but as the original condition of all signification. Speaking is first of all speaking to someone, whose impetus is the address of the Other. It is this address which breaks through the meaninglessness which continually threat-ens the existence of the I. Interpellation gives to the world its human face.

If the feminine goes less far than language it is because the woman, is associated with this absurdity and equivocity which speech dispels. In this moment, it is evident that the feminine is enclosed within the division of the sexes defined by the masculine ideal. In other words, it ceases to have an 'extraterritoriality' which passes between being a woman or a man. Why does the feminine cease to have a general signification, why does it no longer have the proper status of alterity? Because to grant it this status would mean that the Other would be almost indistinguishable from the 'there is'.[12] For the meaninglessness and absurdity which is dispersed by the presence of the Other in the words they speak, is the 'rumbling of the there is', and the presence of the feminine cannot be separated from it (Levinas 1969, 261). The idea of the feminine must be restricted to the specificity of being a woman, so as to prevent the ethical relation from being contaminated by the 'there is'. The ideological content of Levinas's descriptions, therefore, supports a meth-odological necessity, and not the other way around. By limiting the ambiva-lent relation of the Other and the 'there is' to the woman, sexual difference, in a restricted sense, infiltrates ethics. For if the improper alterity is feminine, then the proper alterity must be masculine, and rather than the relation to Other (as is almost promised in the description of habitation) breaking through the mutual opposition of gender defined by a masculine ideal, it falls backs within the self-same opposition.

The idea of the feminine is excessive within *Totality and Infinity*, because of its ambiguity and ambivalence. The feminine is neither present nor absent, neither transcendent nor immanent, neither interior nor exterior. If Levinas excludes the general idea of the feminine from ethics proper, from the signification of the Other in the straightforwardness of speech, this is not for merely ideological, but for systematic reasons. The general idea of the feminine undermines the exclusive separation of the terms in the relation, where the difference is subordinated to the prior self-identity of the terms, even if this identity is not determined by the idea of totality.[13] We might distinguish this conception of difference from a differential relation where difference expresses itself through the relation, rather than in one of the terms in the relation. The self differentiation of the terms of the relation would be a product of the differential relation, rather than its condition. This would detach the meaning of the Other from the other person. It is not the other person that bestows meaning on the Other, but it is the relation which transforms the other person into an 'other'. The relation of speech constricts the meaning of the Other to the presence of the other person who is already distinguished from the person that he or she interrogates. The idea of the feminine, on the contrary, as long as one does restrict its meaning to the content of the woman as she is defined in opposition to the man, is a differential relation, for its generality exceeds the opposition between the sexes. It is productive rather than denominative. It does not merely name a difference between terms that are already constituted, but produces the difference between them, and passes between this difference. If we associate the ethical relation of speech with the masculine ideal, then the generality of the feminine dissolves the absolute separation of the terms of the relation. This does not mean that it causes the difference between these terms to vanish, as though the generality of the feminine were exactly the same as the idea of totality. The inclusive separation of the terms is still a relation of multiplicity, but one where the multiplicity is not determined in advance by the identity of terms. This is not to say that this relation of inclusive separation is not more ambiguous, equivocal and ambivalent than exclusive separation, and this perhaps is the reason why Levinas does not give it the proper status of alterity. In the inclusive relation, the absolute distance between the terms is crossed, and it is this abolition of the distance between them which precludes multiplicity from being determined by the identity of the terms in advance. Interiority cannot be opposed to exteriority, because interiority is already exteriorized, presence cannot be contrary to absence, because it is already haunted by absence, and immanence cannot stand against transcendence, because at the heart of immanence there is already transcendence. 'I is an other,' Levinas writes elsewhere, repeating Rimbaud's enigmatic phrase (Levinas 2003, 60). It is this second relation, rather than the first, which, after *Totality and Infinity*, becomes increasingly the definition of alterity as substitution, the 'Other-in-the-Same'. This change also means that the emphasis on speech begins to diminish, because it is inseparable from the presence of the Other as a person, and the possibility of an interconnection between writing and ethics opens up.

Notes

1 The source of much confused misunderstanding of Levinas is the belief that alterity describes the property of a person, just as the colour 'red' is a property of a red stain. If alterity were a property, there would be no possibility of a singular relation to the Other, since it is clear that properties invite comparison between individuals, whether persons or things. As Jeffrey Dudiak rightly argues in *The Intrigue of Ethics*, '"Otherness", whether absolute or not, is not [...] a property that belongs to individuals, but already a relational term' (Dudiak 2001, 72).

2 Jean Luc Marion's influential critique of Levinas's ethics in *The Idol and Distance*, as merely a reversal of ontological difference, confuses alterity with a term in the relation, rather than then relation itself (see previous footnote). 'In a word,' Marion writes, 'the dominance of being over Being undoubtedly does not suffice to pass beyond ontology toward the Other, because that dominance presupposes, again and in its own way, the ontological difference (Marion 2001, 219).This already begs the question that the only possible relation is an ontological one. It is interesting to note that in a much latter essay he feels himself subjected to the same criticism that he himself accused Levinas of. 'When, in a recent work,' he writes, 'I pointed out this ambiguity [concerning Heidegger's notion of being], some critics believed or wanted to believe that I attempted to reverse the Heideggerian position: in place of privileging the call of Being, I thus would have - imitating the ambiguous gesture of Levinas in favour of the appeal *à-Dieu* - privileged the appeal of God.' (Marion 2000, 229-30). Levinas's 'gesture', ambiguous or otherwise, is not the same as that which Marion imagines his critics accuse him of. Whatever Levinas might mean by the Other, it is never a matter of evoking the priority of a being (God or some other being) over Being.

3 There is a mistake in the English translation here. Levinas writes: 'La *quis-nité* du *qui* s'excepte de la quiddité ontologique du *quoi* recherché et orientant la recherche' (Levinas 1978, 46). Translating *qui* as 'what' completely misses the sense of this sentence.

4 It is better to translate 'rapport sans rapport' as 'relation without relation', rather than as 'unrelating relation' (Levinas 1961, 271).

5 In the section 'Transcendence' pp.10-15.

6 The indefinite article is missing before the second 'relationship' in the English translation (Levinas 1961, 190).

7 'Le philosophe aura-t-il la force de transcender finalement la transcendance elle-même et de tomber vaillamment dans l'immanence sans laisser perdre sa valeur à son effort de transcendance?' [Will philosophy have

the force finally to transcend transcendence itself and fall valiantly into immanence without losing the value of its effort of transcendence?] (Wahl 1953,
721). The key section of the *Traité de métaphysique*, for this discussion is 'Le
Transcendant' (Wahl 1953, 642-9). The word 'transcendence', Jean Wahl argues, does not describe first of all an object, but a movement, and only then
goes on to signify the term towards which this movement ends. It is in the
thought of Heidegger, inspired by Husserlian phenomenology, that transcendence as movement is rediscovered. Wahl underlines precisely what Levinas
finds to be the most important in phenomenology: the idea of an immanent
transcendence. Transcendence is not an exterior term but a movement of the
ego outside of itself. And yet, Wahl hesitates to follow Husserl completely in
this direction. It is important to go beyond the opposition of transcendence
and immanence; but in making the ego the origin of transcendence, would not
transcendence totally disappear in immanence, as perhaps has always been
the case with idealism? Rather than attempting to find a solution to this problem in philosophy, Wahl turns to religion. In Judaism and Christianity, we are
faced with a different relation between immanence and transcendence. In one
sense, God is transcendent, but in another, immanent, since 'we live and
move' in him. The paradox of monotheism is, therefore, to maintain the transcendence of God in His immanence. Elsewhere in *Traité de métaphysique*,
Wahl will refer this paradox directly to the incarnation of Christ (Wahl 1953,
548). Although Levinas follows Wahl in this direction of an immanent transcendence there are two important differences: Firstly, he does rediscover in
Husserl this paradoxical meaning of transcendence, whereas Wahl does not,
and secondly, quite obviously, it is stripped of any association with the divin-
ity of Christ.

8 In this sense, despite Levinas's mistrust of mysticism (see, for example, his comments in *Difficult Freedom*, where he stresses that the authentic
Jewish practice ought to be separated from any taint of enthusiasm, passion
and mysticism (Levinas 1997, 14-16)), his description of creation, in *Totality
and Infinity*, is similar to the Jewish mystical tradition of *tsim-tsum*, where
creation is the result of the contraction of God, allowing room for the world,
rather than the act of bringing this world into being. The classical account of
this mystical idea, which through the Christian mystic Jacob Boheme had a
profound effect on the later writings of Schelling, can be found in Gershom
Scholem's *Major Trends in Jewish Mysticism* (Scholem 1941, 260-64).

9 So, for example., he writes to Mersenne on the 24 December 1640,
concerning the *Meditations*, that 'it should be noted that throughout the
work the order I follow is not the order of the subject matter, but the order of
reasoning (Descartes 1991, 163).

51

10 'She is defined,' Simone de Beauvoir writes, 'and differentiated with reference to man, and not he in reference with her; she is the incidental, the inessential as opposed to the essential. He is the Subject, he is the Absolute - she is the Other.' And in the footnote that follows, she continues, 'he deliberately takes a man's point of view, disregarding the reciprocity of subject and object. When he writes that woman is mystery, he implies that she is mystery for man. Thus his description, which is intended to be objective, is in fact an assertion of masculine privilege' (de Beauvoir 1988, 16).

11 The most thorough and critical reading of Levinas and the feminine is Stella Sandford's *The Metaphysics of Love* (Sanford 2000). I agree with her criticism of the feminist appropriation of *Totality and Infinity*, but she seems to be on less certain ground in her interpretation of *Otherwise than Being*. This is because she understands Levinas's idea of transcendence only as a repetition of Plato, and ignores the Cartesian structure of alterity outlined in this chapter. This overemphasis on Levinas's Platonism perhaps explains her less than convincing interpretation of maternity in *Otherwise than Being*, which follows the Cartesian model of immanent transcendence, and which will be discussed in the following chapter. For a good account of the different feminist positions in relation to Levinas's work as whole, see Tina Chanter's introduction to *Feminist Interpretations of Levinas* (Chanter 2001).

12 For still the most thorough, clear, and illuminating explanation of the 'there is' in both Levinas and Blanchot, see Simon Critchley's *Very Little...Almost Nothing* , which is indispensable (Critchley 1997, 31-83).

13 The source of this exclusivist logic is undoubtedly Rosenzweig. For an excellent account of the influence of Rosenzweig's philosophy on Levinas, see Robert Gibbs' book *Correlations in Rosenzweig and Levinas* (Gibbs 1992), and for Rosenzweig's philosophy itself Stéphane Moses' book *Système et Révélation: La philosophie de Franz Rosenzweig*, which has a preface written by Levinas (Moses 2003). The first work also demonstrates that one of the sources, beyond Plato, for the emphasis on speech in *Totality and Infinity* is the second part of *The Star of Redemption*. Nonetheless, where Gibbs sees a creative repetition between these two authors, as the word 'correlation' in the title appears to suggest, I see a subtle divergence. If we read Levinas through Blanchot, then the importance of speech over writing is undermined, and the difference between the Saying and the Said, which is so important to Levinas's later philosophy, ceases to be merely a description of speaking, but of language in general in which no priority is given to the spoken over the written word.

3

Substitution

It is not the metaphysics of language which acts as the bridge between *Totality and Infinity* and *Otherwise than Being,* but fecundity. In fecundity, the self is dispossessed of its identity from within, which Levinas describes as a 'transubstantiation' (Levinas 1969, 271). It is a 'transubstantiation', because in the erotic, the self is opened up to a future which is not its own. Nonetheless, this 'other' future is not totally separate either. The substance of subjectivity changes, but it does not become another substance opposed to the previous one. Or better still, it ceases to be a substance, if substance is defined in terms of identity. It is a substance other to itself from within itself. The Other takes my place, or this dispossession becomes my subjectivity. The future which is not my own, but which is inescapably tied to my future, is the future of the child, who is 'mine in a certain sense,' Levinas writes, 'or, more exactly, me, but not myself' (Levinas 1969, 271). This identity of the subject, Levinas tells us, takes us outside of the 'classical categories of logic' (Levinas 1969, 272). The self is not itself, but it has not become something other either; rather, it is both other and the same at the same time.

It is true that within Western philosophy the self has been understood as a split being, where one side of the self, like Socrates' *daimon* or Freud's unconscious, speaks to the other. But this split within the being of the subject defines the temporal unfolding of its identity in activity and thought, rather than its rupture by another's future more future than its own. The fold of subjectivity is not subjectivity's own, but the 'Other within the Same', a trans-substantiation of subjectivity's substance from within. This does not mean that the subject loses its identity, but it is defined precisely as this 'Other within the Same'. How is the interiority of the subject invaded by the exteriority of the Other? It is because the child both belongs to and does not belong to me. It is 'coveted' in the erotic relation, but its future is not *my* future. Unlike any other project which belongs to the course of my life, my child has a life of its own which I cannot anticipate and recuperate.

We shall see the same structure of subjectivity repeats itself in the description and analysis of substitution, which is at the heart of the argument of *Otherwise than Being*. We have, therefore, acting as a counterweight to the metaphysics of language, a sequence of models of alterity beginning with the idea of infinity and ending with substitution. Fecundity acts as the switching point of this sequence. What is placed at the margins of *Totality and Infinity*, to the extent that many commentators (including the most important, Derrida) can ignore it, becomes central to *Otherwise than Being*. This shift marks a movement in Levinas's work away from an emphasis on speech, and the separation, distance, and exteriority of the Other from the self, to the inclusion of alterity within subjectivity.

The child

No doubt there are some who do view their children like any other project, but this is only because they refuse their children lives of their own. They live their lives, their failed ambitions and wasted talents, through their children, but only so their children can disappear in their hopes and expectations, which are really only hopes and expectations for themselves. What concerns Levinas in the relation between the parent and the child, however, is not just that the child has a life of its own, and so cannot be said to be a project like any other, but that this life somehow comes to substitute for the life of the parent. The existence of the child displaces the life of the parent from within. To the extent that the child is granted its own life, and does not just become a mirror for the needs of the parent, it takes over the life of the parent. The parent is a hostage to the child. This is why Levinas can compare the relation between the child and the parent to the idea of the infinite (Levinas 1969, 267). The child haunts the parent from within, even before the parent speaks to the child, just as in Descartes, the idea of the infinite exists within the finite mind, even before it is thought. I still carry my child's life within me even after they are born, though this life does not become my life and we do not become one. The future of the child is not my future, but the future of an other. True this future, in a certain sense, belongs to my future, since I care what happens to my child, but it only belongs to my future because it is *their* future. If their future were only mine, then there would be only one future, and the future of the child would be obliterated.

Fecundity means that the recommencement of time is not merely the repetition of the same. The child is not the avatar of the parent, but a new beginning. One, however, which is also a continuation. The time of subjectivity is not just the inner time of a solitary ego, but the time of the relation to the Other. This relation is not determined by a time that would somehow lie outside both the terms of the relation, either the eternal time of the heavenly spheres, or the time of consciousness, or even as it is made concrete in the temporality of existence, but it is the time of the relation itself, the time between the self and the Other, a time that would come from the Other, from a future which would not be the same as the future that belongs to the present. The child interrupts the time of the parent, because it introduces another future into time, a future which is not continuous with the parent's time, with their own hopes and disappointments. The span of generations is not the repetition of the same, but the continual interruption of old age by youth. It is the rhythm of birth which breaks with the unity of being, for human existence is not closed in on itself, but already opened out to the Other from within. The relation between the parent and the child is the possibility that my own existence can contain within itself more than it is possible to contain, that it can contain another's existence without reducing this existence to its own. 'We thus,' Levinas writes 'leave the philosophy of Parmenidean being' (Levinas 1969, 269). We do so not through the power of thought, through inventing a concept of non-being which does not contradict being, as Heraclitus did, but because human life is already multiple. Sociality precedes thought, even the thought of existence, and I do not live alone first of all, and then in a second moment, live with others; rather, my life is already in the place of others. Solitariness is a contraction of being, not its emanation.

The descriptions of fecundity in *Totality and Infinity* marginalise language as the expression of ethics. In speech, the self is interpellated by the Other, which as a separated term constitutes, in its co-presence with the words spoken, the relation in advance. It is only to the extent that the alterity of the Other overflows the signification of language in general, in the assistance given to the spoken word, that there can be said to be an ethical moment at all. Yet fecundity is not speech, but time. Even before speech, the time of the child interrupts the time of the parent. If we examine this change with respect to the order of Levinas's work, then a strange displacement occurs. If fecundity follows the description of the ethical relation in the idea of the infinite, then the idea of the infinite also, despite Levinas' intentions, breaks with the metaphysics of language, since if the idea of the infinite and language were the same, then fecundity could not reassemble the idea of the infinite. It is for the sake of the unity of *Totality and Infinity* that Levinas links together speech and the idea of the infinite, but as argued in the previous chapter, they are a completely different relations.[1]

The difference between language and the idea of infinity, and the latter's reappraisal in fecundity, however, is not just a question of methodology, but also a matter of the interrelation between writing and ethics. We have already seen that in language writing can have no ethical significance. This is because, if ethics is defined in terms of language, and this language in turn, by the presence of the Other in the words uttered, then writing cannot be ethical, because the written word is read in the absence of its original author. In writing, language is not animated by living presence of the interlocutor, but remains the dead letters on the page, and even these letters, if they are to be reawakened, require the spoken word. And yet, just as the language of ethics closes off the relation between ethics and writing, the idea of infinity, and its reprise in fecundity, opens up the possibility of such a relation. A hint is given in the announcement that fecundity breaks with the philosophy of Parmenidean being. Levinas writes that 'philosophy itself' could be understood through the temporality of the idea of infinity and fecundity, because philosophy is addressed to another. Importantly, however, Levinas does not refer this address to a spoken word, as he would everywhere else in *Totality and Infinity*, but to a written one. 'Philosophy itself,' he writes, 'constitutes a moment of this temporal accomplishment [the splitting of being into the multiple], a discourse always addressed to another. What we are now exposing is addressed to those who shall wish to read it' (Levinas 1969, 269).

This statement cannot, first of all, be understood within the ethics of language, because writing, even the writing of *Totality and Infinity*, cannot be 'addressed to another'. One way of situating it within the overall argument would be to subordinate the relation between a book and a reader to the interpellation of the self by the Other. Levinas might claim that it is because the self is addressed by the Other, before any written word, that it can write a book addressed to an Other. This is what Levinas means when he argues, elsewhere in *Totality and Infinity*, that representation, thematisation and narration are secondary to interpellation (Levinas 1969, 204-9). Yet what Levinas describes here does not seem merely to be a secondary act of representation pure and simple, but a writing which is straight away already an address to another, obsessed by the Other, even before it has become representation, thematisation and narration, and which can be read in that way.

In fecundity, alterity goes beyond the Other of speech, and this is the peculiar status of the last section of *Totality and Infinity*, where the relation to the Other is no longer a relation to the presence of the Other in person, but opens onto a time which exceeds the immediacy of the face-to-face relation of speech. In the relation to the child, the desire for the child opens out to the child's desire. It is transcendence for the sake of the transcendence of the child. As Levinas will say in his later writings, I am not just responsible for the

Other, but responsible for the Other's responsibility. I am substituted for the Other. The Other takes my place. In being substituted for the Other, I do not simply carry myself along to the other locale unchanged, as though I were going on a journey from which I would return the same as I had begun, but my subjectivity becomes something other to itself. It is no longer something which I possess, but something which dispossesses me, and yet, this disentitled subject is the very possibility of my individuality and uniqueness.

Fecundity is the reversal of the meaning of transcendence, which is no longer an inside existing without, but an outside existing within. The self is not first of all solitary, then proceeding outside of itself towards the world and other selves which are equally solitary (a process whereby society would be merely be the addition of separate beings in a 'General Will) but from the very beginning its existence is already plural. The existence of the child belongs to my interiority, but that very status ensures that this existence can no longer be thought of as a self-identity which precedes the world. My self is occupied by the existence of the child prior to any choice or decision. I do not exist for the child in the sense of making the child part of my activity, plans and projects, rather existing for the child is *my* existence. The different future of the child interrupts the transcendence of my possibilities of my being. It goes much further than these possibilities, because it is not just one more possibility amongst others, but another existence which takes my place, usurping it, and opening me onto another time than my own. In so doing, the life of the child extends me beyond myself. It is a distention of my inner life which begins not from myself, but from the Other.

There are many things, certainly, I can choose to be or not to be, and there are other possibilities which I cannot avoid at all. All these possibilities are also an extension of my existence beyond a simple point in the present, but they are included within this present. My existence is dilated to include both my past and my future. The existence of the child, its own future, the future of another, rather than my own, expands my life in another sense and direction. It dilates it from within to the extent that the child is not merely added to my other possibilities, but completely transforms them in their totality. They are lived through the life of an Other. This is what Levinas means by saying that existence is itself plural, rather than plurality being added to existence as one attribute of social existence. In living *for* the life of an Other, this life does not just become one more added part of my life. There is not a unity between my life and the life of the child, rather the life of the child inserts itself within the very interstices of my life, such that my whole life is coloured by his or her life. Being weighed down by the life of the child is not something chosen, if by choosing we mean deciding between different possibilities. The preciousness of the life of the child means that she or he is not one possibility amongst others, not part of my existential drama. The life of the child is more important to me even than my own death. I am responsible for this life, which obsesses me, beyond my death. This is the meaning of future beyond my future, one which actually interrupts my future, extends my existence beyond its limits and boundaries. I fear not for my own death, but the death of the child, even to sacrificing my own life for him or her.[2]

Otherwise than Being

Levinas is already using, in the descriptions of fecundity in *Totality and Infinity*, the vocabulary of *Otherwise than Being*. He employs the very same language of election, uniqueness and substitution (Levinas 1969, 279). We ought not, however, to interpret this as a continuity, as though both works merely express the same form of alterity. The change of language in the depiction of fecundity is the displacement of one relation of alterity by another. The last section of *Totality and Infinity* does not complete the book as a whole, as we argued in the first chapter, but disrupts its unity.[3] Similarly, *Otherwise than Being* is not merely a continuation of *Totality and Infinity*, but an extension of the latter's own self-interruption and disruption. There are two different forms of the ethical relation in Levinas, which are *mutually incompatible*: the first, where the Other is opposed to the self through language, and which on the whole dominates the conception of Levinas's ethics, whether critical or appreciative, and the second, where the self is occupied, substituted, or displaced by the Other from within, and which, on the contrary, is almost absent in the reception of his work.

Despite Levinas's intentions, these two relations cannot be thought together. The structure of the 'Other-in-the-Same' is not the same as the composition of the ethical relation in speech. The difference between these two relations is the translation or inversion of the interval or distance between the terms in the relation from an exteriority to an interiority, and from an exclusive to an inclusive difference. In *Totality and Infinity*, it is the feminine which marks this difference in the relation. This is not to deny the ambiguity of the feminine in this work, because the meaning of ethics, in *Totality and Infinity*, is, by and large, expressed through the exteriority of language. As we have already seen in the previous chapter, this ambivalence is most forcefully present in the descriptions of the Eros.[4] Fecundity, however, takes this argument one step further, because the uncertainty about the feminine (perhaps because Levinas can now describe fecundity in terms of the relation to the son), is dropped. Fecundity is not an addition to the metaphysics of language, but expresses a completely different meaning of alterity. Thus, the temptation to avoid it completely in the explanation of *Totality and Infinity*, since it undermines the completeness, exhaustiveness, and coherence of the metaphysics of language as the legitimation of alterity. And yet, it is fecundity, not the metaphysics of language, which is the precursor for *Otherwise than Being*.

Care is needed here not to take this internalisation of the difference between the Other and the self as being the same as its abolition, negation or destruction. We have already seen the Other does not disappear in this relation in the analysis of fecundity. Though I am my son, in the sense that my life is substituted by his, this does not mean that he and I become one. '*To be* one's son,' Levinas writes, 'to be I in one's son, to be substantially in him, yet without being maintained there identically' [author's italics] (Levinas 1969, 278-9). It is for this reason that the relation of fecundity breaks through the alternative of *Totality and Infinity*, which seems to offer only two options: either there is the relation to the Other which respects the exteriority or distance of the Other above the self, or one which denies this interval by making the Other part of the self. In fecundity, the Other does become part of the self, or better the self becomes part of the Other, but this does not lead to them becoming one and the same. Perhaps this exceeds the idea of ontological unity to a greater extent than the exteriority of the Other, for the latter, to some degree, in the designation of καθ' αὐτό, is still thought of in terms of identity. The Other is defined in advance as opposed to the self, since it absolves itself, in language, from the ethical relation differently than the self. The I's relation to language, on the contrary, objectivity, representation and reason, is dependent on this prior relation of the Other to language in speech. In the relation of exteriority, the terms that are opposed to one another, the Other and the Same, are still described as being identical to themselves, as though they were separate substances, an ethical dualism which takes the place of an ontological one. There is a tension, in *Totality and Infinity*, of conceiving the Other only in a relation to the self, and vice versa, but also as conceiving both terms as self-identical to themselves outside any relation. The relation itself, therefore, rather than the terms in the relation, can end up being thought of through identity rather difference. Thus, although the terms are thought of as separate, different from one another, the relation between them is not. Their difference is determined by their self-identity of terms and not the other way around. It is only with the idea of infinity and fecundity that Levinas begins to elaborate a different kind ethical notion of substance or unicity, and he does

59

so by re-interpreting the difference of terms of the relation not through their own self-identity, but through the substitution of one by the other. I am who I am only to the extent that I am already Other, but equally the Other is only Other to the extent that it is the rupture of this self-identity. Alterity is no longer the designation of a term separate from the self, but is the very meaning of subjectivity transformed by alterity from within. Rather than understanding Levinas's work as the destruction and annihilation of the self for the sake of the Other, which tends to repeat the form of the Hegelian dialectic it is meant to escape, we should see it as the creation and invention of a new way of thinking about the subject. Ethics is a re-interpretation of subjectivity, of what it might mean to be a self, not one more sign of its demise.

Fecundity does not arise from a discourse between the Other and the self, but the substitution of the self by the Other. This means that the alterity of the Other no longer lies on the side of the other person, but *within* the interiority of the subject. It is this relation, rather than the former, which is the crux of *Otherwise than Being*. What is marginal in the overall argument of *Totality and Infinity* becomes central to the second work, and rather than just being the description of a particular and specific relation of the father to the son, it becomes the *general* description of ethics. There is no priority, in *Otherwise than Being*, given to the face to face relation, to conversation, speech or dialogue, as the expression of the alterity of the Other. Ethics, rather, now becomes an archaeology of a subject older than, and therefore on the other side of, consciousness.[5] The separation of the self is now no longer fundamental to the ethical relation. Unlike *Totality and Infinity*, we do not first go through a description of the existence of the self, whose enjoyment of the world, is then, in a second moment, interrupted or disturbed by the interpellation of the Other. On the contrary, my subjectivity, right to its very core, is already occupied and obsessed by the Other *before* intentionality, or even concrete existence which would be its condition.

This obsession for the Other is not a relation to others which surround me, either in my immediate, or distant environment, but is the extension of my subjectivity beyond myself to include these others. To include these others at the heart of my subjectivity does not make them just one more content of consciousness, or even one more aspect of my world, but means my subjectivity is replaced, displaced and substituted by them. I am never alone, not because I wish to be with others, but because my life is already implicated and involved with them, prior to any decision on my part, or need on theirs. My subjectivity, older than any conscious act or representation, and thus not dependent on whether I recognise it or not, is this knot of myself and others. Ethically speaking, I do not begin from myself and move outwards towards others; rather I begin from others back to myself, and I can only do so, because my subjectivity is already, prior to any decision or choice, involved with them. To begin from the side of others back to the self, rather than from the self to others, does not mean that I simply decided to change my orientation in the world, for even this alteration of my viewpoint would still belong to my will. To truly begin from the side of others must mean that there is a beginning other than mine, another time than the time of the freedom of a subject which has made up its mind before acting, even if this certainty can only be an ideal and endlessly deferred.

Responsibility for responsibility

In his Talmudic commentary, 'The Temptation of Temptation', Levinas writes of the Jews accepting the Torah prior to understanding it (Levinas 1968, 91). They did not decide *not* to understand the Torah, which would be just one more form of slavery, but their acceptance *preceded* their understanding. As Rav Simaï teaches in the *Chabat* itself, 'the Israelites committed themselves *to do* before *understanding*' (Levinas 1968, 68). This, Levinas says, runs entirely counter to our usual understanding of action, where we weigh the pros and cons of a situation before making a decision. To act is to act through some kind of knowledge, and even though we can never be certain we have acted well, every action is already the announcement of a judgement. Even to decide not to judge, to act recklessly, is still to make a judgement not to judge. This forever seems to be the comedy of revolt. It is parasitical on the very order it seeks to overthrow. But is there a disorder or anarchy which is not merely the opposite to order, which is defined internally within the system? Is there a derangement more than any arrangement, more than the unruliness which any system can accommodate, and indeed even feeds from? Is there, Levinas asks his listeners, a 'different relation between being and knowledge' (Levinas 1968, 80)?

Let us compare the Levinas's notion of responsibility with the traditional Kantian account. First of all, for Kant, it is not enough simply to be responsible. Rather one has to have the responsibility to be responsible. This responsibility for responsibility he calls duty, which he differentiates from merely acting responsible out of coercion or habit. To be responsible for others and for yourself, you already have to have this responsibility to be responsible. What is this first responsibility? Is it the same as the second? We might imagine duty is first of all imposed by force from the outside. Be responsible or else! Thus, we could have a picture of childhood, where the child is initially irresponsible and lawless and needs to be educated and disciplined. True adulthood arrives, however, only when then child realises that the law she believed was imposed from without by her teachers in fact comes from within, since the moral law is merely an outward expression of our inward rationality. Freedom, rather than being antithetical to the law, is one and the same. I am not so much substituted by the Other, but I and the Other become one. In Hegel, this moral law becomes translated into social being. My individuality is nothing other than the manifestation of my social being, but in the same way the Other also belongs to this social being. I and you become we. The social does not stand above us, but affirms our common identity. It overcomes the difference between the self and others by internalising this difference in each one us. Our own individuality is the expression of social being, just as our social being is the expression of our individuality. Social being is not something added on to what it means to be a human being, rather social being *is* what it means to be a human being.

Ethical substitution, on the contrary, is quite different from this social substitution of the I and the Other, where the difference between the terms in the dialectical relation is sublimated in the identity of the 'we'. Rather than the Other being substituted by the I (I recognise myself in the Other and the Other recognises themselves in me), the I is substituted by the Other. The personal pronoun 'we' is the plural of the first person, and this is why I retain my identity in the Other, for the Other's identity is the same as mine. In my substitution by the Other, my identity is not expanded to include all the others who are just like me, but contracted to a knot or a node in which the Other as Other is already involved in my existence, such that my identity, which is the beginning point of the movement of recognition, is in fact always a second moment dependent on the repression of this internal split.

If identity is secondary, rather than primary, then responsibility for responsibility could be interpreted in a different way than respect for or duty towards the moral law. The responsibility which comes before responsibility is the relation to the Other which precedes any categorical imperative, because it is an invasion of my subjectivity before any decision or choice. This is not the same as the naïveté or spontaneity of a will which refuses the moral law, for even this refusal is the result of a mind certain and made up, which willfully sets itself against the ethical community. The conflict between reason and desire does not include the relation to the Other, for this antinomy is internal to the self, who is both the source of the subjective impulse and the law which could transform it into a moral imperative. Even the respect for the others is a decision made by the self, and like any decision can be rescinded, for the rationality of the morality is higher than both the self and the Other as individuals. To reject this antinomy cannot, therefore, be to fall back to senti-ment and feeling, as though the relation to the Other were just another kind of immediacy. This would be to remain on one side of the antinomy of rational morality. What is irrational is not truly the opposite of rationality, but ration-ality's opposite. 'Naïveté,' Levinas writes, 'is an ignorance of reason in a world dominated by reason' (Levinas 1968, 83). To be responsible for respon-sibility is not to be irresponsibly responsible. Rather this first responsibility arrives before any act of the will, rational or otherwise. It is to bear the weight of a responsibility you have not chosen.

Not to confuse the absence of choice with not choosing demands a completely different structure of subjectivity than the strife between imme-diacy and reflection. We need to get beneath, or at the heart of this self in order to see how it can be inverted by the Other. Beyond the to and fro of subjective impulse and objective thought, the ultimate horizon of subjectivity is time. Self consciousness is the possession of time. To be able to make oneself a theme for oneself, to be able to speak to oneself, as Plato defined thinking, means to be present to oneself, to gather up the dispersion of one-self in time. To be a theme for oneself, and to recollect one self in the present, are two sides of the same process of identification. To be a self is to identify oneself. Subjectivity is a doubling up the self, in which the self is both subject and object, form and content. Identification is not just a figure of speech, but the very process through which the self becomes a self. And yet it is the insurmountable paradox of the language of individuality that it can only be expressed through the official language of the universal. I am I only to the extent that I am like everyone else. As soon as I open my mouth, I speak the same words which everyone else speaks, but these words are the only words which I can use to say who I am. The more original, unique and special I think I am, the more likely that it is that I am the same as everyone else. My individu-ality is a cloak which hides a nothingness at the heart of my existence. I am an empty cipher filled by the countless words said before me.

My relation to the Other, however, is not a theme of self discovery. The Other is not an image or concept which I grasp first of all in my mind and then apply to my experience so as to unify it. Primarily, my relation to the Other is contact, proximity and obsession before it is a thought or a word. This would mean that the Other must have a totally different signification than any other experience mediated by a sign which signifies it in advance. If the Other cannot be thematised, this is not because of a failure on the part of our consciousness to adequately grasp its meaning. The Other is not something mysterious or unknowable on the other side of our knowledge of the world. In this sense what is said to be 'other' is merely a projection of our own consciousness alienated from itself, where there is always the possibility, in a second moment, of the realisation of this false consciousness, and so the ability to overcome this alienation by proclaiming that all that is *is* the subject. The difference of the Other is not the same as the externalisation of the other in the dialectic of self-consciousness. It announces a wholly singular meaning. The possibility of such a meaning lies in the structure of subjectivity itself. It is only because the subject is *not* just an identity that there is a possibility of a signification otherwise.

As Levinas writes at the beginning of the essay 'Without Identity', published eight years before *Otherwise than Being*, this desire to save a meaning for subjectivity does not fit easily within the intellectual fashion in which the death of the subject is seen to be the *sine qua non*, at least in Paris, of the human sciences (Levinas 2003, 58). In this death, the whole of the inner life of the subject is placed outside of itself. All the singular desires, thoughts and words of an individual are instances of higher structural forms. To think otherwise is to be guilty of a naive humanism, which is, Levinas quotes Blanchot, to be '"more repugnant than all the nihilist vulgarities"' (Levinas 2003, 59). Nonetheless, the human sciences are just as much caught up with metaphysics as any other discourse. Their formalism expresses a nostalgia for the certainty of mathematics and the reduction of experience to number, a possibility which Socrates himself had already spoken of and hoped for at the end of the *Protagoras*.[6] Interiority is lost precisely to the extent that the subject is reduced to these formal structures. There is no secret fold inside of yourself in which you might hide. Everything is visible, everything is known. 'All that is human,' Levinas writes, 'is outside' (Levinas 2003, 59).

For Levinas, at least, the loss of an interior life of the subject begins with the philosophy of Heidegger. The self is not the origin of being, rather being is the origin of the self. The language of the self belongs to this history, rather than being its prime mover. Being speaks through us, rather than we speak being. We are the herald of a message which has already been spoken, though it has been spoken by no-one in particular. Even the interior world of the subject belongs to this language which is spoken by no-one; it is a fiction that it makes possible. The status of subject is attacked from two sides: from the impersonality of the discourses of the human sciences, in which the subject is merely a formal position within a system, to the post-metaphysical language of philosophy, where it is merely a cipher for the history of being, of which it is neither the origin nor the creative force. How then is it still possible to speak of a subjectivity which is not merely the repetition of naive humanism that these attacks have already defeated?

In both discourses, the interiority of the self is opened out onto an outside which precedes the self, either in the general structures of the sign or the historical forms of Being. Such a dispersal of the inner life of the self 'among things or in matter' (Levinas 2003, 62), without any remainder, supposes that this interiority is without idiosyncrasy or eccentricity. The self can be converted to an outside, because it has always already only been a container for it. But to say that the self is more than a receptacle for an outside, is not to lay claim to a fold of interiority that escapes it, an inner citadel that remains closed off from the forces without. It is rather to imagine a different relation to exteriority. The quirk of subjectivity which ensures that it is not swallowed up, like a pebble on a beach, in the impersonality of discourse, is not a uniqueness which comes from itself, but from its relation to the Other. The self is more than a sign or more than an emissary for being, because it is more than just a self. The Other is precisely not one more thing or one more piece of matter which lies indifferently outside of me, rather it belongs to the interiority of the self. It is an exteriority which inhabits my interiority, an itch that you cannot get rid of. 'Behold the impossible interiority,' Levinas writes, 'that disorients and reorients the social sciences of our times. An impossibility that we learn neither from metaphysics nor the end of metaphysics' (Levinas 2003, 67).

It is not as if the theory of intentionality is unaware of the exceptional and unusual, but it is always anticipated and welcomed in advance as the exceptional and the unusual. Even what is non-thematisable is reduced to the *idea* of the non-thematisable, for every content of consciousness is an idea for that consciousness, belongs to the reflection of the self to itself, however extraordinary that content might be. The question is whether this self-reflection of consciousness exhausts the meaning of subjectivity, whether it too has a condition. If consciousness is an act, then it is an act of someone. It is true that in idealism, the subject and the activity of subjectivity are said to be the same. Subjectivity is nothing less than the act of self-positing. To separate the subject from the activity of being a self is to fall into the error of treating the subject as though it were an object, as Kant had already diagnosed in the paralogisms of the *Critique of Pure Reason*. Yet he had already decided in advance that the reverse side of the objectification of the subject is a pure activity. Again we are faced with two alternatives: either the subject is pure interiority or it is a pure exteriority. What if there were a meaning of the self that was neither the activity of thought or the inertia of the thing? The principle of individuation is not the presence of myself to myself, either in thought or deed, where I am both actor and spectator, but the inversion of my self in my 'assignation' to the Other. I am who I am in my response to this call. This assignation, however, should not be seen as something that comes from outside of the subject, towards which it maintains its own hardened identity, rather it is the complete inversion of the self through the Other. It is not that I decide to put myself in the place of the Other, rather the Other has already taken my place, but in so doing produces a subjectivity beyond or on the other side of consciousness. The individuality of a consciousness is not a self-production, or auto-affection, as is the case in idealism, rather it is the effect of an introversion of an outside.

Maternity and sensation

In a footnote to the same essay, 'No Identity', Levinas draws our attention to the etymological link in Hebrew between the word for 'mercy', *Rakamin*, and the word for uterus *Rekhem* (Levinas 2003, 75). The uterus is not just a biological designation of the difference between the female and male sex, but a general signification which is true of subjectivity in general. 'It means,' Levinas writes, 'mercy that is like the emotion of the maternal entrails' (Levinas 2003, 75). By *Otherwise than Being*, Levinas is much less concerned to treat this as an image, metaphor or symbol. It is not that carrying a child in the womb it is an image of the ethical relation, rather the *experience* of the woman is the closest expression of the structure of 'Other-in-the-Same'. Rather than starting with the experience of the man in relation to his son, as is the case in fecundity (and fecundity likewise is not a metaphor) which is then generalised to cover every human relation, Levinas begins with the experience of the woman. It is important to say that maternity 'starts with the experience of the woman', rather than being simply a metaphor. For if maternity were just that, we would not, as Catherine Chalier argues, escape the subordination of women to men.[7] It would be a false ethical substitution of two terms which are still opposed to one another. It is not that the woman becomes the metaphor of the man's experience, re-appropriated and therefore alienated from her own body, but her experience replaces, displaces and disturbs his. Maternity does not just define the difference between the male and the female, biologically or psychologically, but crosses between this difference. If maternity were only a metaphor, then it would be a metaphor of a neutral relation, which on closer inspection would in fact operate through the masculine ideal. It would then operate in the same way as the famous Platonic metaphor of the birth of truth, where Socrates acts as the midwife. Here there is no recognition of the experience of the woman, rather it completely disappears in the sublimation of the erotic in the search for truth. The whole of our physical and sexual life disappears in the universality of reason, which cannot be separated, as we know, from the masculine culture of Athens.[8]

Maternity, in Levinas' text, on the contrary, comes from the side of the experience of the woman undermining the universality of the masculine ideal. It stubbornly resists its evaporation in a metaphor. The woman does not live her body as though it embodied justice, reason and the state. She lives it as she can. Thus, maternity does not simply replace the masculine ideal determining the opposition between the sexes, but is the experience of the self as the unraveling of the self. The woman lives substitution as she bears the child within her womb. This is not an image, metaphor, or symbol for Levinas. She lives this in her 'entrails'. To be possessed by the Other is not to be possessed by a thought. It is not to feel pity, empathy, or sympathy for the Other, rather it is to have the material conditions of your life changed. It is this experience of the woman which crosses over the difference between the sexes, but it is important here not to lose the woman's experience as the starting point of this movement, otherwise it would be re-appropriated by the masculine ideal. The 'extraterritoriality of the feminine', to use Levinas' expression, comes from the side of the woman, from the experience of her body, and not from the side of the man, from his practice, embodied, as it is, not in his physical life, but the institutions of the state and power, which is then universalised in reason, justice and truth, so as to retrospectively justify his supposedly natural superiority.

Unlike fecundity, what is stressed in maternity, is not time, history and generation, but pain, flesh and the sheer physicality of the relation to the Other. This part of the whole shift of emphasis from *Totality and Infinity* to *Otherwise than Being* from conversation, dialogue and the interpellation of the Other to the suffering and vulnerability of the flesh. Contact with the Other is first of all contact with the skin. I do not decide or choose to be for others, through an act of generosity putting their existence above my own. Rather, before any decision or choice, I am already substituted by others to such a degree that my very flesh, sensibility, and sense of self, has already been taken over by the Other. The relation of child to the mother within her body, more intimate than any caress, is something that which occurs beyond any conscious act. The woman's body does not bear the child in the same way that the act of thinking contains a thought, even though we might use metaphors of birth to describe this relation. In thinking, the thinker constitutes the thought. In thinking, the object of thought is immanent to the thought itself, they are two sides of the same act. But the child is not a unity with the mother's body and their union is one of difference prior to identity, the 'Other-in-the-Same', and not a fusion of two parts within a whole.

The metaphorical subordination of the woman's experience to the masculine ideal is part of the general subordination within philosophy of sensation to thought. For this tradition, sensibility has always interpreted through consciousness. Sensation's meaning comes only from the thought animating it. The touch of flesh against flesh, the movement of the child within the womb, only has an import because of the concept associated with it, when the mind turns to the flesh stirring within. Flesh without consciousness, the contact of skin against skin is inert and lifeless. It has no more meaning than the wall has for the chair which leans against it. Sensation is the same as the consciousness of sensation. Of course this does not mean that the meaning of sensation is the same as a thought or a judgement, but nonetheless it is still an act of consciousness, and outside this circle it is not only meaningless, but absent. To recognise that nothing could have any meaning for me without the intention animating it, is to understand that consciousness engulfs and surrounds my whole world. My world is the horizon of my consciousness. It goes no further than this.

Yet even this model of sensation distinguishes between the two moments. On the one hand, there is the sensation, and on the other, the conscious act of meaning which animates it. Meaning has to have some matter it holds or grasps onto, even if it is something meaningless. There is a teleology of meaning. Sensation moves toward or can even move away from meaning. To save sensation from consciousness would therefore be to hold these two moments apart, to hesitate between sensation and its fulfillment in consciousness. This is to argue against a prejudice of philosophy, which sees sensation merely as the material for a consciousness, and which for Levinas has its apotheosis in Husserl's interpretation of subjectivity, where, in the priority of the 'doxic thesis', every non-theoretical act has its foundation in theoretical assertion. Even if I desire I must know what it is that I desire. Of course, Husserl is not denying that sensation has a content outside of the representation of that content, but this content is utterly meaningless. It can only have a meaning when it is animated by intentionality. The absence of meaning of the content of sensation is the correlative of its subordination to thought, rather than the granting of any positive content to sensation. Levinas's position, on the contrary, is quite different, and is not caught between distinguishes between sense and non-sense, but between two kinds of senses. His argument is not whether there might be some content to sensation which is beyond representation and about which we can say nothing, but whether there is a meaning to sensation which is not the *same* meaning given to it by intentionality. This would imply a signification of sensibility, which would be different from its intelligible and manifest meaning. This signification would not be an intentionality specific to sensation, but sensation's signification.

68

Sensation is not a thought without feeling, still less a feeling without a thought, but the contortion of the interiority of the self around the Other. We need to be careful not to confuse Levinas's attempt to redeem sensation from the intellectualism of the Western philosophy with a 'banal psychology' which believes there is a taste beyond the thought of taste, or within touch a content beyond the thought of touch. The attempt to find a content true to sensation is just the opposite side of the intellectualisation of sensation. For Levinas, sensation names the relation to the Other. It does not name contact with others (as though Levinas were simply arguing that the relation to the Other was first of all primarily physical, rather than intellectual) but the convolution of interiority. This convolution is not the result of an act of thought, as though I decide to place others before myself, but the fact that my interiority is already a fold of an exteriority, the 'inspiration of the same by the other', prior to consciousness,or even the intelligibility of Being (Levinas 1991, 67).

This is why Levinas immediately relates sensation to psychism. If sensation is more that just the empty content of a feeling outside of a thought which would animate it, if the self is more than just consciousness, manifestation or intelligibility, it is because its interiority has already been disturbed by the excessive signification of the Other, which occupies and obsesses me beyond any thetic position I might take towards it. If sensation is not just the material base for intentionality, but is a signification in its own right, then it is only so because of the structure of pyschism. When Levinas speaks of the vulnerability and exposure of the body to the Other, he is not speaking of a physiological reaction, nor are they metaphors which would take such a reaction as their starting point. Physiology is not the opposite to consciousness, but merely its dead twin. Sensation, on the contrary, has an ethical signification beyond the opposition between the mind and the body. The ethical body antecedes the parallelism between the body and the mind, even if this body is thought as having more meaning than inert matter.

Here we begin to understand the true import of maternity for Levinas. The maternal body already bears the weight of the child, already carries this child within her, an obligation which goes beyond any idea of obligation, before this child has become a theme, a story or a narrative. In the same way, the psyche bears the weight of the responsibility for the Other. I do not start from my own situation and work out towards others, rather my own situation has already been usurped by others. It is this usurpation which is the meaning of responsibility. It is not enough to think that others have rights, and I have duties and obligation towards them, but to know that one's own rights are already an injustice. To start from an interiority that is closed in upon itself, that possess itself, is already to have closed yourself off from the injustices of the world. It is to have to uttered the first word as 'I'. But why not start from the side of the others, from the side of injustice rather than the idea of justice, from the outside and work your way back, rather than from the inside and work your way out? From the vantage point of an interiority wholly in possession of itself, the outside is always just one more inside. It never gets to any experience which is not already a reflection of how it experiences the world. Its idea of justice is to make the world the same as itself. But to start from the outside is quite different, as though from a disturbance of the surface of the water made by a stone that has been thrown into a pool, you could work from the furthest ripple back to the concentrated point of entry. It would be to begin with the injustices in the world which call into question my superiority, and not from the idea of injustice which supports it. It would be to see that injustice belongs to your very existence, and that you are already implicated in the injustices of the world, before you had any idea, thought or solution for them. Substitution is not the idea of justice, but its condition. I am responsible for the injustices of this world not because I think that I am, but my very existence already implicates me. '"That is my place in the sun",' Levinas quotes Pascal in the exergue to *Otherwise than Being*, '"This is how the usurpation of the world began"' (Levinas 1991, viii).

The unicity of the self does not exist in its own self-constitution, rising up like a miracle from the earth, but in this implication with the suffering of the others. Outside this relation, the self has no more meaning than the content of what it says. Its existence is inserted within the general significance of a system of signs. The unicity of thought is an illusion, since thought by definition is universal. What is the content of 'I' but the same as any other 'I'? The uniqueness of the self lies not in thought, but in what lies outside thought, just as the individuality of the thing lies outside of its concept. There is a density to a thing, which perhaps poetry tries to grasp in a sensitivity which lies outside ideas, and which no concept can explain. Poetry and sensation are not wholly apart. My individuality beyond the concept of the 'I' exists only in the passivity of sensation, as though there were a whole world of feeling which the sharpness of a concept could not capture. A passivity, moreover, which is not merely the reverse side of intentionality, as though the only significance of sensation were to be the receptacle of thought. It is a passivity exceeding even its opposition to thought, and which Levinas marks by its written intensification in such expressions as the 'passivity of passivity more passive than any passivity', where only the superlative could do it justice (Levinas 1991, 15).

It is not enough simply to refer to the body as the opposite to thought, for the body is thought's opposite, its matter and material in which it constructs its own world. The body can only be other than thought, if the body has its own meaning or significance which is not thought's. This body is the ethical body, the maternal body. It is in this body that the 'I' has its unicity, but paradoxically only because it is not an I, or at least not an I as it is represented in thought as the unity of the self in time. For the I is only unique as 'me', as that subject which is accused from the outside by the injustice of suffering *before* it has represented this injustice to itself and inserted it within its world order. Accused, therefore, not because it has chosen to take up its responsibility, but in that its very existence is already implicated and interwoven with the suffering of others. I cannot choose against this fate, for such an intertwining of the self and the Other has already taken place in a time older than any memory or hope that I have. Levinas writes:

> Here uniqueness means the impossibility of slipping away and being replaced, in which the very recurrence of the I is effected (Levinas 1991, 56).

Of course, this does not stop me from acting as if I were not so involved, and the whole of Western philosophy might be said to be the justification of the arrogance of the self, whether this pride is beneficent or not, against the reality of my complicity.

The individuality of the I is not a substance which would be separate from the content of thought, whether this substance is the act of thinking itself, or the body that sustains it, but a psychism preceding the dualism of the mind and the body, in which the existence of the self has already been invaded by Other, both because my existence already implicates the Other, and because I am already accused of this complicity before I have assumed it. A strange individuality, for I am only individual to the extent that I am not myself. This invasion of the self by an exteriority is not the same as the populating of my mind by the thoughts of others, for it is through these thoughts that I constitute myself. This is the paradox of idealism. The possibility of subjectivity is only in its objective representations. I am only an I to the extent that I become an I, which means that I take on and live the thoughts of others. But substitution does not 'begin with consciousness' (Levinas 1991, 57). It does not begin at all, if by beginning we mean a conscious act. Prior to any thought, my subjectivity is already an usurpation, and I already stand accused. Maternal pyschism does not name a substance which would mysteriously stand behind the substance of thought, rather it points to the guilt of thought, to the guilt of any thought. Guilt here does not signify a heavy and morbid meditation wallowing in its own pure expression of feeling, but that thinking itself, in its totality, is guilty. Thinking is the illusion that consciousness is a commencement, rather than an arrogation. But it is an illusion for Levinas. Tyranny is parasitical on the life it crushes.

The Name of God

In *Totality and Infinity*, the relation to the Other is presented through the straightforwardness of speech. The Other is present in the words spoken, though no word expresses this presence. It is the assistance added to language, the non-linguistic essence of language, which signifies the Other. But in substitution, there is no Other which is opposed to the self from on high. The Other does not present itself in speech, but has already inverted the existence of the subject before any word has been spoken, and thereby before the opposition of speech and writing has taken place. Speech conceals an opposition between the Other and the self, which the anti-Hegelianism of *Totality and Infinity*, and the works that precede it, cannot completely rid itself, despite Levinas's insistence that 'transcendence is not negativity' (Levinas 1969, 40). The Other constitutes and determines my reality in opposition to me. Without the interpellation of the Other, my existence is mute and soulless. Would I address nature, if I had not already been addressed by the Other? I do not constitute and determine the reality of the Other, but the Other constitutes mine. I am dependent, whereas the Other is independent, absolute, καθ' αὐτό . This does not mean that the relation between the Other and the self is suspended in an objective point of view in which the difference between them would be abolished, where the identity of the terms in the relation would arise only from their difference, and the Other would only be Other, because it was not-I, the I only an I because it was not-Other. Rather, the Other is more than the I, and the I less than the Other. Nor is this relation of 'more or less' between them reciprocal. The Other is more than the I, not because the I is less than the Other; rather the less of the I has its source in the more of the Other. The more precedes the less. 'The idea of infinity,' Levinas writes, 'designates a height and nobility, a transascendance' (Levinas 1969, 41).

The neologism 'transascendence' expresses the inequality of the relation of creation which we have already discussed in the previous chapter.[9] Ontologically, the distance between God and the creature is thought within the same totality. Thus, being precedes both God and the creature. This leads to a theological aporia. For how can God be both absolute and infinite, but at the same time be identical to that which He creates? Not a problem for Aristotle, whose God in *Metaphysics* contains no notion of creation, since it is immanent to the cosmos as its final and not efficient cause, but a great difficulty for a philosophy inspired by monotheism. The solution lies is freeing transcendence from immanence, freeing it from the categories of being. The transcendence of God is a transcendence beyond being, and there is no bridge that would join or link them together. For Levinas, although this dilemma has its source in theology, the significance of this transcendence which transcends the interdependence between transcendence and immanence, a 'trans-ascendance', has an origin beyond theology in the ethical relation to the Other.

It is wrong to argue that by applying the idea of creation to the ethical relation, Levinas is thereby fleeing philosophy to the more certain shores of theology, as though it were possible to separate these discourses from one another, inextricably bound as they are in their history. Rather than appealing to theology beyond philosophy, Levinas is leaping beyond their opposition by appealing to ethics. The idea of creation in *Totality and Infinity* is, therefore, not ontological, but ethical, and if theology is still ontology, then it cannot be said that Levinas's philosophy is theological, in any traditional or simple sense, when he affirms this idea.[10] The ethical idea of creation cannot be thought through either efficient or final causality, where both God and creation are bound together. The ethical idea of creation, on the contrary, maintains the separation of the relation. This is why the idea of creation, paradoxically, for Levinas, is synonymous with atheism. For in the ontological idea of creation all beings share in the being of God. There is no separation between the God and creation, transcendence and immanence are one. But if the ethical idea of creation expresses the separation of the terms in the relation, then atheism must be the necessary corollary of creation, for it merely states the necessary truth of the idea that the creature is *not God*. Again for Levinas, none of this is of any interest ontologically, the idea of creation proves nothing, let alone that God has created the universe. He is only concerned with the ethical significance of the idea of creation: the separation of terms in a relation which do not mutually determine one another. Only to this extent does the Other 'resemble God' (Levinas 1969, 293).

And yet the terms are not equally separate from one another. The Other has priority over the self. We can understand this asymmetry linguistically. The Other is the 'first intelligible', because discourse is first of all apology. I speak only because I have first of all been addressed, and what I speak is not contemporaneous with this address. The address is of a completely different order than the response which it demands, just as in the idea of creation, God is of a completely different order than the creature. The separation of the creator is antecedent to the separation of the creature. Strictly speaking, atheism would therefore be a creation of God, for I am atheist only to the extent that I am created in His image. In the same way, the essence of language is subordinate to the address of the Other. I only speak, because I first of all have been addressed by the Other, and I do not address the Other because I first of all speak. This is what Levinas means when he argues that the relation between the terms is asymmetrical. Although both terms are separate, the separation of one term depends on the separation of the other. In this sense, we might speak of the ethical relation as a one-sided dialectical relation, rather than a purely non-dialectical relation, since the I is dependent on the Other, even though it has a separate existence, whereas the Other is the only *absolute* term. 'In the conjunction of creation,' Levinas writes, 'the I is for itself without being *causa sui*' (Levinas 1969, 293-4). This means that it is dependent on God for being itself. In the same way, in the ethical transformation of the idea of creation, the I is dependent on the Other for speech. I only speak because the Other speaks to me first of all. I speak not because of what these words say to me, because what they signify hold us in common in the system of signs which make up our shared culture, but because of the very fact of speaking itself, which is irreducible to any word. The origin of language is the address, which cannot be spoken by any word, but nonetheless inhabits every word, as this turning towards the Other.

The idea of creation is held within the opposition of speech and writing, because only speech can do justice to the superiority of the Other, the asymmetry between the Other and the self. Substitution, the structure of which we have been trying to describe in this chapter, where the Other inhabits the self from within and does not address it from afar, this priority of speech disappears, and strangely enough is closer to the Rabbinic conception of God, than the more Platonic emphasis of *Totality and Infinity* will allow. For in Judaism the priority is the written not the spoken word.

In the Torah, it is the written word of God which is the first act of creation, even before the creation of the heaven and earth.[11] Hebrew, as the religious language of prayer and the synagogue, is sacred first of all as the written, and not the spoken word. For the names of God, as Levinas explains in his short essay, 'The Name of God according to some Talmudic Texts', are known only through their written form. They are, Levinas writes the 'letters traced upon the parchment' (Levinas 1994, 117). These letters themselves are so sacred, Levinas tells us in a footnote, that the Talmudic Tractate *Shebu'oth* (35a) tells us that whenever we write down the names of God we must not efface them, even if the name has been incorrectly transcribed. Any such erasure demands that the whole leaf must be buried in the ground, as though it were a dead body (Levinas 1994, 212). These letters are, therefore, not simply a sign signifying a concept or an idea. Rather they embody, in the written letters themselves, the transcendence of God. We must not interpret this transcendence as a mystical or magical power. In the same treatise, a distinction is made between those names that cannot be effaced and the substantive attributes which can. This is not a difference of supernatural power, but thematisation. The substantive attributes treat God as any other being, even if He has these attributes to the highest degree, whereas the names that cannot be effaced are proper names, which announce only that God is 'unrepresentable and holy, that is, absolute God, who is beyond all thematisation and all essence' (Levinas 1994, 120). This excess beyond thematisation and being can only be found in the written, and not the spoken word. In the name of God, Levinas discovers the possibility, which elsewhere he will deny, and especially so in *Totality and Infinity*, of a writing *bearing* alterity rather than representing it.

'Bearing', however, is not the same as 'signifying'. The name of God does not signify alterity, for then it would make of alterity an idea, a concept, or an essence. It would turn the proper name back into a substantive. The name of God preserves the alterity of God in announcing it. It is because the written word preserves the alterity of God, rather than representing it, that it must be not be effaced. It can only be the materiality of the word that pre- serves this alterity and not any idea which it might contain. For as soon as one jumps beyond the written word to the idea that it expresses, then the alterity of God is lost. It becomes one more essence, however great, within our world. This is why Levinas draws our attention to the fact that it is not only the effacement of the word which is forbidden in this treatise, but even the first letter. It is the word itself, as a written word, rather than as a sign, which preserves and keeps the alterity of God. 'The square letters,' Levinas writes, 'are a precarious dwelling from which the revealed Name is already with- drawn' (Levinas 1994, 121). These letters do not carry an idea, but the impos- sibility of an idea, and they do so as the very materiality of writing, as the very ink on the page which some hand has traced and copied.

This precedence of the written word over speech is emphasised in the one name of God that has precedence over the others. The Tetragrammaton is vocalised differently from the way that it is written.[12] The significance of the name of God is its effacement. In withdrawing in the very moment it is uttered, it breaks the parallelism between the signifier and signified. Such a rupture, which is the only way that the transcendence of God can enter language, is only possible in writing, in the difference between what is said and what is written on the page. It is this difference, which can never be spoken, which 'puts into words' the transcendence of God. This explains further the prohibition against effacing the Name which is already an effacement. It is not the written word which is sacred, but the *difference* between the written and spoken word. What is unpronounceable can only be written, can only be an effect of writing and not speech. The prohibition against effacing the Name of God is not because it contains the idea or concept of God, for in this case it would be a word like any other, but because it is already the effacement of the idea of God. The written word is an effacement prior to any effacement. It already rubs out the Name of God. It already makes the name of God less than any concept or idea, but in doing so preserves the transcendence of the Name. God is barely legible in the Name of God, but it is only this illegibility which is sacred. Only because the Name of God is illegible, should it not be made more illegible.

Levinas turns the prohibition of the effacement and obliteration of the written word in Rabbinic Judaism against what he has written. He asks, at the end of essay, whether he has not been guilty of the same thematisation when he argues that what the withdrawal of God in the Name of God expresses is not a mysterious essence or substance, as in negative theology, but the ethical relation to the Other. Is this interpretation not the same as saying that the Name of God *signifies* the ethical relation? Not if this thematisation is made illegible by the very relation it is attempting to describe. 'The language of thematisation,' Levinas writes, 'that we are using at the moment has perhaps been made possible by this Relation, and is subservient to it' (Levinas 1994, 128). The relation, then, between Levinas's text, and what this text attempts to describe, is the same as the relation between the Name of God and the transcendence of God. The name of God only announces the transcendence of God by not naming it in the difference between the written word and spoken word. What is written can never be said. Transcendence can enter language through the written word, but only as a double illegibility, where the illegible is made present only by being more illegible. In the same way, Levinas's text can only describe the ethical relation by not describing it. Yet it is only the written word which allows him to do so. This is why we should not take the Name of God to be a metaphor or symbol of the ethical relation. It is not that the ethical relation is like writing, but that its excessive signification can only be said by entering the written word, where what is written can say more than what is said, just as the prohibition against speaking the Name of God can only be written and not spoken. The ethical pronounces the transcendence of the Other, and philosophy, as writing,

Notes

1 In the section 'Descartes', pp.37-40.

2 These are themes that Levinas makes transparent in a conference contribution late in his career, 'Dying for...', where he underlines, once again, his divergence from Heidegger's analysis of being-towards-death in *Being and Time* , when he writes that 'the death of the other comes before care for self' (Levinas 1998, 216).

3 In the section 'Beyond the face', pp.20-4.

4 See the section 'The feminine', pp.40-9.

5 There is a time of the subject that is older even than the unconscious, which Levinas views as merely the reverse side of conscious life. 'It is not a question here,' he writes in a footnote, 'of descending toward the unconscious, which defined in a purely negative way with reference to the conscious, preserves the structure of self-knowledge' (Levinas 1991, 194).

6 In the calculus of pain and pleasure (355e-357a).

7 Catherine Chalier's work is very important, because she is the first to recognise the importance of maternity in Levinas, but she disables its force to undermine the traditional sexual hierarchy by interpreting it as a metaphor, symbol, or 'analogon', to use her expression. She argues that it can only repeat the marginalisation of the feminine in Western discourse. 'La femme doit aussi entendre son nom dans la utopie éthique, là où se dit le langage comme justice et résistance au Même. Pour cela il incombe d'en finir avec un effacement d'elles-mêmes derrière des métaphores qu'elles n'ont pas choisies' [The women must also hear her name in the ethical utopia, where language as justice and resistance to the Same speaks. For that it is necessary to break with their own self-effacement behind metaphors which they have not chosen] (Chalier 1984, 48). I am not certain that maternity is a metaphor in the traditional sense. It is not question of the woman's experience disappearing in the metaphor as it goes onto signify something else. As John Llewellyn notes in *The Genealogy of Ethics*, Levinas is fond of Bruno Snell's statement that we should not think of the metaphor as opposed to the literal, rather there is a transformation of meaning on both sides of the metaphor. When the Greek phalanx, in Homer, is compared to a rock, we should not just think of the rock in a human way, but human beings as rocks. Likewise, when the ethical relation is described as maternity, we should not just think of maternity as a metaphor for ethics, but ethics as maternity. In other words, maternity changes the very meaning of ethics and does not just disappear (Llewellyn 1995, 88). The same transformation of ethics by maternity is present in Lisa Guenther's subtle and attentive reading of its biblical source in '"Like a Maternal Body":

Levinas and the Motherhood of Moses'. 'Perhaps Moses' responsibility,' she writes, 'for the people requires him to be *feminized* and *maternalized* by this responsibility, to be altered in such a way that he becomes *like* a maternal body' (Guenther 2004).

8 See the section 'Philosophers and Others' in Dover's admirably succinct paper 'Classical Greek Attitudes to Sexual Behaviour' (Dover 1973, 70-1).

9 In the section 'Atheism', pp.35-7.

10 For the most influential criticism of Levinas's philosophy being too theological, see Dominique Janicaud's book *Le tournant théologique de la phénoménologie*. (Janicaud 1991, 25-37).

11 There is a Midrash which says that the first act of creation is the creation of language, since the first Hebrew word after the verb 'he creates', in the first verse of Genesis, is אֶת, which although it only has a grammatical function of a direct object marker, is actually made up of the first and last letters of the Hebrew alphabet.

12 The Tetragrammaton is written with the Hebrew letters יהוה but it is always pronounced אֲדֹנָי, 'my master'. The Masoretes (Jewish scholars in Tiberias) added vowel notation to the original consonantal text in the 9th and 10th centuries A.D. To remind the reader not to pronounce the written Tetragrammaton as it is written, they placed the vowels of the word אֲדֹנָי beneath it. This explains the mysterious existence of the words 'Yahweh' or 'Jehovah', which are all attempts by non-Jewish readers to read the Tetragrammaton with the vowels of אֲדֹנָי rather than replace the written word with a the vocal one in speech.

4

Friendship

To have recourse to Blanchot's reading of Levinas is not to make him useful, as though by employing his work we might arrive at a clearer and more orderly understanding of Levinas. On the contrary, his reading of Levinas should make the latter (as any truly productive and creative reading must do) more unfamiliar and strange to us. It forces us to address those questions which appear at first glance to be furthest away from the intentions of the author. To follow Blanchot's reading of Levinas is not to attempt to uncover or discover some common theme or bridge between them. If we can argue that Blanchot's reading challenges us, undoubtedly by a certain violence, to address the question of writing in Levinas, then this does not mean that we would have discovered, after all, they were involved in the same search, investigation and enquiry. Let us avoid the temptation of agreement and reconciliation and maintain the violence of Blanchot's reading. It is this violence which opens up Levinas's text to an interpretation which it cannot assimilate or incorporate.

Our strategy, then, should be quite different from Françoise Collin's, in *Maurice Blanchot et la question de l'écriture*, which is perhaps the most important book on the relation between Levinas and Blanchot, when she writes, for example, that 'le thème de l'autrui et le thème de l'écriture littéraire peuvent voisiner' [the theme of the Other and literary writing can be placed side by side] (Collin 1971, 116). Her argument rests on the uneasy analogy between the disappearance of the author in Blanchot's description of literature and the unseating of the self in Levinas's portrayal of the ethical relation. The analogy is awkward because ethics, at least at the time of writing of *Totality and Infinity*, which is the period to which Françoise Collin is referring, language for Levinas is deeply personal, following the Platonic tradition of dialogue and intercourse, whereas for Blanchot, literature exposes us to what is profoundly impersonal and anonymous in language.

There are many passages in Blanchot's work that demonstrate this difference between the two authors, but let us take one in the opening pages of his essay 'The Experience of Proust' in *The Book to Come* (Blanchot 2003, 11-24). We are taking this example because nothing would seem to be more personal and individual than Proust's writing. It would seem natural to suppose that the narrative of *In Search of Time Lost* runs parallel with Proust's own life, that the artifice was merely a repetition of what really had happened, and the book no more than a journal of one man's life, so that in reading it you might really find who the real Proust was by discovering that event which defined his life, as though every individual existence has the one event which marks its own uniqueness, and from which everything else that happens in that life, every twist and turn, must unravel. But this circumstance, profoundly personal and intimate to Proust, the famous taste of the madeleine, is the beginning also of something else which is not a life or an existence. It is also the possibility of the narrative which narrates it. It is not just the secret of Proust's life, but also the centre of the book which is written about it. The narrative is a journey towards this incident, the explanation and discovery of its many ramifications and reverberations.

And yet, in terms of the life already lived, this journey has already taken place, for without the incident it could not have been written. Is *In Search of Time Lost*, then, just an autobiography, the simply telling of a life? It is not really that simple, because what is known about this event only becomes known through the writing of it. For Proust this paradox is the paradox of time. The event only becomes real to me after the narration of which it is meant to be the narrative's own origin. It is, therefore, after what is meant to be posterior, and which now becomes anterior. No doubt this thing really happened, but it is only realised in the recollection and writing down of it. Here is a curious reversal. It is the narrative which makes the remembrance of the event possible and not the other way around. This would mean that the narrative is suspended in thin air. For what is meant to make it *possible* is now what *it* makes possible. The narrative becomes the origin of itself. The real existence of the event in the past, if we can call it 'real' at all, can only exist in the written word. If Proust speaks of the 'living present', he can only do so with words which are neither, in relation to the event, living or present, and which belong, Blanchot remarks, to an 'other time' (Blanchot 2003, 13). The time of narration makes possible the time of the past which we imagine is real and substantial. This would reverse the natural order of things. It is not reality which is the origin of the narrative, but narrative, reality.

When Proust writes of the instant annihilation of time in the stumble on the irregular paving stones on the way of Guermantes with a similar trip at the

Baptistery of San Marco, whose time is he writing about? Is it the time of the 'real' Proust, the son of Adrien Proust, who lived and died as the rest of us live and die? If we pay special attention to the description of this stumble, however, it is much stranger than we first might think. It is not an account of the psychology of memory, even if Proust sometimes himself might call it that, but the experience of pure time, and the possibility of writing, which for Blanchot are irrevocably intertwined. In the stumble on the irregular paving stones, time is annihilated, because the distance between the two events is abolished. One is not the echo of the other. It is not the latter incident which recalls the prior, but both are experienced in the same instant. It is not just these two similar situations which Proust experiences, but time itself which connects them. Such an experience of pure time is for Proust to be outside of time, outside of the 'order of time', in which one event comes after the other. This experience of time as being outside of time, Blanchot adds, is also the possibility of writing. For it is in the taste of the madeleine that Proust is convinced beyond doubt of his own literary talents. Not that we should understand this moment merely as the sentiment of a vocation, when one utters the immortal words, 'Now I will write. Now I will become a writer.' Rather, Proust, in the taste of the madeleine on his tongue, touches 'the very essence of literature' in which he, the living, breathing man disappears (Blanchot 2003, 14).

The pure time outside of time is the time of the imaginary in which all events become interspersed and commingled. The imaginary should not be confused with an interiority of the self, but is its opposite, when the self becomes externalised in words. In the experience of pure time, when the distance between events is abolished in an instant, my interiority is placed outside of itself in time. Time is not a form of the subject, but the subject a form of time. To view this experience as a real event which somehow, mysteriously and enigmatically begins Proust's writing career would be to forget, Blanchot reminds us, that it is described after Proust had already published the first volume of *In Search of Time Lost*, 'Swann's Way', and much of the rest of the work had already been written. Is then Proust a liar to say that this experience was the start and the impetus of his writing? Yet he can only make this event 'real', Blanchot writes, by placing it *inside* the very work which it is meant to make possible. This is the necessity which belongs to every work. It is the moment in which the 'I' of the writer becomes the 'I' of the narrator, which in this case is 'no longer the real Proust, nor Proust the writer who has the ability to speak' (Blanchot 2003, 15).

If writing, its very possibility and reality, only happens because the real events of one's life have been displaced and neutered by the written word, and this life itself is only an illusion which words make possible, then it seems to be a difficult task to show that Levinas and Blanchot are involved in the same endeavour. I am called into question by speech, by the direct address of the Other, by interlocution, not by the anonymous appeal of the written word. Only by the most cursory glance at a common vocabulary could we be convinced that literature and ethics were the same. And yet, Françoise Collin is not completely wrong. For this is precisely what Blanchot will argue in his most substantial engagement with *Totality and Infinity* in *The Infinite Conversation*. But he will make the connection not through a similar mistrust of the arrogance of the subject, but in the anonymity of language itself. He will want to discover, in the ethical relation, which is meant to be what is most personal, direct and straightforward, the impersonal and unknown. It is here where the link between their work lies, and it completely changes our understanding of Levinas's ethics, and allows us to read his philosophy in a complete different fashion, moving us away, perhaps, from the more sentimental, schmaltzy, and evocative reading, to one which is complicated, dark and uncertain.

Writing and friendship

Levinas's essay 'The Servant and his Master' begins with the anonymity of language at the centre of literature. 'Artistic activity,' Levinas writes, 'make the artist aware that he is not the author of his works' (Levinas 1996, 140). In every other experience, our activity appears to be intimately connected to an agent. Indeed, it does not seem possible to make sense of action at all without an agent. And yet what we ordinarily call inspiration seems to suggest that the work speaks for itself in the place of the author and has its origin beyond them. We are content to allow art to be impersonal as long as it does not invade our normal experience. Art is a special case. We can separate the different uses of language. On the one side, there is art, where the author of the work disappears in the activity, and on the other, communication, where, in every case, language is the medium of intention.

The meaning of inspiration in Blanchot, Levinas tells us, does not easily fit within this simple and straightforward opposition, because it reverses the polarity between art and everyday activity. Rather than activity being the norm and art a special case, beneath our everyday experience lies the impersonality of language. Words make possible what we speak, but they do not have their origin in our speech. They have a history which is older than the history of consciousness, older than any 'commencement or end' of a project or task, and we are trapped in this language like an insect in amber. In this sense, speaking, as it is envisioned in *Totality and Infinity*, is the interruption of this impersonal language, re-activating hidden and lost meanings by the warmth of the human voice. Yet even the intrusion of the voice in the endless stream of language requires words which have been used endlessly before by other speakers. How can I add my originality and personality to language? Every speech, it would seem, is just the continuation of what has already been said, and only gives us the illusion of individuality. Such an impasse, the impossibility of escaping the condition of language, explains the suffocating atmosphere of Blanchot's novels and narratives, where you have the sensation that language has broken down, because the same words are spoken over and over again until they cease to have any meaning, signification or intent, separating themselves from the characters which speak them.

The splitting of language from the intention of the speaker could not be further away from Levinas's own description of speech as the direct address of the Other in *Totality and Infinity*. There is no ambiguity or obscurity. The Other is absolutely present in the words they speak. The ethical demand is nothing else than this presence. How different are the conversations in Blanchot, where between the speakers, Levinas writes, 'an unspoken understanding – without mystery for the interlocutors, but opaque with its own emptiness – slides by (Levinas 1996, 144). It is perhaps for this reason, in a footnote to this essay, that Levinas can write that in the 'modality of transcendence' in Blanchot's work, 'no moral element intervenes' (Levinas 1996, 184). Yet even here Levinas will not go as far as to say that Blanchot's work is unethical, and his latter essays this will be even more apparent.[1] Literature is not just a species of the genus art. It is, Levinas writes, 'inseparable from the verb, it overflows with prophetic meaning' (Levinas 1996, 185). The anonymity and impersonality of writing, then, would not be so far away from the ethics of speech, as we might first suspect.

We must resist, however, the temptation, alluded to earlier, to take the proper names of these authors and create some kind of identity or unity, as though all along they were involved in the same project, enterprise and endeavour. Rather than basing our interpretation on unity, would it not be more productive and creative to start from the position of disunity and dissension? I am interested in how Blanchot's reading of Levinas's philosophy makes it more difficult and opaque, not how it might solve an interpretive problem. Is this not how Blanchot describes their friendship in 'Our Clandestine Companion' (Blanchot 1980, 79-87)? They are friends not because they share the same goal, but because each has the power to disrupt the other, and dispossess their work of its ownership. Blanchot's thought is inseparable from his reading and interpretation of Levinas, but this 'Levinas' is not the same as the

Levinas who writes the books which bear his name, and who wishes us to read his work in a certain way.[2] Moreover, this other 'Levinas' can be a way for us to read these works more fruitfully. This is far more significant than any titillation, however tempting and attractive, we might feel in finding out some biographical fact about their lives, or academic security in tracing their footnotes and references to one another. There is a different meaning of friendship than merely the bringing together of two people through a sharing of the same ideas, thoughts and beliefs, where a friend is only someone in whom I can recognise myself, and not that one who makes me a stranger to myself.

In a collection of his essays called *Friendship*, Blanchot writes about another of his friends Dionys Mascolo in a review 'On One Approach to Communism' (Blanchot 1997, 93-7). Blanchot informs us in a footnote that this review was published in the same year as the publication of Mascolo's book *Le communisme; révolution et communication ou la dialectique des valeurs et des besoins*, 1953. Thus, before *Totality and Infinity*, and a long time before 'Our Clandestine Companion'. You might think, considering the title of the book which he is reviewing, that the subject matter of the review would be Mascolo's interpretation of communism, but like all Blanchot's reviews it is not that straightforward, for what he ends up writing about is the relation between communism and friendship in a way that is never mentioned in Mascolo's book.[3] Friendship, which is a word that both ties and keeps apart Blanchot and Levinas's writing, is, therefore, not a recent term in Blanchot's work. It is there from the very beginning, and it's importance in understanding Blanchot's reformulation of Levinas's ethical relation cannot be underestimated.

Mascolo argues, throughout his book, that what is at the heart of communism is the primacy of needs above values. Human beings, even in a century in which everything has become meaningless, still search to satisfy their needs, but this search hits against an immovable wall of economic necessity. In their ingestion of things to satisfy their needs, human beings have become the very things they consume. No doubt, Blanchot writes, in our world this transformation of human beings into things bought and sold like any other is concealed and dissimulated through values, which promote freedom, happiness and equality. These values, however, are perfectly ridiculous, for they refer to a time that no longer exists, when people were not things. We live in a society which completely masks our true relation to things by idealising it. The aim of Marxism is not to deny the power of things, but to reverse it. Things no longer have power over us, rather we have power over them, and in this moment we rediscover our lost humanity. Blanchot writes, qualifying that this is a '*restrictive* understanding' [italics in the original],

The essence of Marxism is to give man mastery over nature, over what is nature in himself, by means of the thing (Blanchot 1997, 94).

The pivotal position of the alienated workers is that they prevents us, precisely because they have lost their status as human beings, from falling back into a nostalgia. The worker is not better than us, because they are more human, but the impersonality of the economic necessity is more visible in their lives. Only when we recognise ourselves as the things we have become is it then possible to rediscover a new humanity, one which cannot be the same as proclaimed by the false humanism of ideology. Our religion, ethics and morality allow us the luxury of believing that we are truly human and above the sway of economic necessity, but the truth of alienated labour is that against the wall of this inevitability all our values are shattered. We really have become things bought and sold like the very items that we produce and this impersonal power has taken over our whole reality, even those values that we think are its opposite. The worker is the truth of reality and we are all proletarians now. Only when we recognise the barbarity we have become can we overcome it. This struggle is immense, because it is impossible to know in advance what this other humanism would be, since the only humanity we know is either what we have become under alienated labour or the unreality of the idealisation of humanity. 'We absolutely do not know,' Blanchot writes, 'what man could be' (Blanchot 1997, 95).

Is the choice between the reality of disillusionment and the melancholy of idealism, between need and value, or is their another relation? With respect to the current state of society, which only offers these alternatives, this other relation can only be said to be impossible. It bears the name of friendship. Blanchot writes,

> *Man can become the impossible friend of man, his relation to the latter being precisely with the impossible* [author's italics] (Blanchot 1997, 95-6).

This is not a friendship, then, in which both partners are considered equals, the idealisation of friendship, but in the friend something impossible remains, which is beyond both friends, and therefore, can only emerge between them without their knowledge or foresight. What is it that is impossible about friendship, since we all think we know what this is? Friendship, as this relation to the impossible, first of all breaks with economic need. I do not use a friend as I would a tool, or expect her to furnish a satisfaction which needs to be filled. But equally, friendship is not part of recognition. In the friend I do not find a mirror in which to construct the full image of myself. Friendship does not belong to the completion of the self, rather it breaks with its self-sufficiency. The danger here is idealising friendship and reducing it to an ideological value. On the contrary, Blanchot argues, we must, however difficult that might be, live two lives. One is a relation to a future; one which for Blanchot bears the name of communism, in which the relation between human beings is not a relation between things; but to do so means to engage fully with the world of things and the political injustice and wickedness of alienated labour. The other more difficult and fragile life is the engagement with what is impossible in friendship, for this cannot be appropriated and possessed by economic necessity.

In the novel *Atomised*, Michel Houellebecq describes the world of need dispassionately. Our society is nothing but the destruction of human relations, and we are only beginning to understand what this means. But he also very briefly alludes to another possibility, a possibility which he knows is impossible, that stands as an indictment precisely because of its impossibility. 'In the midst of nature's savagery,' he writes 'human beings sometimes (rarely) succeed in creating small oases warmed by love. Small, exclusive, enclosed spaces governed only by love and shared subjectivity' (Houellebecq 2001, 103). Of course it is possible to read these sentences with too much sentimentality and nostalgia. Perhaps it is only the word 'rarely' that holds us up short. For perhaps we believe we all live in such sheltered places away from the brutal storm of capital which seems to destroy all we cherish and hold dear. Our private lives have become so invaded by economic necessity that we no longer have any idea what love might or could be. Our intimacies might be nothing more than a flight from the reality, a flight whose condition is the very world it flees. Neither Blanchot or Houellebecq are idealising friendship or love, but reminding us that in them something impossible happens. This impossibility is outside the world, but not in the same way as the 'outside' of idealism. It does not rest on the illusion that there could be a realm of values somehow completely separate from need. As such, this impossibility is always fragile and momentary, always at the instant of collapsing back into the routine and sentimental.

At the end of the same book which contains this review bearing witness to his friendship with Mascolo, Blanchot writes of another friend, Georges Bataille, in a few pages called 'Friendship' (Blanchot 1997, 289-92). We might believe or even hope this is a personal testimony, since we know Blanchot knew Bataille well, and avidly read to discover some facts we did not know before, so as to add them to our insubstantial image of these writers. Right at the start Blanchot warns us off from such expectations. It is not about truth he writes, if that is what you think the truth is when remembering a friend. For what he is trying to remember cannot be captured by the memory of facts, details and data. What is essential about that person is what cannot be made present in any portrait. It is only those who do not matter to me that I can describe as 'persons'. The one who is my friend, who exists for me in the intimacy of friendship, escapes the objectivity of any description, and the experience of their character becomes something more than merely a list of character traits. The truest friend is not merely a reflection of myself, rather the friend opens me out to what is not myself. The intimacy of friendship should, therefore, not be confused with any social order. The friend is not a social agent revealing a common world with me. Rather, true friendship opens both friends to that which is unknown between them, and to a world which is outside this world. This is why Blanchot can write about friendship that, in some measure, 'there are no witnesses' (Blanchot 1997, 289), if we imagine that to witness something is only to witness what can be remembered, labelled, and objectified. To witness a world outside this world would be, on the contrary, to witness what cannot be remembered, what we cannot quite put into words, because it escapes us. In remembering his friendship with Georges Bataille, Blanchot bears witness, therefore, to what cannot be remembered and this is the greatest testimony to the intimacy of their relationship. It is a work of memory in which we attempt to remember what is so personal that it escapes any designation, description or classification. This is why the first thing that Blanchot refers to, when explaining his friendship with Georges Bataille, is not Georges Bataille himself, whoever that might be, but his books. For it is easy enough to remember Georges Bataille the man, as there are numerous biographies about him, which would tell us any number of facts we might wish to learn. But what is the strangest, the most unknown, affair of this life are the books, which although they are inseparably involved with this existence, are in no way wholly reducible to any fact, item or event of it. It would be laughable, though we could be sure many might have been tempted by it, to explain these books in terms of some personal reminiscence, whether his own or others. For the very reason that this life has become something very different is because of these books. Every biographical approach to literature imagines the life being used to describe the meaning of the books is itself something exterior to them, immutable and changeless, and yet this life has become a literary affair.

The Bataille of the books is not the same as the Bataille who lived and worked in Paris as a librarian, just as the Proust of *The Search of Time Lost* is not the same as the son of Adrien Proust. The real Bataille, whom we would like to anchor the writing, someone whom we might meet, and who might tell us face to face what all this means, is just as much a creation of words, as the

Bataille who is the character of *Inner Experience*. We start with the books and this is why we are interested in the life of Bataille the real person, but this life has already been radically changed by literature, such that it could never be the unambiguous starting point of an external and supposedly objective reading of the work.

Books communicate to us what is most unknown about the author who writes them, which we would find impossible to insert within the narrative of a seamless biography. Even if the writer, as Bataille certainly does, uses the first person personal pronoun often, this does not tell us anymore about them, for who does this 'I' refer to? Is it not just as a much a creation of words as any fictional character? Does it make it any more definite when we say that this personal pronoun refers to Bataille? For when we read *Inner Experience*, for example, which seems on the surface to be about the author, what he writes and describes is what is most difficult and unknown about himself, which properly speaking does not belong to him, nor to any person at all, if we think 'belonging' is what is proper to a stable and fixed identity, something we carry, for example, in our passports and other identity papers. Of course Bataille, like anyone else, can be such a person in the eyes of those institutions which require it, but this image is just as much a fiction as any other, and moreover tells us nothing about his work, even when he is part of it.

When Blanchot refers to his friendship with Bataille this is not an attempt to reconstruct this personality from the outside and then use it to interpret the body of work which bears his name, as though this friendship gave Blanchot an intimacy with Bataille other critics did not have, and thereby a greater access to the meaning of this work. What is at the heart of friendship is not knowledge of someone, but the absence of this knowledge. Only those who are indifferent to what officials, functionaries and bureaucrats know about us can be our friends. For the others our lives are only a series of facts and dates. To speak *about* a friend is no longer to be friends with them, but to speak *to* a friend is something quite different. In speaking, what passes between us is what is unknown to both of us, and which Blanchot calls a 'common strangeness' (Blanchot 1997, 291). In speaking about a friend, on the contrary, I merely inform everyone what I already know about my friend, which does not trouble or disturb me at all, and most of all does not touch on what troubles and disturbs me about myself in this friendship.

There are two kind of distance which are very different. There is the distance of the objective gaze in which a life is reduced to a series of events and dates, and there is the distance intimate to friendship which prevents me from finding a mutual recognition and shared interest, where my relation to friendship is neither one of need nor value. In my relation to a friend, my very self is turned inside out in speaking to them. I offer myself to them, but not as a bundle or parcel of knowledge. In the intimacy of my exposure and vulnerability, I offer to them what is not myself, what is unknown to me, but which lies at the very heart of who I am. The conversation of friendship is not really a speaking about oneself, if you think of it is as a giving and receiving information about yourself and the other. This is to confuse conversation with cross-examination.

To speak to a friend, as opposed to speaking about a friend, is to proffer yourself in the conversation, to leave yourself behind, let yourself go, and sacrifice yourself. Intimacy is not the recording of data about yourself, but losing yourself, such that you are no longer sure who you are speaking about when you are speaking to a friend. It is not that something unknown about yourself becomes known when you speak to a friend, as though friendship were a form of analysis or therapy. What is unknown remains unknown. It is this that is communicated through friendship. To be intimate with someone is not to know someone, but to be in relation to that which they do not know about themselves, and equally in that relation, to relate to that which you do not know about yourself. This is the distance which is necessary to friendship, which does not at all contradict intimacy but belongs necessarily to it. For the relation of knowledge is precisely not intimate. It is only those who do not affect me, whose presence I am wholly indifferent to, that I know. I cannot say who my friend is, or even who I am in this friendship. In this relation, both you and I have become something unknown to ourselves and to the other. Only when I speak about myself or my friend outside of the friendship, can I inform some third person about some fact or trait of their character. But at this moment I am no longer a friend, and this intimate knowledge is no intimacy at all.

Blanchot's friendship with Levinas does not give him a knowledge of his work which would be lacking to the rest of us. Still less does it mean that what they write must be held together in a common theme which they might have spoken about in a cafe in Paris, which some assiduous biographer will find out at some later date. Blanchot could not be more clear that the opposite is the case than when he writes that if it were philosophy that brought them together in friendship then it was this friendship which made philosophy 'lose its name' and become 'difficult' (Blanchot 1980, 80). In this instance, philosophy and friendship come into contact with one another, but only because they have lost their habitual significance. Their friendship names the most demanding thought which passes between them, which perhaps it is not possible for either of them to think without the other. When Blanchot writes that philosophy 'loses its name', he immediately adds after this phrase, 'by

89

becoming literature'. Philosophy is what lies at the heart of their friendship. It is, Blanchot writes, 'their clandestine friend'. It is the friend of their friendship. In being at the centre of this friendship, however, philosophy ceases to be what it is outside this friendship. It loses its name, and in so doing becomes literature. It does not lose its name in Blanchot's or Levinas's work, through a wilful act of misinterpretation or misunderstanding, but in the intimacy of their friendship, in which one interrupts and disrupts the other. To bring their work together through a common principle, concept or thought, would be to stand outside the corrosive effect of their friendship upon the ownership of their respective work. It would be to restore to the picture what their friendship occluded, and as such, it would be to become their enemy and the enemy of friendship itself.

When Blanchot writes about Levinas, for example, in *The Infinite Conversation* or *The Writing of Disaster*, we need to be very careful. We need to avoid two pitfalls: one that these interpretations are predicated on the secret knowledge of a personal and intimate history, or two, that they are purely objective and impersonal interpretations. In each case, the work would remain stable. It would only be a matter of displacing its equivocal surface to find the true meaning beneath. In the first instance, through an appeal to a life which stands outside the work, and in the second, in the objective reference of the work, the body of knowledge and information on which it stands. Blanchot on the contrary, writes of their work losing its name in their friendship. On the side of Levinas, philosophy becomes literature, but equally, on the side of Blanchot, literature becomes philosophy. Just as much as the meaning of Levinas's work changes in Blanchot's reading of it, 'becoming literature', so we too must reconvert this alteration back into philosophy.[4]

The thought of the outside

Blanchot tells us, in 'Our Clandestine Companion', that what Levinas shares with contemporary philosophy is an interest in language (Blanchot 1980, 82-3). This concern, however, is quite different from an interest in its logical, structural or pragmatic aspects. What is ethical about language is not the words which I speak, but my response to the Other who addresses me. A strange place for their thought to meet, since as anyone who has read a word of Blanchot's critical work, knows it is not speech but writing, and in particular literature, which is its question. How do we go from ethics to writing and still preserve the alterity of the Other? The details and particulars of such a journey will be the topic of the next chapter, but for now we need to reach the heart of Blanchot's conception of language to see that such a conjunction between writing and ethics is not as contradictory and incongruous, especially considering what Levinas has written about language in *Totality and Infinity*, as it first might appear. We remember that for Levinas writing is unethical because it is impersonal. It is the petrifaction, fossilisation and mortification of the presence of the Other in the written word, as opposed to its living presence in speech.[5] We also know that this is the essential Platonism of his ethics, at least as it is formulated in *Totality and Infinity*, and we might understand Blanchot's reading of Levinas's work in *The Infinite Conversation* as an attempt to rid it of this last vestige of Platonism. But all of this is yet to come. Let us first make a detour through thinking of language as a whole.

What is common to every analysis of language is its division, separation and partition into objective and subjective spheres. The former corresponding to universal forms or structures of language, and the latter to its use. These two parts can either be thought together or apart. Either the formal aspects of language are affected by the use of language or they are not, and visa versa.

Language is both the personal expression of an individual, where the creativity and abundance of meaning has its source, or it is the dispassionate object of a scientific analysis. The only question is what has precedence, the subjective or the objective. Take, for example, Chomsky's argument in *Cartesian Linguistics*.[6] What cannot be accounted for by the mechanistic explanations of language is the creative aspect of its ordinary use. What is decisive here is not the use of speech or sounds or written marks on the page, or even the ability to reproduce them, but the possibility of producing new meanings. Language is not merely communication in the sense of a response to stimuli, but the production of new ideas, content and impressions, which have no natural cause, and can only have their source in the over-abundant imagination of the subject. This is why Chomsky writes that the essence of language is poetry (Chomsky 2002, 61-2). Ironically, this is not because of language itself, but because of the subject which precedes language. Creativity is not in language, but is the power of self-expression, of which language is merely the tool. 'Speech,' Chomsky writes, 'is an instrument of thought and self-expression' (Chomsky 2002, 63). Linguistics, as a science, merely informs us about the universal features of a 'deep grammar', which probably have their source in the brain, and are therefore common to every human language. These aspects, however, tell us nothing about the creative, productive and prolific power of language, which is probably its true meaning.

The French linguist Emile Benveniste, in his seminal essay 'Subjectivity in Language', will also argue that the subject is essential to language, but, unlike Chomsky, places it within language, rather than outside (Benveniste 1971, 223-30). Language is not an instrument or tool of the subject's imagination, which is exterior to language, but its condition of possibility. Rather than language being dependent on the subject, the subject is dependent on language, and without it there would be no subjectivity at all. The idea that language is exterior to the subject rests on the fiction that sometime in the past human beings were without language, as though on one distant day, beyond memory and recall, two of our ancient and venerable ancestors met, and in this encounter miraculously learnt to speak to one another. There is no human nature without language. It makes no sense whatsoever to speak of human beings without language. To learn to speak one already has to be able to speak. 'We can never get back to man,' Benveniste writes, 'separated from language' (Benveniste 1971, 224). Rather than being a tool, language is first of all speech, and it is speech which is the condition of communication and not the other way around. What speech first of all constitutes, even before any information, content or data is exchanged, is the *relation* of speech itself. In this way, Benveniste's argument is no different from the priority given to speech in *Totality and Infinity*. Objectivity does not determine language, but language objectivity. It is not what is said which is primary, but the relation of speech which makes the said possible. Yet there is an important way in which Benveniste and Levinas are different. For what the relation of speech essentially constitutes for Benveniste is not the demand of the Other, not the response of responsibility, but the subjectivity of the subject. 'It is in and through language,' he writes, 'that man constitutes himself as a *subject*' [author's italics] (Benveniste 1971, 224). What is meant by subjectivity here is not some metaphysical substance, which was perhaps already destroyed by Kant's critique of Descartes in the paralogisms of the *Critique of Pure Reason*, but the possibility of placing oneself in the position of the subject, of saying 'I'. 'I' is the first word of language, the meaning of the relation of speech, without which no exchange would be possible. Such an 'I' has nothing to do with the feeling of being a subject, but is more a transcendental *discursive* condition of unity, which makes such a feeling possible. Such a unity is not first of all constituted in a thought outside of language, but is made possible by the relation of speech. We have here, then, a kind of linguistic Kantianism, where the function of the transcendental unity of apperception is taken over by the subject position of speech, which any empirical individual can occupy in order to become a subject. It is only because I can say 'I' that there is an 'I' at all. There is no 'I' before this possibility.

If the first word of the relation of speech is 'I', then the second word is 'you', because I only use the word 'I' in addressing a 'you'. There can be no

'I' without its twin 'you'. This is quite the reverse of Levinas's description of speech, where the 'I' is only possible through first of all being addressed by a 'you', rather than addressing a 'you'. I only speak because I am first of all addressed by the Other, whereas for Benveniste, you only speak because you are first of all addressed by an 'I'. The relation of speech is also reversible for Benveniste. The 'I' becomes a 'you' in responding to the 'I', and in this response the 'you' becomes an 'I'. For Levinas, on the contrary, speech is never reversible. I do not become the Other in responding to the Other's address to me. Rather, the 'I' always remains, as Levinas will argue in *Otherwise than Being*, in the accusative. He writes,

> Not strictly speaking an ego set up in the nominative in its identity, but first constrained to....
> It is set up as it were in the accusative form, from the first responsible and not being able to slip away (Levinas 1991, 85).

The reversibility of speech, in fact, for Benveniste, implies that the true position of language is always the first person. It is not because there is a 'you' that there is an 'I', but because there is an 'I' there is a 'you'. The reversibility of the relation does not suggest an equality of the terms, but the priority of the subject. Only because there is an 'I', and I take myself to be this 'I', could there be anything other than the subject. 'The *ego*,' Benveniste writes, 'always has a position of transcendence in relation to *you*' [author's italics] (Benveniste 1971, 225). Exactly the opposite, then, of the relation of speech in *Totality and Infinity*, where the *irreversibility* of the relation has its condition in the transcendence of the Other.

What is remarkable about language is the existence of personal pronouns. It is impossible to conceive of any language without them. Their existence proves the priority of the relation of speech over what is said. Their unique property, Benveniste states, is that unlike any other word in language *they do not refer to a concept or to an individual* [author's italics] (Benveniste 1971, 226). 'I' is not a concept which refers to unity of 'I's', such as the concept tree refers to individual trees. But nor does it refer to an individual person, otherwise 'I' would not be able to relate to any individual who speaks, and at the same time just pick out this one individual here and now. It can only refer to the relation of speech itself, to 'instances of discourse', Benveniste calls it, which can have no actual substantial or objective reference at all (Benveniste 1971, 226). The 'I' designates the speaker who addresses the 'you' in the relation of speech, and this is a possibility which any individual can take, but it does not refer to any kind of objective property of the speaker.

One is not an 'I' because one has brown hair or blue eyes, but only because one says 'I'. Without this saying, there would be no subjectivity. *Subjectivity is enacted, not predicated.* From this subject position all the rest of language follows; indexicals, demonstratives, adverbs, adjectives, and verbs which are the organisation of space and time in relation to the subject which speaks 'I'. So for example, in relation to time, every language, though through different means, distinguishes between the past and the future, but such a distinction only makes sense through reference to a present, and this present can only be thought as the coincidence of what is said and the event of saying it. The present is the same as the 'instance of discourse' and cannot be understood outside of it.

It is not that there is first of all the subject outside of language, which then in a second moment speaks. Rather only through speaking does the subject come into existence. 'Language,' Benveniste, writes 'is accordingly the possibility of subjectivity' (Benveniste 1971, 227). Having, however, announced the dualism of subjectivity and language, Benveniste then adds something quite remarkable which appears to undermine the priority of the subject in the relation of speech. We have already understood that the 'I' refers neither to an universal or individual I, but an 'instance of discourse' where someone says 'I', but rather than relating this instance back to the subject, Benveniste now links it to the 'empty form' of language. It is as if having argued for the priority of the subject all along, he now puts language before the subject. It is the 'empty forms' of language, which refers to no-one, which is the condition for the possibility of saying 'I', and not the other way around. Benveniste writes,

> In some way language puts forth 'empty' forms which each speaker, in the exercise of their discourse, appropriates to himself and which he relates to his 'person' (Benveniste 1971, 227).

He presents the situation as though it were the subject which appropriated the 'empty forms', but it could equally be the other way around. It is the 'empty forms', in the sense of making possible, which appropriate the subject. It is only because of the empty form 'I', which refers neither to everyone, nor to any single individual, but to no-one in particular, and this is why it is 'empty', that an individual can say 'I', and thus become a subject. Thus, we end up with precisely the opposite than Benveniste intends: subjectivity and language are not co-equal in the 'instance of discourse', but the former is dependent on the latter.

If what is common between Benveniste and Levinas is the emphasis on the relation of speech, and the priority of the 'instance of discourse' over what is said, then the difference between them, as we have already noted, is the relation of precedence between the 'I' and the 'you'. It is not the speaking subject which is the origin of language, but the address of the Other to the I. Just as with Benveniste, it is not the individuality of the Other which determines the form of the relation, but the relation itself. This is a subtle distinction, and one that is difficult to understand. If it were the individuality of the Other, then this would subvert the ethical difference between the terms in the relation. For the category of individuality is common between the I and the Other. Both the Other and I are individuals. Personhood would be an ontological category predicated of both terms in the relation. The reversal of the ontological order into the ethical takes place not through a term of the relation, which would merely be a dialectical reversal of the same logic, but through the relation itself.[7] Nonetheless, in the emphasis on the relation of speech, Levinas undermines this priority by placing the Other in the position of the speaking subject. This completely unravels the ethical relation. The form of language takes precedence over the ethical relation, and subverts the difference between the terms. The Other attends the words they speak exactly in the same way that the subject does. It is true that Levinas speaks of the Other and not the self, but he does so no differently than the tradition has always spoken about subjectivity. Moreover, by placing the assistance given to discourse at the heart of the ethical relation, he subverts the irreversibility of the relation. Why when I respond to the Other do I not become the Other to the Other, and the Other an 'I' to me in exactly the way that Benveniste describes? The emphasis on the personal pronouns of speech focuses our attention on the terms in the relation rather than the relation itself, and as such prevents any movement from the ontological to the ethical order. Alterity becomes a category of discourse, which would be a predicate common to both terms in the relation, rather than the expression of the *difference* between the terms of the relation which precedes their identity.

There seems, therefore, to be only two possibilities: either the subject is exterior to language, as its creative source or principle, as in Chomsky, or it is interior to language in the 'instance of discourse', as in Benveniste. Levinas's analysis of speech in *Totality and Infinity* appears to follow the latter. This is the reason why, without a careful reading, it can appear to be no different from speech act theory, which also prioritises the subject over the structure of language, but places it within the activity of discourse, rather than outside of it.[8] And yet even in Benveniste's description of the subject in speech, a third possibility emerges, which is a clue to Blanchot's critique of Levinas's use of language, and the emergence of his own notion of the neuter. In investigating the status of the subject, Benveniste ends up in the opposite position than the one he sought. It is not the subject which supports language, but language the subject. Without the 'empty forms' of the relation of speech, which are indicated by the use of personal pronouns, there would be no subjectivity at all. If the forms of language precedes or 'proposes', to use Benveniste's expression, the personal pronouns, then language is not first of all personal, but the condition of selfhood from which the other pronouns follow. This would mean that the impersonality of language, the emptiness of Benveniste's 'empty forms', antecedes personal existence, as though there were an 'it speaks' at the heart of every 'I speak'.

Can we approach the impersonality of language directly without the mediation of personal pronouns? Here we might turn to the opening pages of Foucault's celebrated essay on Blanchot, 'The Thought of the Outside'. It also begins with an 'I speak', but rather than discovering a subject speaking in the first person, it comes up against a language which no-one speaks, encircling the subject, rather than issuing from its initiative or act of freedom. Foucault begins with two utterances: 'I speak', and 'I lie' (Foucault 1990, 9). The second utterance is a reference to the famous Liar's Paradox, whose full form is as follows: 'If I am saying that I am lying, am I telling the truth? If I am, I am lying and uttering a falsehood; but if I am not telling the truth I am lying, and so I am telling the truth. So my utterance is both true and false.'[9] It is a paradox because the statement is the object of itself, and it can be dissolved simply by a hierarchy of levels. Foucault knows this, but he is not interested in solving this paradox. Rather he thinks there is something much stranger at its heart than a logical puzzle. Take for example the simple utterance 'I speak'. There seems to be no paradox here between what I say and what is said in what I say, between the statement and the propositional object of that statement. Nothing could be simpler than asserting that when I say 'I speak ' I am speaking. And yet, Foucault argues, language is not that plain and simple, even in this case. The reference of what is said in the phrase 'I speak' is the fact that I am speaking, but as such it is fragile and momentary. It exists only in the moment in which I speak it, and as soon as I fall silent it disappears into the absence of language from which it emerged. What is first, then, is not the subject which speaks, but the formless and inchoate expanse of words, which this subject must break in order to speak, and which it falls back into as soon as it stops speaking. Every word I have spoken has existed before me and will exist after me. I am surrounded by words, words are everywhere, I am lost in words, and rather than speaking them they speak through me.

Literature is the experience of, or tries to approach, this swirl of words before it is occupied by a speaking subject. It is language, which is anonymous or neutral, the 'it speaks' as opposed to the 'I speak', that is first and not the subject. The empty subject position of language, which is the possibility of there being a speaking subject at all, is a function of this anonymity. It is the words which make me, not I them. There is nothing but words, and there is no end or beginning of them. Any commencement is arbitrary, and always a recommencement. We are all in the endless stream of words which come from no one. Without these words we are nothing. At the moment they stop, we stop. When I speak, behind my words, there is always this endless murmuring and rustling of words, a constant chattering and noise, which my speech interrupts momentarily, but falls back into as soon as it is silent. Rather than resisting this chaos, literature attempts to communicate it. This is why it is not the author's voice which is expressed in the work, even when it is at its most autobiographical, but the dizzying, stubborn, and brute fact of language.

Kafka

Literature has a privileged position, because it is the pure statement unbidden by the proposition and the phrase, which are its derivations. Blanchot describes the anonymity of literary language, in perhaps one his most important and significant essays 'The Narrative Voice', as the movement from using the pronoun 'I' to the 'he' in the telling of the story in the modern novel (Blanchot 1993, 379-87). There is a moment, and Blanchot is specifically alluding to Kafka here, where the author no longer writes 'I' but 'he', where the narrative is told from the third, rather than the first person, , as in the opening lines of *The Metamorphosis*: 'As Gregor Samsa awoke one morning from uneasy dreams he found himself transformed in his bed transformed into a gigantic insect' (Kafka 1999, 89). It is important that we do not confuse what Blanchot writes here with any kind of grammatical analysis, which would concern only the structure of language as applied to the literary form, rather than the outside of language which has no substance or structure. Literature is not one more use of language which can be compared to another. Writers do not use language, they suffer from it, from too much or too little. Their aim, if this is at all possible, is to let language speak for itself. This is the meaning of the shift from the 'I' to the 'he'. It is the writer saying to reader, though this had been true all along, 'look it is not me speaking, please do not confuse this with me.'

I can write, Blanchot suggests, a simple sentence like: '"The forces of life suffice only up to a certain point"' (Blanchot 1993, 379). This sentence has a very simple grammatical form. We could also say that it says something about the person who wrote it. Someone who is at the limit of their powers, who if they took seven or eight steps in the street would immediately fall to the ground. The fact, however, that this sentence is written down changes everything. For there is something slightly bizarre, if not humorous, about someone whose existence, if this sentence is not a lie, is so exhausted, and yet they have enough energy, vigour and concentration to write about their distress. What has happened to this limit at the moment that they write about it? It is placed in the interior of the life it describes as exterior. Rather than exhaustion being something which attacks me from the outside, causes me to fall down in the street, I have turned it into an idea or thought which I can write down on the page. It has been translated into meaning. I imagine it happening to someone else, even if this 'someone else' is me. I look down upon them, I describe them falling down on the street.

What occurs, Blanchot asks, if we place the same sentence into a narrative? The difference between them, he responds, would be very great indeed. In the narrative, the same sentence's relation to life is quite different. It neutralises it. This does not mean, he adds, that it no longer has a relation to life, but it relates to it through a 'neutral one' (Blanchot 1993, 380). In this relation, the meaning of life and the meaning of the sentence is still 'given', but only through a kind of 'withdrawal' or a 'distance', which suspends the attachment of meaning to the intentions of a subject.

Already in *The Space of Literature*, again alluding to Kafka, Blanchot had described literature as the transition from the 'I' to the personal pronoun the 'he'. 'The writer,' he writes, 'belongs to a language which no one speaks, which is addressed to no one, which has no centre, and reveals nothing' (Blanchot 1982, 16). But who is this 'he' who tells the story in Kafka's stories and novels? We want to say that it cannot be no-one. It is only a literary device, and in reality it refers back to the author who writes the words on the page, who in real life feels happy, or sad, or exhausted. It is perfectly possible to read literature in this way. Indeed many people do, and there are countless biographical interpretations of Kafka's work, which would interpret, for example, Gregor Samsa's difficulties as merely an allegory of Kafka's own unhappiness. But to read literature this way, in a funny sense, is not to read at all. At the moment where you are tempted to interpret what you are reading through the life of the author, then you have ceased reading a work of literature. It has become an autobiography. This temptation is real, especially so as literature becomes more and more literary, pays more attention to the word and language. For the more empty the novel is, the more it just tells a story, the most difficult problem for the author, the more we are tempted to fill the hole with the full presence of the author's personality. We feel satisfied. We can now insert what we are reading back into the our universe of meaning, into the safe world of the everyday in which everything makes sense, and Kafka vies with the other great writers as being number one on the 'greatest authors of time' list in some Sunday newspaper. But for Blanchot literature cannot be inserted within culture. Literature is not part of culture because it is the great wave of language that inundates the sensible world of meaning and sense where everything has its place, where the word 'cat' really does mean cat and not something else. Literature can become part of culture, but in so doing ceases to be literature.

If Blanchot tells us how to read literature, then it is to stick with it, not to try and find some anchor point against the dizziness in the world outside. So Blanchot says if you really pay attention to the 'he' in the Kafka's work, what you find is that it does not refer to anything outside of the work at all, rather, quite strangely, the narrator ends up belonging to the narrative he or she is telling. Now this is true of literature for Blanchot. There are many devices that the author can use to conceal it. They can write in the first person, for example. Or they can place the narrator outside the events they are describing. But these are all fictions that words make possible. They are not really outside the narrative at all. The 'he' refers neither to a reality behind nor beyond the narrative, but belongs to it. Even if I believe that the narrative voice goes back to someone, the objective voice of the storyteller, who stands above the events he or she describes, or to the personal voice of authors whose narrative is merely the re-dramatisation of their own individuality, then these 'subjects' are what the narrative makes possible, rather than its condition or origin. These narrators are not real, if we think by the word 'real' they are standing outside of the narrative, but are only possible within its circle.

This absorption of the narrator within the narrative is most compelling in the novels and stories of Kafka, which is why Blanchot writes about him so often, where the illusion of the distance between the narrator and the narrative collapses. In Flaubert and Mann, on the contrary, we have the illusion, also made possible by the narrative, of a narrator distanced from the events being told. The reader, then, is easily led into the mistake of thinking the narrator and narrative are separate, and of confusing the narrator with the author. The dissolution of the distance between the narrator and the narrative in Kafka explains the chaotic and nightmarish quality of his work. There is no disinterested narrator who would explain these events to us. Joseph K. is arrested one morning, and we have no more idea why, than he does. Here we have an experience of a pure narrative in which what is recounted is simply what is at stake in the narrative. It refers to nothing outside of itself, even the illusion of reality. Who is speaking in Kafka's novels? Kafka? Joseph K.?

some impersonal narrator? or is it better to say that no-one at all is speaking?
The voice seems to come from outside of the narrative, but at the same time is
part of it. 'The narrative voice,' Blanchot writes, 'that is inside only insomuch
as it is outside', decentres the heart of the narrative or the novel (Blanchot
1993, 386). For to whom could we appeal for authority? Even if we try to
institute another authority, the literary critic for example, to replace the author,
then this power only exercises its influence in relation to the absence it desires to fill. In so doing it kills the very thing it hopes to explain. It is absence,
the language no-one speaks, which is the fascination and compulsion of
literature. It forbids every completion or last word. All this changes radically
our relation to what we are reading. The illusionary distance of the narrator
gave us the security of being at a distance from the narrative. We occupy the
same position as the narrative, recounting the events, but not part of them.
But once the narrator, once the distance of the narrator, has become part of
the narrative, the reader too can no longer be a spectator. The 'he' of narration, beyond the meaning of the personal pronoun, is the experience of this
vertigo, which is the impossibility of any subject position, whether we are
speaking of a real author, a narrator, or a reader.

Notes

1 Josh Cohen, in his book *Interrupting Auschwitz*, gives an excellent reading of the status of art in Levinas, and its uncomfortable relation to Blanchot's writing (Cohen 2003, 71-105). Uneasy, perhaps, because friendship already disturbs Levinas's own certainties.

2 As we outlined in chapter 1 in the section 'Beyond the face', pp.20-4.

3 Except in the conclusion, which might have been the inspiration for Blanchot's review, where he asks the question for whom does one write. 'On n'écrit donc ni pour les vrais prolétaires, occupés ailleurs, et fort bien occupés, ni pour les vrais bourgeois affamés de biens, et qui n'ont pas d'oreilles. On écrit pour les inadaptés, ou désadaptés, ni bourgeois ni prolétaires, c'est-à-dire pour ses amis, et moins pour les amis qu'on a que pour les inconnus sans nombres qui ont la même vie que nous, qui en gros cru comprendre les mêmes choses, pouvoir accepter ou devoir refuser les mêmes silence officiel' [One writes neither for the true proletarian, occupied elsewhere, and really occupied, nor for the true bourgeois starved of goods, who have not the ears. One writes for the mal- or "disadjusted", neither proletarian nor bourgeois; that is to say, for one's friends, and less for the friends one has than for the innumerable unknown people who have the same life as us, who roughly understand the same things, are able to accept or must refuse the same, and who are in the same state of powerlessness and official silence] (Mascolo 1953, 546-7).

4 There is a tendency in the commentaries on Blanchot and Levinas to treat the relation between them as an opposition. Blanchot thus represents 'literature' and Levinas 'philosophy'. Gerald L. Bruns, in his book *Maurice Blanchot and the Refusal of Philosophy*, perhaps best reflects this direction when he describes Blanchot's work as belonging to ancient quarrel between philosophy and literature (Bruns 1997, xiii) and his writings to be '"mystical", even religious' (Bruns 1997, xviii). Their friendship undercuts this opposition. If there is a 'becoming literature' of Levinas's philosophy in Blanchot, then there is equally a 'becoming philosophy' of Blanchot in Levinas. It is possible therefore to read Blanchot philosophically without betraying him; or better, this betrayal is a testimony of his friendship, of the presence of Levinas in his work. A similar approach, though more genealogical than descriptive, is adopted by Marlène Zarader in her book *L'être et le neutre : à partir de Maurice Blanchot*, where she writes that 'il faut se risquer à faire ce qui n'a jamais été fait: prendre ai sérieux, et au mot, la *pensée* de Blanchot' [it is necessary to risk what has never been done: to take seriously, and at its word, the *thought* of Blanchot] [author's emphasis] (Zarader 2001, 21).

5 In the section 'teaching' in the first chapter, pp.16-20. We shall also

describe, in more detail, this mistrust of writing in the last chapter, in the section 'Writing, politics and history', pp.132-8.

6 Why choose this work on language and not any other? Because it expresses in the most clear and transparent way possible a prejudice of a certain conception of language, which perhaps has its origin in such writers as Humboldt and A.W. Schlegel, but which has now become commonplace and ordinary, that language is above all the personal and subjective expression of my own inner world. All linguistics, whether empiricist or rationalist, takes it for granted that language is essentially the expression of the subject. It is this starting point which Blanchot rejects. 'What is first,' Deleuze writes, 'is a ONE SPEAKS, an anonymous murmur in which positions are laid out for possible subjects: "the great relentless disordered drone of discourse' [capitals in the original] (Deleuze 1988, 55).

7 See the first section of chapter 2, 'Identity and multiplicity', pp.28-32.

8 Benveniste summarises speech act theory in his essay 'Analytical Philosophy and Language' (Benveniste 1971, 231-38), and the existence of performatives is offered as proof of the uniqueness of the personal pronoun 'I' at the end of 'Subjectivity in Language' (Benveniste 1971, 229-30).

9 See (Clark 2002, 99), who also gives an excellent, lucid and brief explanation of this paradox.

5

Writing

It might seem that already in the title of Blanchot's book *The Infinite Conversation* a strong alliance with Levinas's *Totality and Infinity* is announced. Does it not already imply the absolute importance of speech which is at the heart of Levinas's ethics? Yet the conversation which begins *The Infinite Conversation* is like no dialogue you would find in the pages of one of Levinas's books (Blanchot 1993, xiii-xxiii). It reads as though it were an episode from a play or novel of Beckett, or even of one of Blanchot's own narratives. Two speakers meet. Or they have met a long time ago. We do not know who they are. They are tired and worn out, and they seem to speak only of the conversation which they are having because they have forgotten the topic at the beginning. What holds them together is not the force of one speaker or the other, but the conversation itself, existing as it does between them, and almost without them. How different this situation is from the straightforwardness and directness of the ethical relation, where it is the presence of the Other which begins and sustains the dialogue. There is no equivocation, awkwardness, and uncertainty in Levinas's ethical relation. Everything circles around the presence of the interlocutor in the words they speak, which dispels any ambivalence or obscurity in what is said. In the conversation which begins *The Infinite Conversation*, the words spoken seem to have suspended their meaning. Nothing could be said which could capture the moment which is about to disappear. Everything which is said is marked by a weariness and fatigue which comes not from the speakers, but from the situation they find themselves in, and cannot quite remember why or how they got there. It is not the speakers who forms the basis of the conversation, as the interlocutor does in *Totality and Infinity*, rather it is the conversation which has taken hold of the speakers in its weary and exhausted grip. It is not the speakers who are tired and worn out, but the conversation. Blanchot writes, at the beginning of the conversation, that one of the speakers waits for 'a confirmation' from the other, waits to see whether they agree about what has been said, but no reply comes (Blanchot 1993, xiii). This is not because the other speaker disagrees, or because they have failed to listen, but because even before anything has been said, they are already in agreement. 'This,' Blanchot writes 'is the condition of their conversation' (Blanchot 1993, xiii). The agreement does not come from one or the other speaker, but from the conversation. It is more of a sentence than a decision or choice: the fact that they are speaking to one another, even though they have forgotten what it is that they are speaking about.

If the topic of their conversation is the fatigue they both feel, this must be distinguished from the very fatigue which is the condition of the conversation. For without this common weariness the speakers would not have come together, but because of it they have hardly the strength to speak. 'What weariness makes possible,' one of them says, 'weariness makes difficult' (Blanchot 1993, xiv). They speak about speaking, but say nothing. Always trying to find out why they are here, why they are speaking in this room, but having completely forgotten. If they were not tired, they would remember, so they would not speak, for they would be quite certain what they were doing and would not have to ask the other. Weariness, one of them says, 'keeps us speaking' (Blanchot 1993, xv). It makes them speak not because it is the topic of their conversation, but they would not speak at all without it. For Levinas too, speaking precedes what is spoken, but speaking is described in terms of the *address*. Speaking is always attached to the speaker, to the presence of the interlocutor in the words they address to me. In this conversation, however, speaking is not directly attached to the speaker. Speaking precedes both the speaker and what is spoken. Speaking places the speaker outside of themselves. Not just because in speaking I am speaking about something else, or even that I am addressing another, but since the event of speaking comes from somewhere else. It does not even come from the Other, if I mean by the 'Other' another person. It comes from the interval between us. The conversation has already begun before I have spoken and before anyone demands that I speak, and its origin is beyond the power of anyone to remember.

Community

The conversation which precedes the speakers is not the same as a community. The latter brings us together, makes us one, and if it comes before us it does so as something welcoming and gives us shelter. It is the 'we' which is the hidden authority of the 'I'. The conversation holds us apart, prevents us from becoming one. Or perhaps, from the perspective of this conversation, it is possible to think community in a different way. In *The Unavowable Community*, published many years after *The Infinite Conversation*, Blanchot again returns to the meaning of communism which we have discussed in the previous chapter.[1] The community which is expressed etymologically in this word is not the same as 'a whole, a group, a council', or even 'a collective', which is usually taken to be the meaning of this word (Blanchot 1988, 1). One way of understanding communism is in terms of equality in which everyone's needs are satisfied. This equality should not be confused with the ideal of a utopia, which still admits of a perfection beyond man's grasp, but is a pure immanence. In this communism, there would be nothing outside man. Everything would be the expression of his needs and it would only be a matter of satisfying them rationally. The fundamental basis of this society would be the individual, since needs only exist at an individual level. An immanent society would be one which allows every individual *equal* rights to their own self-preservation. The other has no rights over me, rather the other is only an individual like me. A purely immanent society would be a society of monads in perfect harmony. Such a communism would be inseparable from the 'sickest totalitarianism' since anything which prevented this harmony would have to be destroyed (Blanchot 1988, 2).

There is another way of thinking communism, and here again Blanchot returns to Bataille. It would be a communism not of reciprocity, but of the dissymmetry of the relation to the Other. Such a communism, however, would have to be thought as the 'absence of community', if what we mean by community is the transparent society in which each is the same as the other (Blanchot 1988, 3). This absence should not be thought in relation to the community of equals, as though it were just its lack. Rather, this absence should be thought in its own right. It is possible then to think the absence of community as a different kind of community, rather than simply the reverse image of totalitarianism. Blanchot asks what is it that really calls me into question. It is not my relation to myself, but the death of the Other who 'absents himself in dying' (Blanchot 1988, 9). It is this death which opens me outside of myself and thereby makes another community possible. Possible only in its impossibility and absence. For this community is the interruption of the community of individuals, whether we think of it as a series of individuals connected together in their equal rights to have their needs satisfied, or as the fusion of all in the whole. It is not another type of community which we might oppose to the community we might have or hope for. It is a community only to the extent that it is not a community at all, but the impossibility of every community. To understand this significance of the death of the Other in

The Unavowable Community, we must go back to the pages of Jean-Luc Nancy's *The Unworkable Community*, which are its inspiration (Nancy 1991, 12-19).

We can consider death in relation to immanence. In this case, death is the return to nature in which 'there is only the continuous identity of atoms' (Nancy 1991, 12). This is why the truth of an immanent society is death. Its ideal is the suppression of every singular life for the sake of a glorious death in which society becomes one. It is also the death of extermination camps where anything 'other', foreign or different is expelled from the inner circle. Nazi Germany is not the exception to the immanent society, but merely its logic pushed to the ultimate extreme. In the end such a logic is impossible to stop. The immanent society is the society of death, for the purest immanence is the death of every human being, whether gloriously or in abjection. There is nothing left but the battlefield and everything is justified in relation to death. The future society, which is infinitely deferred, will only come if I sacrifice my life to the State. The State only exists to the degree that I do not exist. But this future is a lie. It will never come. In fact it is not a 'future' at all, for there can be nothing outside the State. It, Nancy writes, is a 'perpetual past of community' (Nancy 1991, 13). What then of those who have sacrificed their lives for the sake of the disadvantaged, dispossessed or oppressed? All we can say is that they have died, but it would be fraudulent to say that their deaths have been redeemed. 'No dialectic,' Nancy writes, 'no salvation leads these deaths to any other immanence than that of ... death' (Nancy 1991, 13). There is the myth of a secular redemption in modern politics that our deaths are in some way useful, that in some future society they will be redeemed. But death is death, decomposition and cessation, and redemption merely hides this truth. The society of sacrifice is the society of putrefaction and corpses littered on the field or in the concentration camp. This death is not redeemable. Someone always dies for my beliefs.

There is, however, another meaning of death which does not fit with this idea of a collective restitution, and which 'exceeds the recourses of the metaphysics of the subject' (Nancy 1991, 14). This death cannot be put to work, if we mean by 'work' something which is useful or meaningful, when we attempt to justify someone's death, as though there always existed some higher purpose dimly foreseen. This other death is the death of the Other. This brings us to a completely different meaning of community based upon the relation to others, rather than to ourselves. Not others as a collection, unity or assemblage, as though they were merely a totality of egos suspended in a common idea, but others as *singularities*. For if the other is truly other to me, then I am also other for another I. The other is what I am when I am not myself, when I do not consider myself first of all from the point of view of consciousness or a subject . But I am always not 'myself'. I already belong to a 'community of others', if we understand the word 'community' here not as the communion or fusion of egos in a 'higher *We*', but 'what takes place through other and for others' [author's italics] (Nancy 1991, 15). The immanent society is the society of the subject where we begin first of all by considering who we are, rather than from the viewpoint of the others which disrupt this 'we'. We do this by identifying ourselves with a common idea which expresses a common identity and we expel anything and anyone which does not belong to this idea. But this other community is not a community of individuals, but others. Other both to each other and to themselves. It is a community of distance and separation, rather than identity and unity. It is an impossible community because it exists in the impossibility of its own immanence, where each member could become one, whether that one is a nation, race or party. The difficulty is not to fall back into thinking this 'community of others' substantively, as though the word 'other' were just another name for a common identity, which we might express by the phrase 'all humans are others'. The word 'other' is not a substantive. It names a relation in which I am no longer myself, in which I am separated or distanced from myself. The gravity of community is substitution, and not communion.[2]

This 'community of others' is not necessarily one of speech, and this perhaps is the greatest difference between Blanchot and Levinas. 'The community,' Blanchot writes, 'in its very failure, is linked to a certain kind of writing' (Blanchot 1988, 12). Here he is thinking directly of surrealism, but also the more esoteric projects of Bataille, like Acéphale.[3] Yet, reading the opening of *The Infinite Conversation*, we might think that the only relation to the Other which is significant to Blanchot is one of speech. Nonetheless, it is important to see how, in his meticulous reading of Levinas, Blanchot begins to shift the emphasis of the ethical relation away from speech towards writing. This does not entail simply a negation of speech. Rather it is a matter of understanding speech in a different way, one we have already seen in operation in the conversation which opens this book. It is no longer the speaker in the conversation which is given precedence, the Other who attends the words they speak, but the relation of speech, and the interval and distance which separates the interlocutors.

The teaching of philosophy

Let us, then, read the essay which opens *The Infinite Conversation*,

'Thought and the Exigency of Discontinuity', which was originally published in 1963 (Blanchot 1993, 3-10). Although we are quite happy to accept, Blanchot argues, that other kinds of writing have some kind of form or style, such as literature, poetry or drama, philosophy, even though it is written, appears to have none at all. The written word is merely the vehicle of the idea it expresses. The fact that it is written can be easily disregarded. There is, however, even for philosophy, a certain traditional way in which it is constructed, which is determined by the power of the university. No doubt, in our own recent history, there are exceptions to this rule, but however many different styles of philosophical writing there are, what is common to them all is that research is linked to teaching.[4] To practice philosophy is to teach, and to write philosophy is to present the results of this teaching, either directly, for example, in the form of Plato's dialogues, or in a more hidden way. This is a fundamental form or style of philosophy that has been handed down to us by our Greek heritage. This institutionalisation of philosophy is even more obvious in modern times. 'From Kant onwards,' Blanchot writes, 'the philosopher is primarily a professor' (Blanchot 1993, 4).

How then does Blanchot understand teaching? To teach is to speak. The 'interrelational space' of this dialogue, between the teacher and student, or the 'master' and 'disciple' is not symmetrical. It is not a discourse between equals. It is not the master, as such, who is higher than the student, but the relation. It is teaching which determines the asymmetry of the relation, and not one of the individuals in the relation. This is why Blanchot can write that the 'master represents a region of space and time that is absolutely other' (Blanchot 1993, 5). How can we comprehend this relation in greater detail? First of all there is no reversibility. The disciple does not stand to the master in the same way that the master stands to the disciple. If we imagine, Blanchot argues, that the master is point A and the disciple is point B, then the distance, as though we were simply to draw a line between them, between point B and point A is not the same,. Although the space between A and B can be crossed in the words of the master who instructs the disciple, the same space from B to A cannot. Even in hearing the words that the master speaks, there is still an uncrossable distance between him and the disciple. It is quite clear that all of this is written with Levinas in mind, even though Blanchot mentions the 'Oriental tradition' (Blanchot 1993, 6). This is confirmed when at the end of this paragraph he will go on to to argue that this is a description not merely of teaching, but of speech as such. Teaching is not just one kind of speech, but defines the very ethical status of language. Language is not first of all the description or labelling of things but communication to an Other, and this interlocution is not unbidden. Every communication is already a response to the presence of the Other in an address.

All this would seem to work against our argument that Blanchot moves away from Levinas's analysis of speech and its rejection of writing. And yet one of the misunderstandings Blanchot mentions which could destroy the asymmetry of this relation already suggests a subtle difference between him and Levinas. He warns us that if we confuse the transcendence of the relation with the transcendence of the master; that is to say, if we *personalise* the relation of speech, then we threaten to destroy the distance between the terms of the relation. It is because Blanchot depersonalises speech (and this explains the rather enigmatic subtitle of this part of the *Infinite Conversation*, 'the speech of writing) that he steps over the opposition between speech and writing which still operates in *Totality and Infinity*. The relation of language is a relation to the Other who addresses me, and in this allocution the objectivity of the world is founded. Infinity is therefore the condition of totality and not the other way around. Blanchot's account of speech is quite different, even though on first glance, precisely because it makes passing reference to teaching, it might appear to be the same. Speech is not first of all a relation to the Other, but the relation itself in which what is known to me becomes unknown, and when I relate to that person no longer as an individual or even as a person, but as Other. Alterity names a relation, not a person. From this it follows, that rather than being a condition of totality, it is an experience of discontinuity and separation. This is why Blanchot can write that speech, at least if it is understood as the relation to the Other, is closer to the fragmentary writing of Pascal, Nietzsche and Bataille, than to objectivity and representation. Language, whether we are speaking about speech or writing, is the experience of discontinuity. What is important is the difference between continuity and discontinuity, and not speech and writing merely understood as different ways of externalising language. Just as speech could be discontinuous, writing can be continuous. Blanchot makes a passing reference to the very text that we are reading. Is it not made of sentences and paragraphs? Does it not have an argument which the reader can follow so as to arrive at some kind of certain conclusion (Blanchot 1993, 8-9)? Is this not what I am doing in this very moment; trying to communicate to you what I understand these pages to mean? But maybe this continuity is only apparent. One of the strange qualities of modern literature, in such writers as Lautréamont, Proust and Joyce, is that the more they seek continuity and completeness in continuous speech, the more they produce discontinuity and incompleteness. 'An excess of continuity,' Blanchot writes, 'unsettles the reader, and unsettles the reader's habits of regular comprehension' (Blanchot 1993, 9). It is as though through the demand of continuity speech and writing are far apart, but in discontinuity they come together. There is not so much difference, Blanchot is suggesting, between this discontinuity of writing, in which normal patterns of knowledge are disrupted, and the interval of speech, where the other person becomes someone unknown and enigmatic to me. In both cases, it is a matter of disrupting the unity of the terms in the relation. In speech, it is the interval between the speakers which cannot be crossed. In writing, the written page and the reader. Such a proximity allows Blanchot to write something very strange at the end of this essay, which cuts through the very heart of Levinas's philosophy, that 'the exigency of speech' is 'in advance always already written' (Blanchot 1993, 10). 'Written', because it follows the other law of discontinuity, rather than continuity. What is important is not the difference between speech and writing, but the discontinuity which disrupts them both, and which the unity of thought is constantly concealing or avoiding.

Plato

What strikes anyone immediately about the essays concerning Levinas in *The Infinite Conversation* is their form.[5] All, except the last two, which were published a few years later, are written in the style of a conversation. This should not surprise us from what we have already learnt. If there is a profound connection between the interval of speech or conversation and fragmentary writing, then it would be perhaps strange for Blanchot to write about speech in continuous prose more suitable to the journal article or academic book. Of course, this makes it all the more difficult for us, since this work has been written in the form more suitable to the university. We must then, and this can only be a kind of disservice or betrayal, translate Blanchot's discontinuous prose into a continuous one, and ignore the fact that different statements about Levinas are made by different voices. The plurality of the voices subverts the temptation of retracing what is said back to an authorial intention. What can save us from a complete betrayal, but only to a certain degree, is that discontinuity and continuity are two sides of writing. 'These two directions should impose themselves,' Blanchot writes, 'in turn' (Blanchot 1993, 7). This means that no writing is either purely discontinuous, or continuous, even if it imagines itself to be so. This is as true of the most extreme logical writing, which believes in the perfect expressibility of ideas almost to the extent that the symbols themselves no longer matter, as as it is of the most excessive experimental writing, such as the automatic writing of the surrealists, which searches for a pure discontinuity.

The first essay, 'Knowledge of the Unknown', opens with a discussion of philosophy (Blanchot 1993, 49). Philosophy begins in wonder, not fear, and fear of the unknown. To practice philosophy is to open yourself up to what you cannot think, to what shakes the very foundation of your world. To do philosophy is not to defend common sense, as some might think, but to exceed it. This fear is not fear of something specific, for such a fear would still belong to a known world in which I could differentiate between that which is harmful or beneficial to my own self-preservation. Rather, it comes from my own being. I am fearful of my existence in the world as a whole, and not something *in* this world.[6] One of speakers says that this fear or anxiety, in which the philosopher is exposed to the unknown, is like a 'presentiment of the Other' (Blanchot 1993, 51). I cannot remain the same in this encounter, otherwise what is other is not really other at all. It still has a place in what I know about my world. The unknown is not a lack or an absence, if we mean by this simply a hole or interval within our comprehension, much like Kant's famous 'thing-in-itself'. For this deficiency is defined in advance by what it fails to complete. Even for Kant, the 'thing-in-itself' is only an idea of reason, and thereby *knowledge's* limit. This would mean that in relation to the 'unknown', if it is truly to remain unknown and not just thought's image of the unknown, I must become unknown to myself, 'shamefully transformed,' one of the speakers says, 'into something other than myself' (Blanchot 1993, 51).

How would it be possible to write about this relation without betraying it, making comprehensible what is meant to be incomprehensible, and at the same time avoiding an empty mysticism which merely reveals in its own irrationality, and which is, paradoxically, merely the inverse image of the reason that it despises? It is at this point that the name of Emmanuel Levinas is introduced, and more specifically *Totality and Infinity*. 'It is as though there were here,' one of the speakers says, 'a new departure in philosophy and a leap that it, and we ourselves, were urged to accomplish' (Blanchot 1993, 52). It is important at which point or place in the argument Blanchot situates the question of the Other. He does not focus on the phenomenological description as such, as though it were obvious that such a description could be done, but on its possibility. How can we write a phenomenology of that which escapes any phenomena? Does not the very notion of phenomena, from Kant to Husserl, already presuppose a relation to consciousness, and thus the unknown to the known? For Blanchot the question of the Other is from the beginning a question of method and writing, and thus a question of the history of philosophy. How has philosophy as a whole faced the question of the Other, and why is it possible now, in Levinas's book *Totality and Infinity*, able do so in a completely different manner? It is not just the relation of speech which is the experience of the Other, but also the description of this relation. For if writing were not also exposed to the Other, there would be no possibility at all of philosophy thinking differently about the Other, not constantly absorbing it into its own discourse without harm or hindrance. The experience of the Other is not just a question *of* philosophy, but a question *to* philosophy, as though Levinas's work both remains within, and steps outside of, the orbit of philosophy, and it can only step outside of philosophy by writing it in a different way. One of the strongest aspects of this book, one of the speakers says, is the logic of the relation between the self and the Other, which they call, though disparagingly at first, 'the philosophy of separation' (Blanchot 1993, 52). They elaborate with the idea that we must approach this relation through 'four paths', though it is difficult, for certain, to reconstruct them, since we are never presented us with a simple list: the re-appropriation of the Cartesian idea of the infinite, the re-interpretation of thought as desire, the face to face relation, and ethical speech. It is upon the last that we need to focus our attention, for it is here that Blanchot voices, through one of the speakers, disagreement with the emphasis on direct speech in *Totality and Infinity*. The 'philosophy of separation', as Blanchot calls it, exceeds the opposition between speech and writing, as Levinas presents it (following the Platonic metaphor) when he argues that only direct speech can be ethical, and writing never.[7]

Speech in *Totality and Infinity*, is 'interpellation' (Blanchot 1993, 55).[8] What comes first is the demand of the Other, which signifies its height above the self, and not the words spoken. It comes from the Other not because of what the Other says, as though the interpellation Levinas were describing were merely grammatical, but from the logic of the relation. Interpellation expresses the separation of the relation. The demand always comes from the side of the Other and not the self, and it is always the self which responds first of all to the Other and not the Other to the self. Interpellation, command, injunction are all words to describe the asymmetry of this relation. Language, before it is a relation of equals, is first of all, a relation of superiority. The presence of the Other in the words they speak is absolutely important to this asymmetry, for without it there would be only the relation of equals, and as Levinas seems to suggest in the preface to *Totality and Infinity*, war (Levinas 1969, 21-2). Yet this presence of the Other in speech, which prevents conflict and strife, has nothing to do with words. It is the *pre-linguistic* condition of language. This is why one of the interlocutors can speak of 'the presence of speech', which has nothing at all to do with any words that have been said (Blanchot 1993, 55). This presence is associated with two themes of Levinas' work, which both speakers appear to be equally suspicious of, and which they claim can be detached from the main thesis of *Totality and Infinity*: theology and the Platonic denial of writing. Let us leave aside the worry about theology, and examine why they are uneasy about this emphasis on speech and the refusal of the written word in Levinas's work.[9]

Why does Plato reject writing? At the end of the *Phaedrus*, Socrates tells Phaedrus of the myth of the Egyptian god of Thoth, whose invention, amongst other things, were written letters (τά γράμματα) (274c-277c). When asked by the god Thebes what was the use of this invention, he answered that it would improve the memory of the Egyptians and make them wiser. To this answer, Thebes responded that it would have the opposite effect. The Egyptians would become so reliant on this tool that they would forget how to use their own memory. What is important in this little dialogue is the distinction between a proper and improper memory. Writing is improper because it is external (ἔξωθεν). Its memory lies in the written characters, and not within (ἔνδοθεν) the memory which is proper to our own souls. Moreover, this false memory, embodied by writing, gives the illusion of knowledge or wisdom that simply through reading these letters we can gain understanding, even though our souls are completely empty. The only proper function of written letters can be to remind us of what we already know. This second memory must be clearly distinguished from the first, which is the memory of knowledge and truth, when for example, in the *Meno*, the slave boy 'remembers' through Socrates' questions, the solution of the mathematical problem (82b-85b). In explaining the necessary mistrust of writing for those who seek wisdom, we come to the very genesis of the doctrine of assistance which is at the heart of Levinas's analysis of speech. Socrates says that writing is very much like painting (274d).[10] Both create an image of the real which is separate. Nonetheless, however much the painting might seem real to me, the portrait cannot answer back. In the same way the letters on the page are mute. Whatever question I might ask them, they cannot answer. Moreover, when something is written down, it goes from one mouth to another, being uttered over and over again, but nobody really knows what these words mean. Against writing, we can distinguish 'the living and breathing word' (λόγον ζῶντα καὶ ἔμψυχον), where the speaker is present in the words they speak. The speaker's difficulty with Levinas's appropriation of Plato's argument against writing, is that the presence of the speaker in the words they utter would be true of both speakers, and therefore, it would annul the difference or distance between them. There is conflict between the doctrine of assistance and the asymmetry of the ethical relation. Such an antagonism does not arise in Plato's texts, because the speakers of a dialogue are equal, at least ostensibly so, in relation to truth. Truth is exterior both to the teacher and the pupil, and although the teacher might direct the pupil towards the truth, this does not mean that it resides in the teacher, for the teacher was once a pupil too. The danger of Levinas identifying ethical speech with the Platonic dialogue is that the ethical 'relation without relation' becomes subverted by the introduction of a linguistic relation which both precedes and determines it. Now as one of the speakers notes, this linguistic relation is not asymmetrical, but would be equally true of both terms in the relation. I am just as much present in the words that I speak as the Other. All that Levinas has done is transposed the subject position of language from the 'I' to the 'Other', this 'privilege,' one of the speakers says, 'attributed to the vigilance of the self who speaks in the first person' (Blanchot 1993, 56-7). Levinas's error is to think that there must always be a subject position for language, and it is for this reason that he simply replaces the I with the Other. The avoidance of this error can be found already in the ethical relation. For as we have already understood, it is not a term in the relation which is ethical, which would bring us back to a predicative or substantive logic, but the relation itself. It is not some property of the Other which makes it ethical; its ability, for example, to be present in the words it speaks, which would be no different from the presence of the self in its reply to the Other, but the peculiarity of the ethical relation itself, in which the difference between the terms precedes their identity, so that we can no longer think of the Other as a human being, person, or *alter ego* just like me.

For this very reason, the remainder of Blanchot's pieces or conversations about Levinas in *The Infinite Conversation* concentrate on the interval between the speakers, rather than the speakers themselves. What is the strange presence of the Other in a conversation which makes them different from me? It cannot be that they are present in the words they speak, for I too own and possess my words, but somehow these words become detached from the speaker's mouth, and allude to something more important, and startling, than either of us imagines ourselves or the other to be. It is these words, which neither of us quite command, which maintain the difference between us, and not as Levinas believed when he wrote *Totality and Infinity*, the fact of someone speaking which is common both to me and the Other.

The power of speech

Why is it the words of a conversation, rather than the speakers themselves, which are the testament to the strangeness of the Other? The answer to this question can be found in a small piece in *The Infinite Conversation*, 'The Play of Thought', where Blanchot remembers his conversations with Bataille (Blanchot 1993, 211-17).[11] Blanchot recalls that he had a particular 'power to speak'. This power came not so much from what he said or how he said it, but from the 'fact of being present through his speech' (Blanchot 1993, 211). But how is this different from Levinas's 'presence in speech'? This difference is the crux of the matter. Blanchot writes, and here he refers to the power of speaking in general, rather than just Bataille's own, that the presence of speech has to do with its 'seriousness'. Not the seriousness of what is spoken, as though there were some range of topics you could talk about which were more serious than others, but the seriousness of speaking as such, in the sense that just the fact of speaking to someone were a serious matter. This is why the seriousness of speech can happen at any time, even when you are speaking about the most ordinary matters, and perhaps is less likely to happen when you think you are being serious, because what you are speaking about is thought to be sober and solemn. This is also why we should not think that the seriousness of speech is something heavy and grave. On the contrary, Blanchot writes, 'speaking is levity itself' (Blanchot 1993, 212). The lightness of the seriousness of speech comes from its rarity. It can happen that you are speaking to someone and the conversation suddenly becomes serious, even if you had not decided to speak about something important. The seriousness of the conversation does not come from the decision of any one of the speakers. It does not come, Blanchot writes, from a gesture or an expression, or even anything said, but from the conversation itself. So the presence and power of speech which Blanchot found so remarkable in remembering his talks with Bataille was not his, if we imagine that it belonged to how Bataille acted or what he said, but from the enigmatic and fragile distance or interval between them, which a serious conversation holds open: 'a relation to the unknown,' Blanchot writes, 'that is speech's unique gift ' (Blanchot 1993, 212).

Why is this so different from Levinas's Platonic description of speech in *Totality and Infinity*, where the importance of speech over writing lies in the presence of the speaker in the words they speak? Because the seriousness of speech for Blanchot exists in the interval between the speakers, in the conversation itself which has a power, gravity and force of its own, and not in the speakers. To place the power of speech in the intentions of the speakers would mean that every conversation would be a matter of adopting a position to what was said, and imply that you come to the conversation with a thesis which you would, either in co-operation or confrontation with the other speaker, develop or defend. Conversation, then, would not be an opening or listening to what is unknown, mysterious or serious in what is said, which escapes the calculation, ambition and pursuit of each speaker, but merely the repetition of information. The power of speech, on the contrary, is what both speakers confront within the conversation, and which opens up 'another space where the habitual possibilities steal away' (Blanchot 1993, 213). This means that the presence of speech is in fact an absence or void. It is that point in the conversation where everything that is familiar or comfortable in thought falls away. It also means, contrary to Levinas, that speech is at its most uncomfortable when it is impersonal, rather than personal. The interval of speech does not come from the speaker who attends the words they speak; rather it comes when both speakers, through attention to what is said, are exposed to that which is unsaid and invisible between them. This does not refer to the possibility that my words might be misheard or misunderstood, or that I always say more that what I mean to say, but that within a conversation what is talked about ceases to be a topic or a thesis, as though both speakers were grappling with something which was just outside their reach. The power of speech, therefore paradoxically, is that moment in which extreme concentration is turned into powerlessness and weakness. This is why (and this perhaps explains the opening conversation of *The Infinite Conversation*) speakers who are weary and tired are closer to the power of speech, than those who believe that they are in complete mastery of language, and who, though they declare themselves not to know, do so from certainty rather than uncertainty, exhibiting a ruse of reason, and not a weakness of spirit.

The interval of conversation

'I am necessarily in relation with someone,' one of the speakers continues in 'The Relation of the Third Kind' (Blanchot 1993, 67). I can see this person as an object that I can study and investigate, as some kind of thing which is outside me and towards which I have no feeling or intimacy. Equally, however, I can see this person as more than a thing. I can recognise that they have the same freedom and liberty that I do. I recognise that rather than being something alien and other to me, like the rest of the natural world, they are another self like me. Such a recognition is the attempt to find something common or the same between us which we could both belong to. It is the aim of thought to think this unity, which then mediates or determines our relation. Beyond this recognition, there is a different relation to the Other, in which what stands between us is not a common identity, reason, consciousness, or even humanity, but an unfamiliarity, strangeness and incomprehensibility.

This strangeness is not be thought of as 'separation' or 'distance', which are the very words used previously to describe the relation in Levinas, but as an 'interruption' (Blanchot 1993, 68). Why does Blanchot now let the speakers speak of 'interruption', rather than 'separation or distance'? This is a difficult question to answer straight away, for right after these two speakers agree that the words 'separation' and 'distance' are not adequate to describe this other relation, they will go on using them. But we have to ask ourselves how this other word 'interruption' can bring us closer to how these speakers understand the ethical relation, even if in the end it is not possible to be totally precise or certain about the nature of this relation.

This interruption first of all has to do with speech. 'Communication with the Other,' one of the speakers says, 'is not a transsubjective or intersubjective relation' (Blanchot 1993, 69).[12] True, I can speak to another person about something and even if they misunderstand me it is because we belong to a common culture. I can even treat the relation of speech from the outside, where I might describe the different kinds of speech possible within a society and the different things that can be said. But all these possibilities of speech are dependent on what is said being said, rather than to whom one is speaking. To speak to someone is already to respond to them. What first makes language possible is the address, and the address announces a distance between interlocutors which cannot be bridged by any common bond or tie. All this we know from Levinas and it does not say anything more than we could read in *Totality and Infinity*.

One of the speakers asks who is the Other to whom we address our response? The other responds that this question does not get us any closer to the Other at all, but even more so that this word is something that can trick or mislead us (Blanchot 1993, 70). We think we are saying something when we speak of the 'Other', especially when we capitalise this word. Is there not something too simple about this word, as though we could make comprehensible the interval of speech merely by naming it, as though the incomprehensible could retain its incomprehensibility at the very moment that we labelled it? The greatest danger is that we think that this word names 'a certain type of man' (Blanchot 1993, 70). Now in reading these words, we might think that this is precisely what Levinas does do. Our suspicion might be confirmed when we go on to read that to think of the Other in this way is to precisely to think of it as the 'Most High' (*le Très Haut),* the very same words, we know, that Levinas uses in *Totality and Infinity* to characterise the Other in opposition to the self. How can we begin to think about the word 'Other' so that it does not just become an attribute? First, we need to remind ourselves that I am just as much the Other for the Other as the Other is Other to me. As

Levinas writes, in *Totality and Infinity*, but makes little of it, 'I myself can feel myself to be as the other of the other' (Levinas 1969, 84). This means that in the relation of the I to the Other we can no longer think of these terms as being fixed. Just as much as the Other ceases to have a common identity so too does the I. It becomes, one of the speakers says, 'the unidentifiable, the "I"-less, the nameless, the presence of the inaccessible' (Blanchot 1993, 70). Yet expressed in this way it makes the ethical relation sound suspiciously dialectical, in which both terms in the relation mutually determine the other. I am to the Other in the same way that the Other is to me. Except that the dialectical relation is thought through a synthesis of unity of identity, rather than discontinuity or a double dissymmetry. In dialectic thought, the opposition between the terms is overcome in a higher unity, but in the ethical relation the difference between the I and the Other is maintained. They do not become equal, identical or the same.

This interval between speakers, rather than the presence of a speaker in the words they speak, is not an attribute common between two terms, but names a relation in which any common measure is lacking. Here for the first time, one of the speakers, and this will become perhaps the key concept of Blanchot's writing from now on, will name this relation as the 'neuter' (Blanchot 1993, 71).[13] It is not what is most personal about me which announces the relation of alterity, as though there were hidden depths to my existence that no-one could know, but what is most impersonal. The impersonal does not measure the objectivity of thought which exists only in those elements which are common between things, but what is without any measure or scale. What is singular about me, what makes me strange and incomprehensible to another, is no longer an I or an ego, my individuality or personality, which is the same as everyone else's, but what is impersonal and which belongs to no-one. It is this impersonality, 'this relation of strangeness between man and man' that renders the Other other to the I and also the I other to the Other. Now for Blanchot, the 'strangeness' of this relation, which breaks any common identity that might exist between us, has its origin in writing and not speech, if we conceive of the latter as the presence of the speaker in the words they speak. The experience of this relation, one of the speakers says:

> Originates only in that space and time of language - there where language, through writing, undoes the idea of an origin (Blanchot 1993, 71).

Later, in a commentary to this conversation, which is the only one added to any of the conversations in *The Infinite Conversation*, Blanchot is specific about what kind of writing this is, if 'kind' is the appropriate word here, since this writing does not fit within any genre.

> And herein [with the relation of the neuter], we characterise, perhaps, one of the essential traits of the 'literary' act: the very fact of writing (Blanchot 1993, 73).[14]

How have we moved from ethical speech to the neutral impersonality of writing, which Blanchot describes as literature, both of which are the experience of this strange relation of the interval? All Blanchot's analysis of Levinas's work is set within the conversation which opens *The Infinite Conversation*. He does not approach this work in a formal academic manner. There is no attempt to explain, summarise or expose this work in formulas and definitions. Rather, it is the conversations themselves which express, signify or bear witness to the discontinuity of language. The conversations of *The Infinite Conversation*, which might first appear to be explanations of Levinas's work, are, to use Blanchot's own phrase, 'literary acts'. It is as if for Blanchot, the only way to approach the relation to the Other, without at once returning it to the Same, without being caught in the diabolic logic of the dialectic, is through literature. This explains the confusion of the reader of *The Infinite Conversation*, who is unsure whether they are reading philosophy or literature. This crossing of the distinction between genres or discourses is not accidental. It too expresses the language of discontinuity, 'the very fact of writing'. The point is that these conversations could take place in one of Blanchot's novels or narratives, and there we would probably be quite happy to accept, since we have been conditioned to do so, the enigmatic quality of the writing, whose full meaning and significance would be hidden and concealed from us. We are at ease because they have been placed with the context of a philosophical writing where we expect explanations and certainty. The distance between philosophy and literature, however, is not that great. This is why, straight after the last chapter of the first section of *The Infinite Conversation*, 'A Plural Speech', Blanchot places his essay on the philosophy of Heraclitus. 'One of the first works,' he writes, 'in which thought is called to itself through the discontinuity of writing' (Blanchot 1993, 82). Or perhaps it is better to speak of two philosophies. One which is governed and determined by the idea of unity and identity, and the other by the fragmentary and discontinuous. In the second case, the proximity between philosophy and literature would be almost indistinguishable. What is the difference between Levinas, at least at the time of the writing of *Totality and Infinity*, and Blanchot here? For Levinas the interruption of unity and identity takes place only in direct speech where the self is interpellated by the presence of the Other in the words they speak. Writing, for him, as we shall see in more detail in the next chapter, only re-institutes a relation of identity between the self and the Other.[15] This is because Levinas essentially understands writing as representation. The written word is always the operation of a common term. He can only define writing in this way, because he ignores it as a 'literary act'. But the opening of *The Infinite Conversation*, and the subsequent conversations which address Levinas's work, give lie to the identification of writing with representation. Writing is not just the representation of ideas, concepts, and categories, if we mean by these, the operation of unity and identity. Writing is also, as the act of literature, the experience of the fragmentary and discontinuous.

In Levinas's description of the ethical relation in *Totality and Infinity*, at least in its exclusivist form, it is the Other as such, as one of the terms in the relation, which determines the discontinuity of the relation. It is only because in the speech of the Other there is always more than what is said that a relation of difference and non-similarity is possible. This 'more than what is said' has its origin in the presence of the Other which is totally separate from existence of the self. The Other invades my world from the outside. It is not an item or element within this world. For Blanchot, on the contrary, it is not one of the terms in the relation, even the Other, which determines the relation, but the interval of the relation itself, where both terms are separated from their identity. It is the interval between the self and the Other which ensures that they do not form a common unity or identity. This interval, as it is for Levinas, is an interval of language, but it is an interval which belongs to the word and not the presence of the speaker. As we have already seen, in Levinas's description of ethical language, the word, in *Totality and Infinity*, completely disappears to such an extent that the ethics of language no longer has anything at all to do with language, but only with the presence of the Other.[16] The Other speaks, but it is not what the Other says which is ethical, but only the fact of speaking. What is intrinsically ethical about speaking does not belong to any word. It is the silence of the address - this turning toward the Other who commands me. Only the self which is addressed speaks. This is why Levinas's description of language repeats the familiar mistrust of words, when for example, Plato defines thought as a conversation with oneself (a conversation that no doubt no longer needs words since there is an instantaneous and immediate communication of one thought with an other), an ideal that is still sought in the dream of a purely logical and symbolic language able to express the truth without the messiness and ambiguity of words.

The word vanishes because alterity is placed in the presence of the

Other, which is, to some extent *outside* of the relation. This is why Levinas can, in *Totality and Infinity*, designate both terms in the relation as separate from the relation. There are two ways of interpreting this independence: One externally and the other internally. Levinas's text allows for both. In the description of language, which forms the heart of *Totality and Infinity*, the exteriority of the terms to one another is external to the ethical relation. The self, prior to the ethical relation, exists in its possession of the 'elements', and Other comes to the ethical relation through its own relation to language. In the margins of this text, however, there is a completely different logic of relation. The difference between the terms is not determined by their self-definition, as though the Other possessed certain attributes which the self did not, and vice versa, but through the relation itself, or what Blanchot calls the interval which separates them. This interval, distance or separation does not belong to one of the terms in the relation and most especially not to something that we might call the Other, but it is what makes the Other other, and equally what makes the self other to the Other. In the first case, difference is defined from the definition of identity of the terms in the relation, whereas in the second, the relation of difference precedes the identity of the terms. Blanchot writes that we can imagine two people speaking in a room, and we might speculate from where they might have come, what their dreams and wishes might be. We can create for them a complete personality and identity. Each is a unique existence which bears their name. But the relation to the Other, this 'relation of the third genre', strips them of their subjectivity, and opens them out to a region which goes beyond their mutual self understanding. It is important to be precise here to avoid any confusion. The relation to the Other is not a relation to some other, if we mean by the word 'other', some other human being, personality or individual, since this relation takes from both speakers their personality and individuality. Both terms in the relation lose their identity through the interval or separation. The Other is Other to me, but I am Other to the Other. When Blanchot remembers his conversations with Bataille, for example, it is not himself or Bataille that he necessarily remembers, but the interval of conversation, in which both speakers no longer find a commonality founded on reciprocity and recognition, but a difference preceding any identity. What brought Blanchot and Bataille together in friendship was not that they found something to share, and thus to reinforce their subjectivity, but that in this friendship what was other to them both could emerge, beyond their capacity to identify and objectivity. Blanchot writes:

> This Other in play in the third kind of relation is no longer in one of the terms; it is neither in one nor the other, being nothing other than

relation itself, a relation of the one to the other that requires infinity (Blanchot 1993, 73-4).

The inarticulate voice

All these meditations on Levinas and writing and speech culminate in the penultimate essay of this series, 'Interruption' (Blanchot 1993, 75-9). Interruption, in the rhythm of one speaker addressing and responding to another, is necessary to every conversation. But these interruptions internal to every dialogue can be thought of in two very different ways. First, they are the necessary condition for the exchange of information. Here the ideal would be the Platonic dialogue, where the to and fro of conversation is for the sake of truth which transcends the speakers, eternal and immutable, outliving this and every conversation. But there is another way of thinking about interruption, and thus another way of conceiving dialogue and conversation, which is not Platonic. This is also a matter of transcendence, but it is not the transcendence of truth. Blanchot describes this transcendence as a 'wait' (Blanchot 1993, 76). This wait is a kind of an attention, not to what is being said, nor even to the other speaker, but to what stands between them and cannot be said. How can we describe this other space of conversation or dialogue?

There are three ways, Blanchot writes, that we might commonly think about communication. In the first case, and this has been the predominant aim of philosophy and the sciences, we can investigate it as the condition of objectivity. Language, or symbolisation, is the possibility of knowledge. Before anything has been said, language is the condition of truth. Another way we can think about communication is through social relations. Language is the relation to another self. We might even want to argue that the objectivity of knowledge is subordinate to this pragmatic relation of speech. Although this other self to whom I address these words is different from me, nonetheless this difference is subordinate to a common identity. This is not just because speakers must share a common cultural background, in order that they might understand one another, but also, and more importantly for Blanchot, it is taken for granted in this model of language that the difference between the speakers 'passes by way of a primary identity, that of two beings each equally able to speak in the first person' (Blanchot 1993, 77). Finally, there is a third meaning to the interruption of conversation or speech, where the relation between the speakers is neither a relation to an objectivity which precedes them and structures their dialogue, nor to the pragmatic region of intersubjectivity, but an intimacy and proximity. In all these cases, Blanchot argues, though for very different reasons, the distance between the speakers in annulled. In the first case, in the relation of knowledge, the speaker is reduced to an object of an impersonal gaze. In the second, the other speaker is just like me. We belong to the same community of speakers. We are the same. And finally, in the third, which might be a myth or a dream, I imagine, in the most intimate and delicate moments of speech, that we have become one, 'by the instantaneous union of two souls' (Blanchot 1993, 77).

What would it mean not to think of language under the demand of a common measure? Interruption would no longer signify, excessively or not, the means of communication, but the separation and distance between the speakers. The Other is not me.[17] We do not belong to the same world, circumstances or situation. This distance between us, however, does not have its source in a miscomprehension or misunderstanding which is perhaps true of every human communication. Such misunderstanding would imply that the distance of the Other from the I has its source in the I itself. The distance between the I and the Other is not found in my perception or idea of the Other, but in the relation between the I and the Other. The relation precedes any perception or intellectual act. Alterity is not a property or relation of something or someone. I cannot say that there is something about the other person which makes them different from me. For such an attribute would be a common property. It would be something that could be said of many things and, in this sense, would still belong to the categories of thought and being, for every attribute exists in some being or other. Alterity names a relation and not an attribute. Moreover it names a relation that constitutes '*the interruption of being*' [author's emphasis] (Blanchot 1993, 77). This must be so because it has nothing to do with either the existence or essence of something or someone. Alterity does not define what it means to be something or someone, nor that something or someone is or is not.

For Levinas, this relation to the Other, which is outside of being, is the possibility of ethics, but at this point Blanchot wants to draw our attention to another meaning of alterity by placing it 'under the nomination of the neuter' (Blanchot 1993, 77).[18] Why does Blanchot want to use this other word? Why is he not content with simply repeating the word 'Other'? The reason is twofold. Firstly, is to move away from the interpersonal interpretation of ethics in *Totality and Infinity*, where the Other is synonymous with the human face. This places the force or power of the interruption of being in one of the terms of the relation, and in a quality of this term, rather than in the relation between terms. Secondly (and this follows from the emphasis on the human face), if we hold as Levinas does that only immediate and direct speech is ethical, this tenet itself works to abolish the very difference between the terms that the ethical relation is meant to sustain, since speaking in the first person, being present in the words ones speaks, which has always defined the superiority of speech over writing, is common both to the Other and me. Although it is I who respond to the appeal of the Other, both this interpellation and response are spoken from the position of the first person. If speaking in the first person is common to both terms in the relation, then ethics, as Levinas describes it in *Totality and Infinity*, falls back within the thought of unity. This is why Blanchot immediately describes the neuter as the impossibility of direct communication, which runs counter to Levinas's description of the ethical relation in terms of the address of the Other. The distance between us, what makes us no longer one and the same, is nothing that we say, no quality or attribute that we might possess, but is the shape, form or modality of the conversation itself, which prevents recognition, commonality or even a 'meeting of minds'.

Of course one can always think of a conversation as the communication of information or as an action in the world, but this presupposes that language is always to be understood from the perspective of the first person. Words are nothing else but the intentions or actions of an 'I'. What Blanchot wants to draw our attention to in our conversations is how it is possible at any moment that something is *happening* to the speakers rather than that they have initiatied a thought of something. This is not a reference to some obscurity or mystery of intention or action, where I do not know what you mean, or what actions your words imply. This is still to think of conversation from the perspective of the first person. Rather, in speaking, you and I are taken outside of ourselves and no longer belong to any commonality of thought or action. This is what Blanchot felt in his conversations with Bataille. This is what he calls friendship. A friend is someone who allows me not to be myself. It is also this shift from the first person to a language which speaks through us that brings speech under the power and influence of writing. We are not speaking of speech and writing here as activities, talking out aloud or making marks on a piece of paper, but as a change, as Blanchot writes, 'in the form or structure of language' (Blanchot 1993, 77), in which the impersonality of words precedes and antedates self-expression, and which we described in the previous chapter through the 'thought of the outside'.[19]

We learn from Foucault, Blanchot argues, in his essays on the author in *The Infinite Conversation*, that even in the classical understanding of language it should already be understood through its function, and not in the words which make it up.[20] The function of language is representation, and through representation, the organisation, systemisation and unification of experience. In its ideal limit, such as logic, the material aspects of language can virtually disappear. One consequence of this vanishing, however, is that the position of the first person also dissolves. For this function lies in the unity of thought itself, which precedes any individual utterance. It is as though thought, to quote Kant (whose philosophy, in the table of categories in the *Critique of Pure Reason*, is the culmination of the classical picture of language), thinks through me and not I through it.[21] One way to comprehend this disappearance of the first person is through writing. Blanchot uses the example of Descartes' analytical geometry whose aim is to do away with the visible drawing of figures through the use of written equations (Blanchot 1993, 257). In the same way the personality of the voice is subordinated in the written order of thought. At this moment thought escapes the visible, the real, the physical, and it does so through the power of writing. It is not so much that geometrical figures can now be represented in written equations, but these equations can produce figures that are 'unfigurable'.

It is against this impersonality of writing, and the disappearance of the first person, that we must see the force of romanticism. Some such spirit, argues Blanchot, is inseparable from literature. And yet, it is precisely at this point that we can make a great error. We imagine that the reaction of romanticism against the 'frightful dryness' of rationalism is an appeal to some kind of authentic subjectivity lying beneath or behind the 'it thinks'. The 'voice' of Romanticism, Blanchot writes, should not be confused solely with 'the organ of a subjective interiority'. On the contrary, it is an 'opening onto an outside' (Blanchot 1993, 258).

What is the 'outside' and why is it not the same as the impersonality of thought in the classical representation of language? If the voice of the poet (it is Hölderlin who stands for the most profound elements of Romanticism for Blanchot) were the same as the first person, then it would be inserted within a system, order or unity. The disappearance of the I in classical thought, instanced when Kant writes over and over again in the *Critique of Pure Reason*, that it is impossible to know what the 'I' is, is precisely because the I is now only a part of the general function of language to unify experience. The voice cannot return to the first person, because the first person is not the interiority which it is expected to be. It is merely one more word of order. The only possible singular and unique voice, on the contrary, is inarticulate, a murmur, or cry. Such speechlessness does not come from an interiority which has been concealed or even destroyed by the impersonality of thought, but from further away than thought and speech. So far away that it almost becomes indistinguishable from madness, suffering and pain. All this leads to a quite different experience of writing than the ideal of Descartes' analytical geometry.

What emerges, Blanchot writes, is 'the idea of origin' (Blanchot 1993, 259). The question of origin is occulted in the classical representation of language, because language is reduced to its functionality. Again Kant would say that it is not a serious question to ask why human sensibility is spatial and temporal, or human understanding categorial. It just is. To ask the question of origin is to fall back into theology. In this other writing, however, the question cannot be avoided. From where does this voice come from that does not arise from my interiority, and which appears to emerge before the speech of thought? The impersonality of this writing is neither the functionality of language, nor the speech of the first person; it is, Blanchot writes, on 'the hither side of every subject and even every form' (Blanchot 1993, 259). In this moment, writing ceases to be a mirror held up to reality, but becomes something separate and independent. It refers to nothing but itself. Literature announces itself in one great event. *Don Quixote* and *Tristam Shandy* are no less experimental and excessive than any work by Mallarmé or Beckett. This writing is no less non-figurative than Descartes' equations, but it is no longer attached to the ideals of order, systematicity and unity. There is a disorder, confusion and disunity which haunts the very centre of language, one which is older and more ancient even than the impersonality of the 'it thinks', and which thought attempts to keep at bay, like the fog that swirls around Kant's famous island in the *Critique of Pure Reason*.[22] It is this writing which is close to the ethics of speech, where the interval between the I and the Other shatters any possible community or society of equals or rivals, and where language becomes *'speaking-between,'* Blanchot emphasises, 'or the vacancy of discontinuity' (Blanchot 1993, 260). This is neither the language of 'vocal manifestation' nor the visible written language of representation. The writing of the 'outside', the interval and the fragmentary, cuts through the opposition of speech and writing as it is traditionally and usually thought. This is why Blanchot can write (which sounds completely bizarre, if we think that writing means only the marks on a page) that 'writing has ever and always broken with language, whether it be a discourse that is spoken or written' (Blanchot 1969, 390). This is also why he can say, as we have seen, that in Levinas's description of the ethical relation, speech becomes the experience of writing. For what writing means for Blanchot is precisely what escapes the discourse of unity, whether we are speaking of ethics or literature. The 'discourse of unity' means language as representation, spoken or written. The difference between Blanchot and Levinas, at least at the time of the writing of *Totality and Infinity*, is that the latter is still caught up within the traditional opposition of writing and speech, such that it is impossible for him to conceive of writing as anything other than representation. It follows from this that speech itself only breaks with representation through the first person, which leads Levinas still to think of the Other through the traditional categories of a metaphysics of subjectivity at the very moment that he is attempting to escape it. The Other gives meaning to the world through a subject-position in language. It simply takes over this power that was traditionally granted to the subject. The whole direction of Blanchot's reading of Levinas in *The Infinite Conversation*, is to discover an impersonality which subverts this subject-position of the Other. We would completely misunderstand this endeavour, if we were to think this impersonality, for example, as merely a repetition of the Kantian move of finding an 'it thinks' behind the subject-position. It is the interval between the speakers in the relation which is impersonal and not something deeply hidden in the interiority of one of the terms in the relation. The difficulty is thinking this interval prior to the terms in the relation, of not making it a quality, property or attribute of one of the terms in the relation; of thinking, as Levinas would say, the 'relation without relation'. This relation belongs to no-one, not even the Other, but it is what makes every subject-position a usurpation, arrogation and tyranny.

Notes

1 In the section 'Writing and friendship', pp.82-90.

2 For the meaning of substitution, see the section 'Maternity and sensation' in chapter three, pp.66-72.

3 See Lars Iyer's book *Blanchot's Communism: Art, Philosophy and the Political*, for the importance of Bataille for Blanchot's conception of community. 'Bataille's practice is exemplary for Blanchot,' he writes, 'because he maintains the tension between the possible and the impossible, work and worklessness, in his great communal experiments of the 1930s' (Iyer 2004, 141). In the following pages, he goes on to to describe the specific influence of Acéphale.

4 Blanchot is aware that there are exceptions to this rule, such as with the works of Spinoza, Descartes and Pascal, but they are abnormal precisely because they have no institutional role (Blanchot 1969, 2).

5 'Knowledge of the Unknown', 'To Keep One's Word', 'The Relation of the Third Genre', 'Interruption' and 'A Plural Speech' (Blanchot 1969, 70-116). All these essays were published originally in the *Nouvelle revue française* between 1960 and 1964. See the excellent bibliography by Reginald Lilly (Lilly 2002).

6 This distinction owes everything to Heidegger's phenomenological analysis of the difference between fear and anxiety in *Being and Time* (Heidegger 1962, 228-235).

7 The power and influence of Plato's attack upon writing has been admirably described and diagnosed by Derrida in 'Plato's Pharmacy' (Derrida 1981, 61-171). 'Writing appears to Plato,' Derrida writes, '(and after him to all of philosophy, which is as such constituted in this gesture) as that process of redoubling in which we are fatally (en)trained: supplement of a supplement, signifier of a signifier, representative of a representative' (Derrida 1981, 109). There is a mistake in the English translation here. The original is *signifiant d'un signifiant* and not just *d'un signifiant* (Derrida 1972, 125).

8 Susan Hanson translates *interpellation* in the French as 'address'. I would prefer to stick with the closer English translation (Blanchot 1969, 79).

9 A year later, in the essay, 'Being Jewish', which is also republished in *The Infinite Conversation* (Blanchot 1969, 180-90), Blanchot is not so disturbed by the theological content of Levinas's work, because its Judaism always remains an interrogation of philosophy and not merely a supplement to it, as is the case perhaps with Christian theology. It does so for Blanchot in at least three ways: the affirmation of the nomadic above the sedentary, humanism as the humanism of the stranger or the Other, and the privilege of

speech over vision. It should not surprise us, then, that Blanchot will use the same language to describe Judaism as he will to explain Levinas. For an excellent account of Levinas's Judaism, and its relation to Judaism as a whole, one should read Roger Burggraeve's essay 'The Bible Gives to Thought: Levinas on the Possibility and Proper Nature of Biblical Thinking' in *The Face of the Other & the Trace of God* (Burggraeve 2000).

10 We remember that Levinas also uses the analogy of painting for the written word in our previous discussion of Levinas's dependence on Plato in 'Teaching', pp.16-20

11 This passage, which was first published in 1963, should be read in tandem with Blanchot's remarks about Bataille in *Friendship*, which we also discussed in the previous chapter in 'Writing and friendship', pp.82-90.

12 Susan Hanson retains *Autrui* in the English translation, but it is common, following the translations of Levinas's work, to translate this word as 'Other' (Blanchot 1969, 99).

13 Susan Hanson translates the French *le neutre*, as 'the neutral'. It is now standard to translate it as 'the neuter' (Blanchot 1969, 101).

14 This conversation was originally published in the *La nouvelle revue française* as the first part of 'L'indestructible'(Blanchot 1962, 671-2)

15 In the section, 'Writing, politics and history ', pp.132-8.

16 See 'Language without words' in chapter one, pp.2-10.

17 This is the fundamental break with Heidegger's analysis of *Mitsein* in *Being and Time*, where being with others is part of *my* being. 'In characterizing the encountering of *Others*,' Heidegger writes, 'one is again still oriented by that Dasein which is in each case one's *own*' [italics in the original] (Heidegger 1962, 154).

18 *Sous la nomination de neutre* in the French, which Susan Hanson translates as 'in the name of the neutral' (Blanchot 1969, 109).

19 In the section which bears this phrase as its name, pp.90-7.

20 The essays are called 'Atheism and Writing' and 'Humanism and the Cry' and were originally published in 1967 (Blanchot 1969, 367-393).

21 'Through this I or he or it (the thing) which thinks, nothing further is represented than a transcendental subject of the thoughts = X (Kant 2003, A345/B404).

22 This domain [the territory of the pure understanding] is an island, enclosed by nature itself within unalterable limits. It is the land of truth - enchanting name! - surrounded by a wide and stormy ocean, the native home of illusion, where many a fog bank and many a swiftly melting iceberg give the deceptive appearance of farther shores, deluding the adventurous seafarer ever anew with empty hopes, and engaging him in enterprises which he can

never hope to abandon and yet is unable to carry on to completion' (Kant 2003, A235-6/B294-5).

6

Philosophy

In *Totality and Infinity*, Levinas announces that he has 'left the philosophy of Parmenidian Being behind' (Levinas 1969, 269). The instant that he makes this declaration, he draws the reader's attention to the very book he is writing: 'what we are now exposing is addressed to those who shall wish to read it.' A strange announcement, for elsewhere in *Totality and Infinity*, writing is given no ethical importance whatsoever. In fact, it is, as we have seen, quite the contrary. Writing, exposition, explanation and argument are all seen as the end of ethics. Only in the presence of the Other in the words they address to me is ethics possible. But here it is the written and not just the spoken word which breaks with the neutrality of Being in the address of the book to the reader. On the one side, writing is the desire to totalise. It is the designation and domination of beings, as in Parmenides' poem, in the thought of unity. What happens to writing, however, when it no longer seeks what can be designated and nominated, when it is no longer governed by the final goal of totality and unity? Blanchot has already given us the name for such a writing: it is literature.[1] But is there not a way in which Levinas's writing, through the encounter with the Other, becomes a similar kind of writing? This is not just a question of style, as when we say that Levinas's philosophy has a poetic and literary quality which makes it different from the more severe and austere tone of, for example, Aristotle's lectures. In this description, writing is merely seen as a kind of external clothing of thought, which could be fine or not, but the thought itself remains immune. For this reason it is perfectly possible for the thought to be summarised in a different idiom and lose no content or force whatsoever. The question of writing is much deeper than this. How does one approach, describe or capture the experience of the Other without at the same time betraying it? Undoubtedly, this is not a problem for Levinas in *Totality and Infinity*, where ethics is presented in direct speech, and the paradox of describing this situation in the written word is ignored, but this is not the case in *Otherwise than Being*. The famous distinction between the saying and the said in Levinas's philosophy is not a distinction of speech but of writing. The problem of writing becomes central to the question of ethics, to the very possibility of there being an ethics of alterity at all.

Writing, politics and history

The exclusion of writing in *Totality and Infinity* cannot be separated from the status of history, economics and politics. Each of these discourses represents an anonymous objective discourse which negates the singularity of the Other. The aim of Levinas's analysis is to distinguish between two kinds of exteriority: one which neutralises the singularity of the terms in the relation, and the other which maintains and sustains it. These two kinds of exteriority are expressed through the opposition between speech and writing. Only in speech is the second kind of exteriority possible. When the difference between the terms of relation is represented in, by and through writing, then it opens up the possibility of violence. This difference between speech and writing, and all the political implications of this opposition, are no more apparent than in Levinas's response to Brice Parain's paper, '*La langage et l'immanence*' given at the *Société française de philosophie* in 1963 (Parain 1964, 25-6). Levinas says that what is important about Parain's paper is the diagnosis it makes of the complicity between the language of the universal, which is the basis of philosophical discourse, and violence. This involvement has two parts: one, the conversion of the 'I speak' into a language which speaks me, and two, that this language which speaks me, rather than I through it, is writing. The violence of the universal is the violence of writing. Levinas says:

> Here we are imprisoned in the text that in the instant before we were in the process of writing' [*nous voici emprisonnés dans le texte qu'il y a un instant encore, nous étions en train d'écrire*] (Parain 1964, 25).

The text imprisons the subject because there is an interval or separation between it and the actual activity of the subject which initially produced it. At one moment I am writing the text, and in the next, the text writes me. For in the instant of the reversal, the words with which I describe myself are set down forever. I become what they say, rather than what I intend through writing them. I am what is written about me, rather than what I say about myself. The written text has a life outside of its author. It is in this separation, distance, or interval, that the violence of the written word emerges. The written word, the book, the work, are objects which do not wholly belong to the person who produces them. Writing is the experience par excellence of alienation. The written words circulate, disperse, and disseminate, dispossessing the author of the right to their meaning and sense. All these words, which are alienated from the one who writes them, and are in a certain sense, because they remain inactivated by the living word of speech, dead and anonymous; they then act, as soon as they are in circulation, as a substitute, replacement, and proxy for the original author. The name 'Emmanuel Levinas' no longer names a human being, but a body of work which it represents.

This indictment of writing should be interpreted in relation to the ideal of speech which supports the ethical relation, but it also explains why politics is ambiguous in Levinas's philosophy, because it represents the violence of the written word in the bureaucracy of the state.[2] Political institutions can safeguard freedom through the law, but the same law can remove it. True freedom, which is not threatened by this ambiguity, is only possible in the straightforwardness, directness and immediacy of the face. It is a matter here of the possibility of judging history outside of history, politics outside the political. The judgement which belongs to history, on the contrary, is the judgement of the survivors and not the victims of oppression, injustice and persecution (Levinas 1969, 240). Against this immediacy, an Hegelian would argue that freedom and justice require institutions. An apolitical freedom is absurd and useless, full of good intentions, but having no effect on reality whatsoever. What matters is deeds not words. There can be no interior freedom without the exterior institutions supporting and maintaining it. Even those who speak of pure interior freedom, unconstrained by any external institutions, are speaking an illusion, for it is these very bodies they deny which make possible the supposed freedom they enjoy. 'Freedom,' Levinas writes, 'would cut into the real only by virtue of institutions' (Levinas 1969, 241). It is only because the law is written into statutes, and exists outside the individual, that it preserves itself. For without the transmission of the law in the written word, there would be no possibility of the objective will. Everything would vanish with the passing of generations, and the law would be forgotten. We pay for our individuality in order to ensure the survival of our species. This payment has a reverse side, however, which is tyranny. For in the very moment that the written law preserves us, it also alienates us from ourselves. 'There exists,' Levinas writes, 'a tyranny of the universal and of the impersonal, an order that is inhuman though distinct from the brutish' (Levinas 1969, 242). On the one side there is nature, to which liberty opposes itself, and on the other side there is liberty, to which the 'irreducible singularity' of the individual distinguishes itself. The relation to the Other, which here Levinas is quite happy to call religious, belongs neither to freedom nor nature. Liberty, the judgement of history, speaks from the position of the anonymity and impersonality of the third person. It speaks, rather than you or I speak. But 'It speaks' is not a speaking at all, if we mean by speaking the presence of someone in the words they speak. 'It has already lost,' Levinas writes, 'its voice' (Levinas 1969, 242). The 'it speaks', therefore, is the written word, even if this word is spoken by someone. It is writing before the empirical distinction between speech and writing. Writing is language as impersonal and anonymous discourse, even when this discourse comes from someone's mouth in a command, description, or order. Speech, on the contrary, is language in the first person in which the person who speaks attends to the words they speak. Unlike writing, which can either be spoken or written, this form of language can only be spoken, and in strict sense, exists only in the words of the Other. Not in what is said to me, since this can always be confused with the written word, but in the presence of the Other in the words they speak. What is essential to language, Levinas writes, is 'interpellation, the vocative' (Levinas 1969, 69). This is a pure address outside of the spoken or written word. Writing stands for the word alone, its materiality. It is the word without intention, performance or personality, without the presence of the speaker attending what is said. The price of the word, as Levinas writes, is 'depersonalisation' (Levinas 1969, 243).

Levinas refuses the philosophy of idealism, because it places the word above speech, and even in its defence, externalises the interiority of the subject in the structures, organisation, and composition of thought. Idealism, rather than the culmination of subjectivity, is its disappearance and dissolution. There is no more place for the singular and particular in idealism than in materialism. Idealism is also the reduction of ethics to politics. Politics, in this sense, is the subrogation of the Other and the self by ideal relations. The non-relation of ethics becomes the internal relation of thought with itself. Rather than the multiplicity of the 'relation without relation', we have the plurality of concepts thought within the unity of the system. The individual will only has a meaning to the extent that it has become one with the universal. It is true that the universal has not abolished the particular, but the particular can only express itself through the individual. This means that when I open my mouth, even when I address the Other, what speaks through me is not my own unique individuality, but only the universal, the dead word that everyone speaks, indeed, that someone else could speak in my place. No word we speak is truly individual, for everything has already been spoken, if only potentially, just as the thought of square of the hypotenuse is not dependent on the individual named Pythagoras who thought it, but could have been spoken by anyone. What is truly individual is only the response to the interpellation of the Other, my orientation in speech and not what I speak. Such a refusal of the system and the depersonalisation of politics should not be confused with some kind of arbitrary act of the will. For such an arbitrariness defines itself in opposition to the law. Without it, it is utterly powerless. For how can I revolt unless there is something to revolt against, and then I find myself dependent on the very institutions that I despise. Rather, the refusal of the system exists in the surplus of the social outside the universal, and not its diminution, subtraction or abbreviation. Life as a surplus to thought, and not its self-limitation, and which enters into speech without disappearing in the words which are spoken.

The same distinctions operate in Levinas's description of economic life (Levinas 1969, 175-7). Work is the absence of the speaking subject in its alienation from his or her product. In the activity of work, the product of labour is separated, disconnected and removed from the original producer, because the labourer is no longer *present* in the products they make. Through work the world becomes human, takes on a sense and a meaning, but this world as spirit conceals within itself the threat of violence and destruction. For it is humanity as the impersonality and anonymity of the concept to which any individual life can be sacrificed for the sake of a 'higher' good. The 'ruse of reason' is the cunning of war and the battle to death, which justifies all and thereby nothing. The substitution of the political, where one individual is replaceable by the other, (a transferability that defines above all the economic sphere, since not only am I replaced by the products I produce, but anyone else can do my job) must be sharply distinguished from the substitution of ethics, in which rather than my individuality becoming infinitely displaced by another individual element in the series, it is usurped by the Other in me. The condition for individuality is no longer self-possession, but dispossession by the Other.

It is true that Levinas is not, in privileging speech over writing, just defending the ancient rights of the subject. The presence of the speaker to the word they speak, which is a surplus of anything said, whether written or spoken, comes from the side of the Other and not the subject. Only the other attends the words they speak, not I. Even in responding to the Other, I can speak words that have already been spoken, but in this response my own singularity is saved. In demanding a response from me through the superfluity of their presence beyond what is spoken, the Other breaks through the anonymity of discourse, where every individuality is lost. For the word is the infinitely bad substitution of the thing. The word 'cat' does not just mean this cat here, but every cat, real or imaginary, existing now, in the past or the future. The word marks the disappearance of the living thing, and as the absence harbours the threat of death. We can understand why, therefore, in his response to Brice Parain's paper, Levinas can also describe writing as 'visible from the outside like a monument or mausoleum' [*visible du dehors comme un monument ou un mausolée*], and inseparable from a 'necrology' [*nécrologie*] (Parain 1964, 26). All writing is death.

Such a necrology is inseparable from history. A life which can be integrated into a totality, system or whole, is one which is dead. Only in death is my uniqueness, individuality and singularity extinguished. I becomes like all the others, and all the others becomes like me. In death we become one. This death is not the death of the Other, which stands as a permanent judgement against my liberty and freedom, but the death of those who have lost, surrendered, and been consigned to oblivion. 'The history of the histographers,' Levinas writes, is the history of the 'survivors' (Levinas 1969, 55). In such a history of the victor (and this discussion should be read together with the description of philosophy's fascination with war in the preface of *Totality and Infinity*) all that matters is the *essence* of the individual and not his or her existence. The historian looks from the outside and not from the inside of the ethical relation. They are always spectators. This view from the outside is always associated by Levinas with writing. History is always an histo*graphy* and never a histophony. You can never speak history, for even when it is spoken, you are merely speaking words that have already been written, and will always be written. This means that the second and first person of the subject position in the ethical relation is displaced, transformed and neutralised in the third person. The survivor always speaks of the others as 'they' and never as 'you'. The possibility of ethics, therefore, in authentic speech, rests upon the chance that history can be interrupted, that the written word, the *fiat* of time, is not the last word, since the meaning, significance and orientation of our lives cannot be summed up by the idea of a 'human totality' (Levinas 1969, 58).

Just as much as the Other is present in the words they speak to me, so I absent myself from the works I produce. This absence is the condition for the totality of history. Those who have left no works do not have a history. It is what is left behind when I disappear, and in the works I produce, I have, in a sense, already disappeared even before I am dead. The works bear my name after my disappearance, but in so doing they bear witness to it. This is the price of immortality. I am immortal only to the extent that the name my works bear carries on, whereas my flesh and blood does not. This is the great difference for Levinas between the immortality made possible by fecundity, and the immortality of production, creation and effort. For in the former, I am still *present* in the child, whereas I am forever absent from the works I produce. They gain, in the activity of production itself, an independence from me which is never lost. Such is the alienation intrinsic to every production, whether artistic or economic. Levinas writes:

> In contrast to the transcendence of expression..., production attests to the author of the work in his absence (Levinas 1969, 227).

If writing is associated with death and absence, then speech is entwined with life and presence. The Other as Other, as $\kappa\alpha\theta$' $\alpha\dot{\upsilon}\tau\acute{o}$, is always present in the words they speak to me. The alterity of the Other is not the words they speak, but this presence which is surplus to any spoken word. It is this presence which is abolished in history and writing. 'The face,' Levinas writes, 'is a living presence, it is expression' (Levinas 1969, 66). This living expression is inseparable from speech, for only in speaking can I attend to, and be present in, the words that I speak. It is not so much the empirical distinction between writing and speaking which is significant here. The fundamental difference is not between the spoken and written word, but between presence and absence, life and death. In relation to these oppositions, every word, whether it is spoken or written, belongs to writing. The signified, therefore, whether *empirically* spoken or written, is always writing. For this very reason, Levinas can argue that the work has a meaning, but this is not the same as signifying, which is the surplus of the speaker over anything that is said or written.[3] Although the work says something about me, it says so in the absence of the original author. If it points back to this author, it does so only indirectly through the 'third person' (Levinas 1969, 67). This is because there is always a gap, interval or distance between the speaker, author and what is spoken or written. It is in this interval where history is written, and it is this interval that is replaced, substituted by and ousted by the other ethical interval of the face to face relation. There is a time other than history, which belongs to no culture, society or nation, but calls to judgement, in the straightforwardness of the appeal of the Other, every history, culture and nation. The intersection, interval or hiatus within history is in the presence of the Other in speech. This presence interrupts, deranges and disturbs the dead time of the survivors, who exist in the ruins of victory and triumph. It is only this presence of the Other which can stand as a permanent witness against the conquest of dead time. This presence is not a counter-history, but the interruption of every history, even the history of minorities and the dissident. This year's freedom fighter can become next year's tyrant, and the cry for justice can always congeal into persecution and domination against those who now demand justice from us. The living presence of speech is always a struggle against the dead time of the past in which tradition and our customs are deposited like gold in a stream. Or our moral habits are made further invulnerable by being miraculously translated into universal laws and obligations, whereby we can deny our original responsibility to the Other through the appeal to higher destiny and fate.

It is not a question here of reversing the relation between speech and writing, and accusing Levinas of naïveté and innocence, because there can be no moment outside of history in which we are immersed, trapped and imprisoned, but rather to follow this other logic of inclusive rather than exclusive disjunction. There is a symmetry in how we might consider the relation between writing and speech as we have considered the logic of alterity. We have argued that there are two 'alterites' in Levinas' work. One in which the Other is opposed, exterior and external to the self, and the other, where, through the idea of the infinite, fecundity and substitution, it inhabits the subject, breaking its self-identity from within. Is it not possible, in the same way, to think of the relation between speech and writing as also inclusive and not exclusive? Just as much as writing destroys the ethical moment, it is also disturbed and interrupted by it, such that writing, to use Blanchot's expression, becomes the experience of discontinuity, rather than unity. As we shall see, this inclusive relation between writing and ethics must be the case, otherwise Levinas's own philosophical writing itself would be impossible. It would be a lie to the very experience it demands we all recognise.

The trace

Derrida writes, in 'Violence and Metaphysics', in the midst of his discussion of the priority given to speech over writing in Levinas's work, that the 'thematic of the *trace*... should lead to a certain rehabilitation of writing' [Italics in the original] (Derrida 1978, 102). Only 'should', perhaps, because when we read 'The Trace and the Other' by Levinas, it is not at all certain that the trace has anything to do with writing at all, since its description locates it within the phenomenon of the face. And yet, if we locate this analysis within the context of the essay 'Significance and Sense', where is it published for a second time, as a conclusion, we might be able to see that the trace does not belong to the same conceptual schema entirely as *Totality and Infinity*, even though Levinas is, to some extent, still using the same vocabulary.[4]

The overall argument of 'Signification and Sense' is that the meaning of the Other cannot be located in any history or culture. At the beginning of the section on the trace, which was added on its republication, Levinas announces a very peculiar problem, a problem that will begin to haunt his work from this point onwards. If the Other is outside any culture or history, and thereby, as we have seen, outside the written word, a pure interpellation or invocation, how then is it possible for Levinas to write a description of it which does not immediately betray this separation, distance or exteriority? '"The beyond,"' Levinas asks, 'from which the face comes and that fixes consciousness in its rectitude, is it not in turn an unveiled understood idea?' (Levinas 2003, 38) In one sense, the objective of the analysis of the trace is no different from *Totality and Infinity*. It is securely and firmly to distinguish the vocative from the denominative or predicative. The living presence of the Other is quite different from anything that might be written or said of it, even what Levinas might say or write, for its surplus exists in the presence of the Other in the words they speak, and this presence is beyond any description, precisely because it breaks with any description. Nonetheless, we can also argue that the 'Trace of the Other' begins to develop, precisely with this question of method, a writing of ethics which does not immediately betray the Other, or whose necessary betrayal nonetheless still bears witness to the excessive significance of the Other, and undergoes the very contortion and distortion of meaning which it describes.

The purpose of this description is to distinguish the trace from the operation of the sign. The difference between the sign and the trace is that the sign always points to something beyond itself. It makes present what is absent, even in its absence. The word 'cat', refers to cat, even when there is no cat present. The trace, on the contrary, is the absence of an absence. But how, Levinas asks, is it possible to have a relation to this absence of an absence? How is it possible to have a relation to a trace which does not point to something beyond it? The answer to this question is that the trace has a different temporality from the sign. The time of the sign is the time of the present. Even if the sign points back into the past, or forward into the future, both these times are recuperated, gathered together, and restored to the present. Past and future only have a meaning in the present which orientates them. The time of the trace, on the other hand, is the time of a past without the present, a past more past than the past, 'an immemorial past' (Levinas 2003, 40).

Absence can have a signification as absence without reverting back to a present. This would not be possible if signification were always the correlation between the signifier and the signified, in which the signified is a presence which fulfills the absence of the signifier. The referent which is present in the word 'cat' makes good the word's absence without a reference. Reality confirms the promise of words. The trace, on the contrary, Levinas argues, is the 'irrectitude' of the signifier and the signified (Levinas 2003, 40). The face, as the trace, has no signified, no reference or correlate, not even itself. It is a pure signifying (*signifiance*) without any signified. The trace, therefore, opens up a distance between the signifier and the signified, where signification is no longer returned to the presence of the signified. The 'personal order' of this language is no longer the 'I' or the 'you' of *Totality and Infinity*, in which the speaker is present in the words they speak, but the 'third person' which passes beyond the present through this absence of an absence.

The trace is not a sign without a referent, but that of which the reference cannot be made present. It is certainly possible, Levinas adds, to read the trace as though it were a sign. This is what a detective does when he reads the 'signs' of the criminal, or the hunter when she reads the traces of the prey in the snow. The trace is then an absence of a presence. It is not as though there is no signified, but it has been pulled away from the signifier, like a faint memory which can barely, if at all, be remembered. It has an effect upon consciousness, but it cannot be recuperated by consciousness. If the image of the sign is the tracks which signify some other intention, then the image of the trace is the marks themselves as the very impressions within matter, but without referring to some signified beyond this matter. It 'deranges' the order of the world, without at the same time pointing to some world beyond this world. The trace is the very marks themselves, before the instant of their passing away and disappearing.

Now it is remarkable, in relation to our long discussion of the place of writing *Totality and Infinity*, and all the implication this has on the exclusions of this work, that the example that Levinas gives to elucidate this idea of the difference between the trace and the presence of the sign, is writing. Every sign, Levinas argues, can also be interpreted as a trace, just as every trace can be interpreted as a sign, and the absence it tells converted into a present. The words that are written on the page can be read as signs, and as such they are submitted to an interpretation. Thus the psychoanalyst searches for hidden meanings which even the original writer did not know were present. All interpretation takes this form. It is the translation of the potential presence of words into an actuality. But words can also be read in terms of their tone, which expresses a certain 'sincerity, someone purely and simply passes by' (Levinas 2003, 42).

No doubt we could be tempted to understand this example in the same way we understood the face to face relation of *Totality and Infinity*. Here writing seems to be made identical to speech, since sincerity seems to appeal to the original intentions of the author. Thus, style is the presence of the writer in the words they have written, just as the 'face' is the presence of the Other in the words they speak (Levinas 2003, 42). To attend to the style of the letter therefore is to pay attention to the person who has written it, and thus to a faint echo of their ethical presence. To read sincerity in this way, however, would be precisely to read it through the sign and not the trace. It would be making an absence present, and an absolute past merely past. Writing works as an example of the trace so well here, because it can be read as the absence of an absence. The psychoanalyst would read this sincerity as the sincerity of someone and make them present in the act of the reading. To read ethically is to read completely otherwise. It is to allow this absence to pass without making it present. Levinas adds,

> But that which remains specifically a trace in the graphics and style of the letter does not signify any of those intentions or qualities, does not reveal and or hide anything at all (Levinas 2003, 42).

Is this not exactly what was taken to be evidence of the non-ethical status of the work, the absence of the author, the very condition of an ethical writing, and as Derrida asks, in 'Violence and Metaphysics' (on the very same page that he imagines that the trace in Levinas might rehabilitate writing) does not,

> the writer absent themselves better, that is, express himself better as other, address himself to the other more effectively, than the man of speech? (Derrida 1978, 102).

How is it possible to write about the trace, when it is not a phenomenon which offers itself to thematisation and conceptualisation? To adequately portray, if such a thing is possible, this signifying prior to a system of signs, would it not require a different kind of writing which did not operate at the level of description, designation and objectivity? Yet this seems to be the only conception of writing that Levinas has. On the one hand, Levinas must insist that the trace cannot belong to a phenomenology, for in a very strict sense it does not *appear* at all, but on the other hand, to deny phenomenology completely would undermine the possibility of being able to write about the trace at all. Levinas is left with a kind of negative phenomenology similar to negative theology which endlessly makes statements about that which it claims to be beyond any kind of human knowledge. It is a phenomenology whose only purpose is to write its own impossibility, by 'situating that significance,' Levinas writes, 'from the phenomenology it interrupts' (Levinas 2003,

41). Writing must interrupt itself in the very process of being written. This is not due to any decision, judgement or choice of the author, and it is not primarily, therefore, a question of method, in any ordinary sense, but of the manner in which the written word is already unravelled by the trace of the Other beyond intentionality.[5] Also it would not be possible simply to oppose writing to speech, since if the saying inhabits the spoken word, then it must also do so the written, because the notion of the word in general includes both writing and speech. In *Totality and Infinity*, the saying of the said, and what is said are mutually *exclusive*. By the 'Trace of the Other', through the very idea of the trace, and even more so in *Otherwise than Being*, they are *inclusive*, just as in the example of the letter, the sincerity cannot be separated from the words that are written on the page.

In the essay, 'Phenomenon and Enigma', which was originally published in 1965, this problem of method becomes more explicit (Levinas 1987a, 61-73). The aim of philosophy is to unify experience in the present, both in terms of manifestation and the temporal order of time. This notion of unity is contained in the idea of being. Being is the coming to presence of beings. This is why ontology is the culmination of phenomenology. Even within the history of philosophy, however, there have been counter discourses which appear to escape the domination of the idea of being. Ideas, Levinas mentions, such as the Platonic One or the Good, and the absence of God in negative theology (Levinas 1987a, 62). How is such an excess possible? It is not because of the finitude of human knowledge, as though there were simply some 'beyond' which is on the other side of the limit of our understanding and apprehension, since this very limit, as any good Hegelian will tell you, is posited by the very thought which claims it is so restricted. It has, rather, to do with the structure of knowledge itself which is always the correlation of the sensing and the sensed, the perceiving and perception. The excess of experience over and above the idea of being has to do with the possibility of a non-correlation, of experience *internally* and not externally being out of sync or out of joint with itself. This in turn is only possible because with the idea of Being, in which every being is assembled and unified, there is the trace of the 'beyond Being'. What is important is that this 'beyond being' is not to be understood in terms of negative theology, otherwise we are back to the antinomies of the finitude of the human knowledge, where the Other is indistinguishable from the *noumena*. The Other is not some mysterious phenomenon beyond the reaches of knowledge, which must somehow be postulated as an idea of reason. Rather than an idea of reason, it is the immanent disruption of the correlation between sensibility and the understanding. There is a part of experience, the brute fact of experience, which cannot be inserted within the categorial table of the understanding, and thereby does not offer itself to the systematic grasp of reason. It is important, however, not to translate this discontinuity between sensibility and the understanding into the Kantian 'thing-in-itself'. What resists the unity of knowledge is not some separate sphere of experience, which could only ever be, as Kant himself has shown, an idea of reason, and therefore as much an element of the architectonic of reason as the correlation between the understanding and sensibility. The beyond of reason is *reason's* beyond, and therefore in the strictest sense there can be no 'beyond'. Such is the truth of idealism, which in this sense is indistinguishable from the most rigorous atheism. Rather, what resists knowledge must be immanent to knowledge itself within the correlation of understanding and sensibility. The possibility of the non-categorial experience can only be found in the slippage between sensibility and understanding, without at the same time translating the sensible into an idea of reason, the noumenal or the 'thing-in-itself'. Such a lack of synchronicity between sensibility and understanding is only possible if there is another kind of time no longer susceptible to the schematism of the present which functions as the bridge between sensibility and the understanding.

The problem is that as soon as one refers, indicates or describes this other or different time, one immediately returns it to the presence of the idea of Being in which all phenomena become unified and combined. How can one write about that which escapes the correlation between the sensible and reason except as Kant does through the idea of reason? Everything depends, Levinas writes, on the possibility of a signifying, which though it is part of discourse, nonetheless does not lose its power to disrupt and fragment its order. This is only possible if we reverse the relation between order and disorder and subvert their relativity. Disorder is not merely a moment prior to equilibrium in which order once more re-establishes itself. Rather than being different from order, disorder would only be an element in its own self-fulfillment and culmination. For Levinas on the contrary, the disorder of the trace is discontinuous. This means, paradoxically, disorder intervenes in order before and prior to its recapitulation, repetition and duplication within that order. The knock of the door, to use Levinas's image, which interrupts the peace and tranquility of my home, resounds before I have heard it and can then reinsert it within the thread of my daily life. 'The context,' Levinas writes, 'was given up before beginning, the breaking of contact took place before engagement' (Levinas 1987a, 65). Now the possibility of such a reversal between order and disorder, such that the latter can intervene before the former can re-constitute itself, is given in language. In one sense language is order par excellence, since, in the relation between the signifier and the signified, experience is reduced to a system or relation of substitutional elements. But language is also the possibility of an enigmatic equivocation which cannot be translated into a definite meaning without losing all its power. Words are never just what is said, even when they are just written or spoken. Such enigmatic expression is not merely the collision between two different meanings in the same word, but the way in which another meaning can insinuate itself in the meaning of another without appearing definite. This is why it can never be a matter of choosing one meaning over the other, but of the certainty of meaning being upset by a sense which never quite makes itself present, and can never be made present. Levinas describes this through a new modality of a 'perhaps' which falls through the opposition of the 'is' and the 'is not', or the possible and actual (Levinas 1987a, 67). Equivocation, therefore, should not be confused with the operation of a metaphor where, behind the unfamiliar expression, is discovered the literal term, such that, in the strictest sense, metaphors would never offer anything new to language.

There is not, on the one side, the language of information and communication, and on the other, the language of derangement, disorder and subversion. For this would be merely to oppose one order to another, or to make disorder relative to order. On the contrary, disorder, without ever being internalised, *insinuates* itself within order, in the same way that a word can suddenly have an equivocal, enigmatic and cryptic meaning, whereas before it had none. This is why Levinas argues that the possibility of disruption of order lies not in the fact of the existence of an opposing order, but in that the present itself is already 'fissile', and 'destructures itself in its very punctuality' (Levinas 1987a, 68). In the same way, it is not a matter of opposing the writing to speech, whether as the written or spoken word, but of demonstrating that the word is already interrupted by an exorbitant saying, and of recognising that such a saying only absolves itself from the said through writing. Rather than writing being extrinsic to ethics, it is the only possibility of an enigmatic and obscure signifying which is not immediately identical to the relation between the signifier and signified. We need to be clear here that what we mean by 'writing' is not the written marks of the page, just as for Levinas speech is not the same as the spoken word. Speech is the presence of the Other in the words they speak, which saves the words from equivocation. The trace, on the contrary, is this very equivocation which subverts the unity, coherence and continuity of knowledge. Equivocation is the mark of writing in the spoken and the written word, preventing them from becoming merely elements within a system of signs. It is the surplus of language beyond communication, which nonetheless exists in every act of transference of information, though it cannot be summarised as an item of knowledge, even when it is denied or forgotten. Philosophy, then, for Levinas, becomes the strange paradox of remembering what cannot be remembered, capturing in words what cannot be said, and representing the un-representable. This would be absurd, and a ridiculous task if it were not for the fact words already contained more than what could be said. The aim, through the very analysis, description and account of the approach of the Other (but not reducible to any of them) is to bring back the said to this surplus of language.

In an essay published in 1980, 'Manner of Speaking', which was republished in *Of God Who Comes to Mind*, Levinas writes that his own philosophy is inseparable from the rational pursuit of philosophy as a whole (Levinas 1998, 178). What is irrational is not the opposite of the rational, but the very limit by which the rational constitutes and composes itself. To seek to be irrational is not to confound the rational, but merely to increase its strength and power. So are we merely compelled to repeat what has been said before, and to repeat over and over again with minor variations that there is nothing new under the sun? Has the rational stifled any innovation, creativity and novelty? Even that discourse which contests reason must do so rationally. Such has been, at the very dawn of philosophy itself, the perennial critique of scepticism and sophism. Even the great Plato contradicts himself when he says that the One cannot be designated, nominated or assented to, since it is named in the very discourse which contests its appellation (Levinas 1998, 178).

Such is the power of thought which can reflect upon its own negation and contain, dissipate and disarm it in this very reflection itself. Yet against this potency, Levinas asks whether thought always has the necessary time to immediately catch up with its own negation, and whether the interval between the negation and the reflection is instantaneous. And here it is interesting for our own account of a possible rehabilitation of writing that the example Levinas gives of resistance to the immediate folding back of the negation of thought in its own reflection is poetry. The distance between the thought that thinks, interprets and reads the poem, and the 'matter of the words' that express this thought are not one and the same. Such that there is always a interval, which can never be immediately covered up, between the ideality of meaning and its material base. This gap is not something which is extrinsic to poetry, but belongs to its very expression. In the same way, Levinas suggests, philosophy can be seen as an 'alternation' or 'ambiguity' of sense, which can never totally be made simultaneous or contemporaneous with itself (Levinas 1998, 179). Thus, although no one would question the necessity of writing, even the most sceptical thought, in terms of the strictures of reason (and this is the weapon that the rationalist always uses against the sceptic), this is not to say

145

that reason must be or is the ultimate justification. For in the end reason can only justify itself rationally. It can make no appeal except to itself, and its justification can only be a kind of 'doubling up'. Levinas envisages a philosophy in which, between the two moments of thought returning to itself, there is a kind of delay or interruption. In this hiatus, a different meaning can make itself visible, which is not 'encrusted' in the very rational discourse which makes it possible (Levinas 1998, 180).

This is a difficult and complex relation; far more so than the appeal to the immediate experience of the face in *Totality and Infinity*. This other meaning is not external or opposed to ontology; rather it inhabits, and is implicit within it. Alterity is possible only through and within the ontological order which it interrupts. It is nothing outside of it. The task of philosophy, therefore, is not to appeal to some mysterious beyond, but to the disorder that gnaws and burrows away within every order, and which it must continually expel, exile and dismiss. Levinas names this new task of philosophy a 'reduction'. He writes:

> For philosophy the ontological proposition remains open to a certain reduction, disposed to unsaying itself, and to wanting itself wholly said (Levinas 1998, 180).

Ethical language

The complexity of the influence of the phenomenological method on Levinas's philosophy would require a book of its own to describe, but it is clear that it remains within this tradition.[6] Writing in the preface of *Totality and Infinity*, Levinas tells us that 'the presentation and development of the notions employed owe everything to the phenomenological method' (Levinas 1969, 28). The same allegiance is given thirteen years later in the conclusion to *Otherwise than Being*:

> Our analysis claims to be in the spirit of the Husserlian philosophy, whose letter has been the recall in our epoch of the permanent phenomenology, restored to its rank of being a method of all philosophy (Levinas 1991, 183).

Even this quotation indicates, however (and this would obviously not surprise us considering Levinas's critique of the theoretical bias of Husserlian phenomenology in his earlier work) that this allegiance is anything but straightforward.

The same critique of theory is present in *Otherwise than Being*. The approach of the neighbour is non-synchronisable, representable, or thematisable. Rather than being an object of knowledge, it interrupts every knowing. Thought denies the un-thematisable by translating it into a signifier. Even if it is a signifier of what cannot be signified, its negativity becomes part of the positivity of thought, either as a necessary limit, or as a projection beyond every limit. Thought surprises itself by forgetting its own inventions, creations and work. The approach of the neighbour does not operate at the level of the sign. Its signifying cannot be expressed through the difference between the signifier and signified. The face, Levinas argues, it is not the sign of anything, but is its own sign. It is a signifying as the sign of a sign. How can this signifying be analysed, described or portrayed without it being immediately translated into the relation between the signified and the signifier? The phenomenon of the face signifies the irreducibility of the Other to any concrete form or guise as signified. In describing it, I have immediately made presentable what is meant to be un-representable, synchronic what is diachronic, and thematisable what is un-thematisable.

Perhaps the simplest and easiest response to this difficulty would be to accept that writing cannot capture the surplus of the Other over its description, and therefore we can only make an appeal to that which lies outside, or on the other side, of writing. This is the strategy of *Totality and Infinity*. The excess of the Other lies only in their presence in the words they speak. Even *Totality and Infinity* cannot express this exorbitant signification. This is why it repeats the Platonic mistrust of writing. No true teaching can occur in books. Its proper place is in the oral teaching of the face to face relationship. What is significantly different about *Otherwise than Being* is that it does not repeat this simple response. It is aware of the paradox of describing the indescribable in the very words which announce its impossibility. Phenomenology can follow its own contortion and distortion in the face of this impossibility. There can be a phenomenology of the non-apparent. The absence of the face that conceals no hidden signified, whose absence is the very absence absenting itself, 'requires,' Levinas writes, 'a description that can only be formed in ethical language' (Levinas 1991, 94). We might imagine, after reading *Totality and Infinity*, that this 'ethical language' must be an appeal to the immediacy of the face to face relation. In a footnote to this sentence, however, it is clear that, on the contrary, this ethical language is situated within the phenomenological descriptions themselves, and not in the object of these descriptions, which would be external to them. The difference between the approach of the neighbour, and the system of language in which every sign is the relation between a signifier and a signified, can be signalled in the very writing which describes this difference. It 'marks', Levinas explains, phenomenology's 'own interruption' (Levinas 1991, 193, fn. 35).

Levinas will also use the same expression, 'ethical language', in the following chapter, when he describes communication (Levinas 1991, 120). We think of communication as the transportation of ideas from one mind to another. The ideal of communication is, therefore, paradoxically, an interior monologue. For only in such a monologue can material available for a dialogue be made ready. The highest ideal of knowledge is that this material is already constituted even prior to a dialogue, since any true thought must be true no matter who speaks it, and its meaning external to any mind which thinks it. Levinas's position is not simply to invert the relation between monologue and dialogue, so that the latter has priority over the former, for even the dialogue is merely the coming together of two equal partners in a discourse which maintains their mutual independence. The relation to the Other is not merely the inversion of the hierarchy between monologue and dialogue, an appeal to inter-subjectivity over subjectivity, but the inversion of this inversion. It is a dialogue which comes from the side of the Other, and not from the I who is equivalent to the 'You' it addresses. On the contrary, for Levinas, a dialogue which presupposes the interchangeability of terms is not a true dialogue at all. For such a dialogue would always proceed from the dominant term presupposing its own cultural identity as embodying a universal principle of commensurability. All values are therefore translated through the same language of values, which then begins to discover itself everywhere. They were like us after all. Recognition is always the reduction of the Other to the Same, for it always finds in the Other the same essence it has projected there and which ultimately has its source within itself, whether positive or negative. I speak in order to obtain agreement, but this presupposes there is a common ground beforehand in which something like agreement, or even disagreement, already exists. For Levinas, on the contrary, this common ground is secondary. To be open to the Other already implies that I have stepped outside the limits of what is shared, implicated and equal between us. The condition of the condition of communication is therefore a certain lack of communication, and not universal agreement.

Nonetheless, Levinas is adamant that such a relation of non-communication, in which the self and the Other are not contemporaneous, should not be relegated to some kind of 'special moral experience' which is beyond description (Levinas 1991, 120). The 'ethical language' that Levinas is using in order to portray the approach of the Other, the figures of speech that go up to make its style and content, are perfectly 'adequate', he argues, to the description, without making an appeal to such an experience necessary. This is only possible if the phenomenological descriptions themselves can 'follow out the reverting of thematisation into anarchy in the description of the approach' (Levinas 1991, 121). This would mean that the enactment of ethics is not only in the relation itself, but also in the description of the relation. It is not a question of there being an ethical experience on the one side, which can never be said, and on the other, the said which cannot describe the ethical experience. Writing, however, can only describe the ethical relation through the very interruption of its meaning. It is only to the extent that writing is not just the difference between the signifier and the signified that it can be caught up in the 'reversal of thematisation'. The reversal does not operate outside of the writing through the positing of experience outside of description, but is internal. Writing unravels itself, but by doing so it does not point to yet another signified. On the contrary, in referring back to itself, and reversing its momentum, it points to the absence of the signified. It then becomes for Levinas a 'saying' rather than a 'said'. What it is important and significant is no longer the conveyance of information or facts from one mind to the other, but the testimony of language as language to the difference of the Other, the 'sign of a giving of signs', rather than the signifier of a signified (Levinas 1991, 119).

Ethical terms such as 'substitution', 'persecution' and 'responsibility' are not in Levinas's descriptions expressions of a signified, such that 'responsibility' means the idea of responsibility that I have, but this pure giving: the superabundance of my responsibility over any idea that I might have of it to such a degree that I am even responsible for the responsibility of the Other. What is significant, however, and what makes *Otherwise than Being* quite different from *Totality and Infinity*, is that this superfluity, this overflowing of every concept, idea and object of thought, happens through writing rather than through speech. There is no longer any appeal to direct speech as a privileged site of an ethical experience of the alterity of the Other. Philosophy can indicate what stands outside of philosophy, without at the same time returning it to the norms and criteria of what makes common sense. What is important is not to confuse or tie up the superabundance of the signifying of the giving of signs with some external referent outside the written or spoken word. For Levinas this would be to fall into a theological discourse which imagines a secret reality beyond language, which on further reflection is the very creation of the language it abhors. 'Theological language,' Levinas writes in a footnote, 'destroys the religious situation of transcendence' (Levinas 1991, 197, fn. 25). It does so because it substitutes for the Other the reality of the signified, whose meaning is possible only with the overall system of signs. The transcendental signified is dependent on the very immanent order of meanings which it desires to rise and soar above. The signifying of the giving of signs is not 'higher' than the relation between the signifier and the signified, but cuts through their mutual interdependence, in which every word must refer back to a thing, and every thing back to a word.

The symbolic

Our constant temptation is to attempt to re-translate the signifying of the sign back into the signifier of a signified, as though it were a symbol or an allegory. There is a parallel here with what Blanchot tells us about the art of reading in the essay 'The Secret of the Golem', which was first published in 1955, and republished in *The Book to Come* (Blanchot 2003, 86-92). To read symbolically, especially after the work of Freud and Jung, has almost become second nature to us. We are always trying to look for hidden meanings behind the surface reality of the work. These hidden meanings are the truth of the work, whether obscured or not from the original author. What is striking for Blanchot, however, is that the writer of the work does not appear, when they are writing, to be involved in symbols at all. It is only after the fact that they recognise the symbols in their work. The delay between the writing and the symbolic interpretation attests to a certain resistance *within* the written symbol to the symbolic, a resistance Blanchot is quite happy to call the real. The difference between the allegory and the symbol is that the former is still caught with the horizontal relations between the signifier and the signified, whereas the latter attempts, Blanchot writes, 'to jump outside the sphere of language', towards some kind of ineffable experience (Blanchot 2003, 87). It wants to express what cannot be expressed by any word, even the word that is meant to carry its meaning. There is, therefore, in the symbol, always a surplus of the signified over the signifier. The symbolic word is always attempting to say more that it can say, to point to some ultimate reality which exists beyond words. Unlike the allegorical, the symbolic does not intend to expand meaning through different interconnections and interrelations between words, but to overleap and surmount every word in a region of experience which can never be directly described or represented. If we imagine language as a wall that prevents us from any immediate access to reality, as though we were permanently exiled from the world of things, like Adam and Eve from the Garden of Eden, then the symbol is the surreptitious, stealthy and furtive glimpse over the other side. This is why the symbol is essentially speechless. It says without saying; intimates without disclosure or revelation. But in so doing, rather than offering what it promises, the Holy Grail of

language, its secret source and origin, the mysterious conjunction, conver-
gence and meeting of the word and thing, it becomes the most dense and
obscure saying. In attempting to liberate itself from the chain of words which
distances experience from reality, it becomes the darkest word, almost an
evocation, and thereby, Blanchot adds, opens us up to 'another space' which
has nothing at all to do with what we thought was on the other side of this
wall, but is the materiality of the word itself. In the very density of its saying,
the symbol folds back upon itself and prevents any direct reference to a
signified, either as an idea or as an ultimate reality which transcends every
signifier. Thus, when Blanchot says that it is a resistance within the symbol
that is real, he is not referring to some region, space, or sphere outside of
language, which language can somehow mysteriously summon up, like the
ghosts and spirits of old, but the surprising fact that language can bend back
upon itself without mobilising immediately any signified.

No doubt any symbol can be read as a signifier of a signified, but there
is always a revolt against this transformation in the impenetrability that the
symbol invokes, which, unlike the image, is not the expansion, but the contraction of language. Our understanding of the symbol, Blanchot tells us, can
be applied to our reading of literature. We can read literature as though it were
a hieroglyphics concealing a hidden message but in so doing (though we
imagine we are preserving the work for posterity and heritage), the singularity
of the work is lost and destroyed. It becomes, Blanchot writes, 'a sort of
screen, tirelessly bored through by the insects of commentary' (Blanchot
2003, 89). But we can also read literature as the movement of language back
into itself. Rather than the reference of the work being outside of the work, the
outside of the work becomes its very centre. 'The beyond of the work,'
Blanchot writes, 'is real only in the work, is nothing but the unique reality of
the work' (Blanchot 2003, 90). The work, in the very density and opacity of its
language, seems to refer outside of itself, seems to demand an interpretation
which goes beyond the work, but the more that you follow the labyrinth of the
work, its strangeness, uniqueness and individuality, the more you get lost
within it, such that you are no longer really sure that it refers to anything else
but itself.[7] The distance between the symbol and what it is supposed to refer
to is a distance which belongs to the work, rather than being exterior to it, and
it is within the work that you experience the 'outside' of the work, the limit,
confinement and constraint of meaning, rather than in a region beyond, whether
this realm is considered real or metaphorical.

We must, therefore, distinguish between this interior 'outside' from the
external 'outside'. The latter is the destruction of the work in commentary and
critique, which always finds the meaning of the work in something other than

the work itself. That the work says more than can be said lies in the work, in the turning back of language upon itself, rather than in an interpretation pointing to some information or item of knowledge lying outside of it. Of course, we tend to confuse the one 'outside' with the other. It is just to the extent that the work opens up a distance within itself, in this turning back of language, that a space is opened up within the work which demands to be filled by an interpretation. This is the temptation of every reading, which is not accidental, but necessarily belongs to the work. We are constantly asking what does the work mean, seeking some way to avoid its uncomfortable emptiness, and the more so when the work is pushed to the limit of its genre and style, such that it becomes nothing but this emptiness and this absence.

Certainly we would not expect philosophy to be troubled by such uncertainty, ambivalence and ambiguity. The task of philosophy is simply to announce what it has to say. To be coherent, rigorous and magisterial. Philosophy precisely begins in the moment in which equivocation is refused, since to resist speaking the truth is to deny the possibility of any kind of dialogue, reasoning and argument. Yet Levinas's writing is compelled to betray such a duty by its allegiance to transcendence. The more Levinas allies himself to this spirit of philosophy, the more he betrays the excessive signification of the Other, capturing, enslaving and destroying the ethical relation within the very categories, concepts and ideas it is supposed to transcend. And yet, the more that he remains faithful to this signification, the more he is compelled to remain silent, mute and helpless. The reality of his work, however, confounds this double bind. The existence of his books announces the absurdity of their impossibility. Either you can write about the experience of the Other, and the contention that philosophy cannot describe transcendence is simply false, or you cannot write about the Other, and every word that Levinas has written is ornamental and useless.

The opposition between philosophy and experience, however, might itself be false. The question might be not whether philosophy can describe what is not philosophical, since in the very moment you announce it you contradict your own statement, but that philosophy already *contains* the non-philosophical. It does so in the very way that Blanchot writes about literature. Literature announces itself not in deploying and unfolding its own essence, form and idea, but in resisting them through its own singularity. In terms of philosophy, and this is the closest it ever gets to literature, which has nothing at all to do with some kind of mysterious 'literary quality' (we might speak here of a kind of reversed phenomenology), in which the object described turns against the description from within the description itself. Something stands out within the description which cannot be said, but such an excess of meaning, the unspeakable, indescribable and inexpressible, only has its place *within* what has been written. We must resist the temptation of situating the unnameable, non-categorial and un-schematisable *outside* of language, as Levinas does in *Totality and Infinity,* when he places transcendence in the presence of the Other in the words they speak, exterior to any spoken or written word. In *Otherwise than Being,* on the contrary, the giving of sign, the exorbitant signification of the relation to the Other, is internal and inherent to the sign. This totally retranslates Levinas's relation to philosophy. The written word, just as we saw in our discussion of the name of God, affirms, declares and pronounces the ineffable presence of the Other, which passes by before it is captured in a signified.[8] It does so, however, only in effacing and withdrawing itself before its own proclamation becomes solidified into certitude and irrefutability. Such explains the peculiar rhythm of Levinas's writing, in which every positive statement is undermined by a string of qualifications and modifications - a philosophy of the adverb.

Scepticism

The clearest statement of Levinas's mature method is in a small section called the 'reduction' in *Otherwise than Being* (Levinas 1991, 43-5). Even in writing the statement 'the Other is beyond being', I make use of the copula, in which a predicate is joined to an apparent subject. Even more so, the meaning and sense of the signifying of the sign, the giving of signs, beyond what they communicate, appears to be captured and held within the written word. 'As soon as saying,' Levinas writes, 'on the hither side of being, becomes dictation, it expires, or abdicates, in fables and in writing' (Levinas 1991, 43). Here we seem to be faced with the same opposition which we found in *Totality and Infinity.* On the one side, there is the living presence of the Other in the words they speak, which must be sharply distinguished from these words themselves, and on the other, the dead letter of writing, in which the presence of the Other has been completely extinguished, like the cold embers of a fire which has long gone out. If we want to explain, describe and account for what this saying *is*, then it seems inescapable that we will have to say 'what it is', and in so doing we will have to speak of it in terms of propositional language. The only possible way out of this impasse is to accept that the saying can enter writing without losing its excessive signification, and therefore that the relation between the saying and the said cannot be a simple opposition, in the same way that writing is opposed, contrasted to, and distinguished from speech. There are two necessities: one, that the language of thematisation, knowledge and thought is interrupted by the presence of the Other, which is inseparable from the giving of signs, and two, that this saying can be described in words. This double necessity is not a contradiction, because the laying out, arrangement and ordering of the saying in the said is demanded by the saying itself.

There is an ethical impetus behind knowledge exceeding knowledge. If theory and practice are one, then it is practice that determines theory and not theory practice. But if the saying, this excess of language of the sign, must be said in order to make itself visible, then it is equally imperative that this visibility does not congeal into yet one more category. Ethical alterity is not one more universal determination of the object which we can add to our understanding of the world. Philosophy is neither strictly knowing or mysticism, but the more peculiar, difficult and insuperable task of opening up within knowledge what exceeds knowledge. It is not mysticism, enthusiasm or superstition, because it avoids the temptation of transforming the ineffable or unutterable saying into another signified. The saying is not a signified without signifier. It is the position, standing, or situation of language in which signs are offered as a response to the Other. It is not what I say but that I speak, which is the ethical imperative of language, without which there would be no language at all.

Levinas calls this effort of philosophy to bear witness to the ethical surplus of language a 'reduction'. Now although he is still appealing to the situation of speech as the site of the excess of signifying over the sign, the ambiguity of the interrelation between the sign and the giving of signs, despite what he writes about the 'work of writing', can only be *materialised* in writing. There must, therefore, be two kinds of writing, and not just one as is announced in *Totality and Infinity*. One, in which the written word designates objects, inserting them within a system of elements and relations, and the other, where the word ceases to be tied to any external reference, turns back upon itself, cutting any contact with reality, unsaying and unravelling any direct and immediate communication, saying what cannot be said. Rather than refusing ambiguity, equivocation and ambivalence, Levinas's philosophy (and such is the difficulty of reading and interpreting it), exposes and lays itself bare to equivocation. It suffers from what it cannot say. Not mutely, but in a stammering, stuttering, clumsy and inarticulate style, whose very aphasia attests, and can be the only testimony, to the extension of the saying over and above the said. It is only in writing what cannot be spoken that what cannot be said can appear non-contemporaneously with its appearance. 'Writing what cannot be spoken' - this is the very force of the written word. Here the difference and distance between philosophy and literature becomes blurred, for it is only through a language of tropes that the non-simultaneity of the saying and the said can be expressed, rather than in propositions, statements or judgments.

Levinas explains the non-coincidence of the saying and the said through the perennial opposition of scepticism and reason throughout the history of philosophy (Levinas 1991, 165-71). What concerns him about this opposition is not the relative veracity of either side, such that one could always prove that scepticism was wrong, reason right, or vice versa, but the continual interruption of reason by scepticism, despite the fact that reason's arguments against scepticism seem faultless and flawless. Even though reason has the best arguments, scepticism nonetheless keeps coming back. This is because the real difference between scepticism and reason is not between two conflicting arguments (since if this were the case, scepticism would be just another kind of reason, which has usually been the way of defeating scepticism in the history of philosophy, ever since Plato's arguments against the sophists, through a kind of performative contradiction), but between coincidence and non-coincidence. Scepticism and reason are out of step, erratic, and it is this that explains the continual return of scepticism despite the fact that reason has all the best arguments.

Reason organises all elements of knowledge into a simultaneity. Systematicity is not an additional item added onto our knowledge of the world; it is implied in this knowledge. Even if we come across something novel or not yet understood, it immediately has its place within this system, as though there were already an empty place for it to be inserted. The priority of reason, that it has both the first and last word, rests upon this simultaneity and not the other way around. It is because elements within our experience of the world can be taken up together in a system and unity that reason can always defeat scepticism. It is the unity of time that makes possible the unity of reason and not the other way around. It is not that scepticism offers us another conception of time, for this would be only another reason, and since there can only be one reason, it would be same. Rather it is the relation between scepticism and reason itself which is non-contemporaneous and therefore cannot be synthesised at a higher level. For even this further level will once again be interrupted and disrupted by the return of another scepticism.

We risk the danger, Levinas continues, of confusing scepticism with 'lived experience', as though the non-contemporaneity of scepticism and reason, were the same as the non-simultaneity of life and thought, as though there were always more to life than thought can think. The peril of this appeal to lived experience is that the opposition between life and thought is thought's opposition and not life's. Life becomes the murky depths that reason cannot penetrate, but which promises an abundance of unprecedented meanings. Rather than appeal to some experience outside of philosophy, Levinas appeals to a repetition, recurrence and discontinuity immanent to it. 'Must we,' he questions, 'reinvoke alternation and diachrony as the time of philosophy?' (Levinas 1991, 167) Such a reminder should once and for all prevent us from caricaturing Levinas's thought and philosophy as some kind of naive, childish and immature appeal to experience, reality, or life that we had long ago believed we had left behind. Philosophy cannot complete itself not because there exists some impossible remainder outside of itself which resists totalisation, but because it itself always remains incomplete. It remains incomplete because it is out of time with itself, can never quite catch up with itself, as though the reflection and the reflection upon reflection were always minimally lagging behind one another.

Philosophy, therefore, contains both scepticism and its reason without these two moments becoming synchronous. It is always besides itself, uncomfortable in its own skin, rather than content and satisfied with its own certainty, to the extent that even its own well-being disquiets it. Scepticism belongs to reason, but like an uninvited guest which will not leave. Only if the interval between scepticism and reason is thought from the side of reason, can scepticism be defeated once and for all, because we can see that scepticism must use the very reason which it refutes. But if we view the interval from the side of scepticism, it is always possible that it might return, whatever *reason's* reason is. Such an interval is only possible if scepticism and reason are not one and the same, and the interval between them not a false one. It would be an illusion if scepticism were merely a negation of reason, a negation, of course, that would be absurd, since scepticism must give reasons for its negation of reason. Scepticism, rather than negating reason, haunts and obsesses it. Rather than being the end of reason, without scepticism, reason would have no reason to be rational, and philosophy would come to an end. If philosophy really did have the last word, then there would be no need to philosophise. The truth of scepticism is the absence of the last word.

Levinas applies this very difference between scepticism and its refutation to his own writing. In the one sense, it belongs to the side of reason, knowledge and comprehension - the words it uses are concepts like any others - but in another sense, these words are not frozen in a final and ultimate meaning, but continually renew themselves through different readings and interpretations. This is only because the written word always means more than what it simply says, even the philosophical word. Equivocation is not something that befalls the written word, but expresses its essence. Its essence is to have no essence, always to say more than can be caught once and for all in a statement or definition. Here we have a complete reversal from Levinas's position in *Totality and Infinity*, where it is speech and not writing that expresses the interval between the Same and the Other, precisely because speech is without equivocation in the presence of the Other in the words they speak. Now, on the contrary, it is the interval between the literal and equivocal meaning of the word which holds open the possibility of the Other within the Same, of a language not entirely closed up in what it communicates and informs, a 'possibility,' Levinas writes, 'laid bare in the poetic *said* and the interpretation it calls for ad infinitum' [Levinas's emphasis] (Levinas 1991, 170).[9]

This would mean that language in itself is sceptical, and rather than reason being the true expression of language, it would be its limitation and restriction, or as Levinas writes, 'language is already scepticism' (Levinas 1991, 170). Books themselves, which in Levinas's mind were forever associated with a totalising, unifying and coherent discourse, undo themselves in prefaces, introductions and afterwords. Not because these declarations and professions attest solely to the intentions of the author, but since they are proof of an 'outside' which they cannot account for but must respond to. Not everything can be said. Not even the fact that not everything can be said. Everything which is written interrupts itself in demanding that something more can be said. It is not just what is said that is important, but its interruption. Every book is the interruption of another book, but it too will be interrupted, as though writing were an infinite conversation in which no-one could claim to have the last word and thereby call it to an end. Such a culmination of philosophy, in which reason would be satisfied that it had all the reasons and there was nothing outside of its field of vision, would be indistinguishable from silence. It would not have to speak, or even affirm itself, to what is other, different or opposed to it, since every 'other' would be the same as itself. Everywhere it looked it would only find itself since every possible alterity would be only a 'beyond' it had forgotten, it had previously invented, created and posited. Such a silence and antipathy, however, implies and is dependent upon the prior belief, which is not so certain and rational, that reason itself is infallible and complete.

The scepticism that comes back to haunt reason does not refer to some mysterious region, a world behind this world, from which no-one has returned except the insane and the foolish, but to the deficiency, imperfection and discontinuity which is *proper* to reason. The interval, through which the signifying of the sign slips, and which cannot be captured through any conjunction of the signifier and the signified, between reflection and the reflection upon reflection, is reason's guilty conscience that it has left something unsaid, or betrayed what has been said, such that, as soon as you have finished writing the last word, the book, rather than being a finished product, smooth and perfect, must begin again, ready to be read and interrupted by another. There is no end to these words, and only their inexhaustibility is testimony to the true limit of reason which it can declare and proclaim, but never know.

Notes

1 See Robert Eaglestone's book *Ethical Criticism: Reading After Levinas*, for a sustained engagement with Levinas's approach to literature (Eaglestone 1997).

2 There is also a positive content to Levinas's politics, which is admirably described in Howard Caygill's book, *Levinas & the Political*, as a 'prophetic politics' (Caygill 2002, 128-58).

3 'Signifying', in Levinas philosophical vocabulary, should always be sharply distinguished from the linguistic distinction between the signifier and the signified. The signifier belongs just as much to the order of writing, as the signified, since it requires the existence of a separate system of language. The ethical intention, if we can use such an expression, has nothing at all to do with the word, either from the side of the signifier or the signified. It is surplus to them both.

4 This essay was first published in *Tijdschrift voor Filosophie* in 1963, and then republished in *En découvrant l'existence avec Husserl et Heidegger* (Levinas 1982, 187-202). The same essay, apart from the first fifteen paragraphs and a new opening sentence, was inserted at the end of 'Signification and Sense', which was originally published in the *Revue de métaphysique et de morale* in 1964, and then republished in *Humanisme de l'autre homme* (Levinas 1972, 57-63). Since in this analysis we are primarily concerned with the specific analysis of the trace, we shall use the English translation of the second republication (Levinas 2003, 38-44).

5 So, for example, Levinas can write in *Otherwise than Being*, that the sincerity of the saying already inhabits every spoken word even before it is said. 'The unlocking of sincerity', he writes, 'makes possible the dimension in which all communication and thematisation will flow. The trace of the signifyingness in the making of signs and in proximity is not thereby effaced, and marks every use of speech' (Levinas 1991, 198).

6 The best study of Levinas's relation to phenomenology is John Drabinski's book *Sensibility and Singularity*, where he describes his work as the 'explosion of the horizons of phenomenology from within phenomenology itself' (Drabinski 2001, 14).

7 Blanchot says as much of his own interpretation of Lautréamont, in *Lautréamont and Sade*, 'We would simply like to prove,' he writes, 'to what extent one can follow a text and at the same time lose it' (Blanchot 2004, 49).

8 In chapter three, in the section 'The Name of God', pp.72-6.

9 Italicised in the original French, but not in the English translation (Levinas 1978, 263).

References

Aristotle, *The Complete Works of Aristotle, Volume Two*, ed. J. Barnes (Princeton: Princeton University Press, 1984).

Austin, J.L., *How to Do Things with Words* (Oxford: Oxford University Press, 1962).

Badiou, Alain. *Ethics: An Essay on the Understanding of Evil*, trans. P. Halliward (London: Verso, 2001).

Benveniste, Emile, *Problems in General Linguistics*, trans. M. E. Meek (Florida: University of Miami Press, 1971).

Blanchot, Maurice, 'L'Indestructible', *La nouvelle revue française*, 112: Avril (1962), 671-80.

------, *L'Entretien infini*. Paris: Gallimard, 1969.

------, *The Space of Literature*, trans. A. Smock (Lincoln & London: University of Nebraska Press, 1982).

------, 'Our Clandestine Companion', in *Face to Face with Levinas*, ed. R. Cohen, 41-50 (New York: State University of New York Press, 1986).

------, *The Unavowable Community*, trans. P. Joris (Barrytown, New York: Station Hill Press, 1988).

------, *The Infinite Conversation*, trans. S.Hanson (Minneapolis and London: University of Minnesota Press, 1993).

------, *Friendship*, trans. E. Rottenberg (Stanford: Stanford University Press, 1997).

------, *The Book to Come*, trans. C. Mandell (Stanford: Stanford University Press, 2003).

------, *Lautréamont and Sade*, trans. S. Kendall & M. Kendall (Stanford: Stanford University Press, 2004).

Bruns, Gerald, *Maurice Blanchot: The Refusal of Philosophy* (Baltimore: Johns Hopkins University Press, 1997).

Burggraeve, Roger, 'The bible gives to thought: Levinas on the possibility and proper nature of biblical thinking', in *The Face of the Other & the Trace of God*, ed J. Bloechl, 155-83 (New York: Fordham University Press, 2000).

Carver, Raymond, *Call If You Need Me* (London: The Harvill Press, 2000).

Caygill, Howard, *Levinas & the Political* (London & New York: Routledge, 2002).

Chalier, Catherine, *Levinas l'utopie de l'humain* (Paris: Albin Michel, 1993).

------, *Figures du féminin, lécture d' Emmanuel Levinas* (Paris: Verdier, 1984).

Chanter, Tina, ed., *Feminist Interpretations of Levinas* (Pennsylvania: Penn State University Press, 2001).

Chomsky, Noam, *Cartesian Linguistics*, ed. J. McGlivray (Christchurch New Zealand: Cybereditions, 2002).

Clark, Michael, *Paradoxes from A to Z* (London: Routledge, 2002).

Cohen, Josh, *Interrupting Auschwitz: Art, Religion, Philosophy* (London: Continuum, 2003).

Collin, Françoise, *Maurice Blanchot et la question de l'écriture* (Paris: Gallimard, 1971).

Critchley, Simon, *Very Little.. Almost Nothing: Death, Philosophy, Literature* (London: Routledge, 1997).

Davies, Paul, 'A fine risk: reading Blanchot reading Levinas', in *Re-Reading Levinas*, ed(s) R. Bernasconi and S. Critchley, 201-26 (Bloomington: Indiana University Press, 1991).

------, 'This Contradiction', in *Futures of Jacques Derrida*, ed(s) M. Bal and H. Vries, 18-64 (Stanford: Stanford University Press, 2001).

de Beauvoir, Simone, *The Second Sex*, trans. H. M. Parshley (London: Picador, 1988).

De Greef, Jan 'Skepticism and reason', in *Face to Face with Levinas*, ed. R. A. Cohen, 159-79 (New York: State University of New York Press, 1986).

Deleuze, Gilles, *Foucault*, trans. S. Hand (London & New York: Continuum, 1988).

Derrida, Jacques, *La dissemination* (Paris: Seuil, 1972).

------, 'Violence and Metaphysics', in *Writing and Difference*, trans. A. Bass, 79-153 (London: Routledge, 1978).

------, *Adieu to Emmanuel Levinas*, trans. P. Brault & M. Naas (Stanford: Stanford University Press, 1999).

Descartes, *The Philosophical Writings of Descartes: Volume I.* trans. R. Stoothoff J. Cottingham, & D. Murdoch (Cambridge: Cambridge University Press, 1985).

------, *The Philosophical Writings of Descartes Volume II*, trans. R. Stoothoff J. Cottingham, & D. Murdoch (Cambridge: Cambridge University Press, 1985).

------, *The Philosophical Writing of Descartes: Volume III*, The Correspondence, trans. J. Cottingham, R. Stoothoff D. Murdoch & A. Kenney, (Cambridge: Cambridge University Press, 1991).

Dover, K. J., 'Classical Greek attitudes to sexual behaviour', *Arethusa* 6: 1 (1973), 59-73.

Drabinski, John E., *Sensibility and Singularity: The Problem of Phenomenology in Levinas* (New York: State University of New York Press, 2001).

Dudiak, Jeffrey, *The Intrigue of Ethics: A Reading of the Idea of Discourse in the Thought of Emmanuel Levinas*, (New York: Fordham University Press, 2001).

Eaglestone, Robert, *Ethical Criticism: Reading After Levinas* (Edinburgh: Edinburgh University Press, 1997).

Féron, Etienne. *De l'idée de transcendance à la question du langage* (Grenoble: Jérôme Millon, 1992).

Foucault, Michel, 'Maurice Blanchot: the thought from outside', in *Foucault Blanchot*, trans. B. Massumi, 9-58 (New York: Zone Books, 1990).

Gibbs, Robert, *Correlations in Rosenzweig and Levinas* (Princeton: Princeton University Press, 1992).

Goodchild, Philip, *Capitalism and Religion: the Price of Piety* (London & New York, Routledge, 2002).

Guenther, Lisa, '"Like a maternal body": Levinas and the motherhood of Moses', unpublished manuscript, 2004.

Heidegger, Martin, *Being and Time*, trans. J. Macquarrie and E. Robinson (Oxford: Blackwell, 1962).

-----, 'The Origin of the Work of Art,' in *Basic Writings*, ed. D. Krell, 149-87 (New York: Harper & Row, Publishers, 1977).

Houellebecq, Michel, *Atomised*, trans. F. Wynne.(London: Vintage, 2001).

Husserl, Edmund, *Logical Investigations Volume II*, trans. J. N. Findlay (London: Routledge, 1970).

Iyer, Lars. *Blanchot's Communism: Art, Philosophy and the Political* (London & New York: Palgrave Macmillan, 2004).

Janicaud, Dominique, *Le Tournant théologique de la phénoménologie française*. Combas: Editions de l'éclat, 1991).

Kafka, Franz, 'The Metamorphosis,' in *The Complete Short Stories of Franz Kafka*, ed. N. Glatzer (London: Vintage Books, 1999).

Kant, Immanuel. *Critique of Pure Reason*, revised 2nd ed., trans. N. K. Smith, intro. H. Caygill (London: Palgrave Macmillan, 2003).

Lacan, Jacques, *Seminar II: The Ego in Freud's Theory and the Technique of Psychoanalysis 1954-5*, trans. S. Tomaselli (Cambridge: Cambridge University Press, 1988).

Levinas, Emmanuel, *Totalité et infini* (the Hague: Martinus Nihoff, 1961).

------, *Quatre lectures talmudiques* (Paris: Minuit, 1968).

------, *Totality and Infinity*, trans. A. Lingis (Pittsburgh: Duquesne University Press, 1969).

------, *Humanisme de l'autre homme*. Paris: Fata Morgana, 1972.

------, *The Theory of Intuition in Husserl's Phenomenology*, trans. A. Orianne (Evanston: Northwestern University Press, 1973).

------, *Autrement qu'être ou au-delà de l'essence* (Livre de Poche, 1978).

------, *En découvrant l'existence avec Husserl et Heidegger* (Paris: Vrin, 1982).

------, *Collected Philosophical Papers*, trans. A. Lingis (Dordrecht: Kluwer Academic Publishers, 1987a).

------, *Time and the Other*, trans. R. A. Cohen (Pittsburgh: Duquesne University Press, 1987b).

------, *Nine Talmudic Readings*, trans. A. Aronowicz (Bloomington: Indiana University Press, 1990).

------, *Otherwise Than Being or Beyond Essence*, trans. A. Lingis (Dordrecht: Kluwer Academic Publishers, 1991).

------, *Outside the Subject*, trans. M. B. Smith (Stanford: Stanford University Press, 1993).

------, *Beyond the Verse: Talmudic Readings and Lectures*, trans. G. D. Mole (London: Athlone Press, 1994).

------, *Proper Names*, trans. M. B. Smith (London: The Athlone Press, 1996).

------, *Difficult Freedom: Essays on Judaism*, trans. S. Hand (Baltimore: Johns Hopkins University Press, 1997).

------, *Entre-Nous: Thinking-of-the-Other*, trans. M. B. Smith & B. Harshav (New York: Columbia University Press, 1998).

------, *Of God Who Comes to Mind*, trans. B. Bergo (Stanford: Stanford University Press, 1998).

------, *Humanism of the Other*, trans. N. Poller (Urbana and Chicago: University of Illinois Press, 2003).

Lilly, Reginald, 'Chronology of Blanchot's Writing in French',
http:/lists.village.edu/spoons/blanchot/mb_french_chronological.htm, 2005.

Llewelyn, John, *The Genealogy of Ethics: Emmanuel Levinas* (London and New York: Routledge, 1995).

Lyotard, Jean-François, 'Levinas' logic', in *Face to Face with Levinas*, ed. R. A, Cohen, 117-58 (New York: State University of New York Press, 1986).

Marion, Jean-Luc. 'The voice without name: homage to Levinas', in *The Face of the Other & the Trace of God*, ed. J. Bloechl, 224-42 (New York: Fordham University Press, 2000).

------, *The Idol and Distance*, trans. T. A. Carlson (New York: Fordham University Press, 2001).

Mascolo, Dionys, *Le communisme: révolution et communication ou la dialectique des valeurs et des besoins* (Paris: Gallimard, 1953).

Moses, Stéphane. *Système et révélation: la philosophie de Franz Rosenzweig*, 2nd ed. (Paris: Bayard, 2003).

Nancy, Jean-Luc, *The Inoperative Community*, trans. P. Conner, L. Garbus, M. Howard, & S. Sawhney (Minneapolis & Oxford: University of Minnesota Press, 1991).

Nietzsche, Friedrich, *On the Genealogy of Morals*, trans. W. Kaufmann (New York: Vintage Books, 1967).

Parain, Brice, 'Le langage et l'immanence', *Bulletin de la société française de philosophie*, 22: Février (1964).

Plato, *Plato: Complete Works*, ed. J. M. Cooper (Indianapolis: Hackett, 1997).

Sanford, Stella, *The Metaphysics of Love* (London and New Brunswick NJ: The Athlone Press, 2000).

Scholem, Gerschom, *Major Trends in Jewish Mysticism* (New York: Schocken Books, 1941).

Wahl, Jean, *Traité de métaphysique* (Paris: Payot, 1953).

Wall, Thomas, *Radical Passivity: Levinas, Blanchot and Agamben* (Albany: State University of New York Press, 1999).

Zarader, Marlène, *L'Être et le neutre: à partir de Maurice Blanchot* (Paris: Verdier, 2001).

Žižek, Slavoj, 'Introduction', in *The Žižek Reader*, ed(s) Elizabeth Wright & Edmond Wright (Oxford: Blackwell, 1999).

Index

appellation, 10-11, 145
Aristotle, 1, 2, 17, 25, 131
atheism, 35-37, 42, 73-74, 143
Bataille, G., 86-88, 105, 107, 109, 115, 121, 124, 128
de Beauvoir, S., 42-43, 52
Beckett, S., 103, 126
Being, 12, 27-29, 31, 50, 64-65, 69, 131, 142-143, 153
Benveniste, E., 91-96, 102
The Book to Come, 80, 150
child, the, 53-58, 61-62, 66-69, 137
Chomsky, N., 91-92, 95
Cogito, the, 37- 39
Collin, F., 79, 82
communication, 7, 9, 16-17, 31, 82, 91-92, 108, 117, 120, 122-124, 144, 148, 154, 159
communism, 84-86, 105, 128
community, 18, 62, 104, 105-107, 123, 126, 128
consciousness, 4-5, 13, 27, 33-34, 39, 46, 55, 60, 63-66, 68-69, 71-72, 82, 107, 111, 116, 139-140
conversation, 1-3, 7, 9, 25, 35, 60, 67, 83, 89, 103-104, 107, 110, 114-116, 118-122, 124, 157
creation, 36-37, 51 72-74, 78, 137
Critique of Pure Reason, 5, 65, 92, 125-126
Derrida, J., 26, 54, 128, 138, 141
Descartes, R., 5, 35, 37-39, 51, 54, 92, 125, 128
desire, 7-8, 39, 56, 62, 64, 68, 112
dialogue, 1-3, 6, 9, 15, 16-17, 20, 22, 23-24, 25, 32, 35, 60, 67, 79, 103, 108, 113-114, 122, 148, 152
disorder, 61, 126, 143-144, 146
empiricism, 13-15
erotic/eroticism, 24, 43, 46, 53, 66
ethical language, 120, 146-149
ethical relation, 2-3, 6-12, 19, 21-23, 27-36 *passim*, 41-48 *passim*, 55, 58-60, 66, 73-74, 76, 77, 79, 82, 84, 95, 103, 107, 113-114, 117-118, 120-121, 124, 126, 133, 136, 149, 152
experience, 4-5, 14, 28, 33-34, 63, 64, 66-67, 70, 77, 80-81, 82, 87, 96, 112, 125-126, 142-143, 149-152, 155-156
fecundity, 23, 43, 53-60, 66-67, 136, 138
feminine, the, 26, 40-49, 52, 58, 67, 77
Feron, E., 10-11
Foucault, M., 96, 124
Freud, S., 150
friendship, 1, 79, 81-91, 101, 121, 124, 128, 129
From Existence to Existents, 34
God, 2, 3, 6, 8, 9, 36-37, 38-39, 50, 51, 72-76, 142, 153
Heidegger, M., 25, 27, 51, 64, 128, 129
history, 11, 13, 64, 67, 82, 90, 132-139
Houellebecq, M., 86
Husserl, E., 4, 13-15, 34-35, 39, 51, 68, 111, 146
idealism, 18, 29, 51, 65-66, 71, 134, 143